Authority and Representation
in Early Modern Discourse

Authority
and
Representation
in
Early Modern
Discourse

Robert Weimann

Edited by David Hillman

THE JOHNS HOPKINS UNIVERSITY PRESS

Baltimore and London

© 1996 THE JOHNS HOPKINS UNIVERSITY PRESS
All rights reserved. Published 1996
Printed in the United States of America on acid-free paper
05 04 03 02 01 00 99 98 97 96   5 4 3 2 1

THE JOHNS HOPKINS UNIVERSITY PRESS
2715 North Charles Street
Baltimore, Maryland 21218-4319
The Johns Hopkins Press Ltd., London

ISBN 0-8018-5190-4
ISBN 0-8018-5191-2 (pbk.)

Library of Congress Cataloging-in-Publication Data will be found
at the end of this book.

A catalog record for this book is available from the British Library

Contents

Contents

Preface

This book develops readings and ideas that were first conceived in several papers and essays leading to a German-language book-length study, *Shakespeare und die Macht der Mimesis: Autorität und Repräsentation im elisabethanischen Theater* (Berlin: Aufbau, 1988). But what that book contained in two introductory chapters has here been expanded and developed into an entirely fresh and independent study. Although the ultimate conjunction with the issue of authority in the Elizabethan theater has not been lost sight of, this volume cannot be considered a translation of the German book.

To rework, expand, and constantly go beyond a previously published text, language, and terminology is a daunting, and at times quite wearisome, task. I doubt whether, even over a considerably longer period, I would have been in a position successfully to grapple with it without the help and collaboration of David Hillman. He was a member of my graduate class at Harvard University in 1989–90; as we corresponded over a number of years, my former student became a friend and colleague whose assistance and cogent criticism on every level of this project were of inestimable value. His contribution exceeds what an author has a right to expect from the most generous editor. Going over my manuscripts (some of them foul papers, partially handwritten), he improved my English, gave good counsel on how to structure the flow of my argument, pointed out its weaknesses, and drew attention to secondary literature of which I was unaware.

If my debt to my editor, David Hillman, is immense, this does not mean that others have not also deserved my gratitude. It is a pleasure to acknowledge the important help of Ellen Summers (Hiram College), who helped turn two chapters and an early version of the introduction into printable English. The same introduction received much help from Walter Cohen (Cornell), who further improved and edited that early version. David Margolies (Goldsmith's College, London) was generous enough to read and comment on part 1 of the book, and I have thankfully profited from his expertise. From Louis Montrose (University of California, San Diego) I received profound and heartwarming encouragement that was (and is) invaluable. I have an outstanding debt to Jonathan Fortescue, a former student in my Harvard seminar, that I am anxious to acknowledge. Finally, my special thanks go to Sabine Zimmermann, who set up the index and helped on several levels in the final stages of the project. As the book goes to press I must express my deep appreciation for the work of my copyeditor, Jane Lincoln Taylor, whose eagle-eyed attention and unfailing sense of accuracy, transparency, and balance in the use of the English language were especially welcome from the point of view of one who is not a native speaker.

I have enjoyed the facilities, the support, and the encouragement of several cultural institutions. At an early stage, when libraries in East Berlin responded with yawning shelves to urgent calls for books, I was fortunate enough to have the repeated help and hospitality of Stanley Wells and the friendly librarian, Dr. Susan Brock, at the English Shakespeare Institute at Stratford and Birmingham. At another crucial period in the preparation of this (and its follow-up) project I received significant support from Deutsche Forschungsgemeinschaft in Bonn. After the foundation, in 1992, of Forschungsschwerpunkt Literaturwissenschaft in Berlin, I was able to avail myself of generous help and welcome technical facilities. Here, I found a climate no less congenial than that in the old department, Zentralinstitut für Literaturgeschichte, that had sheltered the writing of the German version of the book. Finally, after dividing my activities between Berlin and California, I was again fortunate to meet with unfailing encouragement and support in my new department at the University of California, Irvine. It is a pleasure to remember and record my indebtedness to all these hospitable schools and friendly places of learning.

Portions of several chapters of this book, invariably in a somewhat different form, have been printed in journals or collections of articles. An early German essay on the Reformation crisis of authority appeared in *REAL* 5 (1987): 109–40. I wish to thank Hans-Jürgen Diller, who, with characteristic generosity, arranged for an English translation on which, in certain places, the present study was able to rely.

I also wish to thank the following editors and publishers for permission to adapt or reprint these materials: *"Fabula* and *Historia*: The Crisis of the 'Universall Consideration' in *The Unfortunate Traveller*," *Representations* 8 (Fall 1984): 14–29, and in *Representing the English Renaissance*, ed. Stephen Greenblatt (Berkeley and Los Angeles: University of California Press, 1988), 181–96; "'Bifold Authority' in Reformation Discourse: Authorization, Representation, and Early Modern 'Meaning,'" in *Historical Criticism and the Challenge of Theory*, ed. Janet Levarie Smarr (Urbana: University of Illinois Press, 1993), 167–82; "Memory, Fictionality, and the Issue of Authority: Author-Function and Narrative Performance in *Beowulf*, Chrétien, and Malory," in *Contexts of Pre-Novel Narrative: The European Tradition*, ed. Roy Eriksen (New York: Mouton de Gruyter, 1994), 83–100; "Authority and Signification: Rabelais and Vernacular Renaissance Prose Fiction," in *Sprache und Literatur der Romania: Tradition und Wirkung—Festschrift für Horst Heintze*, ed. Irmgard Osols-Wehden, Giuliani Staccioli, and Barbette Hesse (Berlin: Arno Spitz, 1993), 87–99; and "'Authority' in Calvinism: The Spirit betwixt Scripture and Polity," in *Heart of the Heartless World. Essays in Cultural Resistance in Memory of Margot Heinemann*, ed. David Margolies and Maroula Joannou (London: Pluto Press, 1995), 33–46.

Authority and Representation
in Early Modern Discourse

Introduction

Representation and Division in Early Modern Culture

This is a book about authority and representation in Reformation discourse and in Renaissance prose fiction, but it is also part of a larger ongoing study of early modern culture, even as that culture unfolded its patterns of unbounded appropriation, circulation, restlessness, division, and "rush to knowledge" (*The Winter's Tale* 3.1.21).[1] From today's angle, we can view the premises of authority in that culture more nearly in perspective, at least from a perspective that is no longer exclusively modern; it seems possible, so to speak, to read early modern discourse more consequentially, from what did and did not come out of it. This approach, precisely because it is conjunctural in the awareness of historicity between the then and the now, cannot presuppose consensus; in fact, the underlying perception of early modern culture is troublesome on more than one level.

At issue, then as now, was and is the question of authority, particularly in regard to such modes of representation as implicate traces of existence in and through an act of world-picturing. The early moderns' turning of the world into a picture met an existential need for self-orientation and control vis-à-vis a bewildering rate of change. Representations that addressed this need were not innocent; we cannot, at this late date, continue unquestioningly to accept the traditional grounds of their validity. Today, the premises on which these

1

world constructions were authorized must appear suspect as soon as certain uses of representation are seen to be inseparable from those of "conquest" and "mastery." To think of the world as a picture, and to project this picture as representing that which is, involves the ancient, altogether resolute "naming power" of Heidegger's *vor-stellen* (to represent): to set the picture before oneself and to set it forth in relation to oneself. Such a "conquest of the world as picture," establishing the measure and guidelines for everything, not only affirms "unlimited power for the calculating, planning, and molding of all things,"[2] but at the same time seeks immeasurably to expand the space of human capability and mastery over things. Thus, ironically, "the more extensively and the more effectually the world stands at man's disposal as conquered, and the more objectively the object appears, all the more subjectively, i.e., the more importunately, does the *subiectum* rise up, and all the more impetuously, too, do observation of and teaching about the world change into a doctrine of man."[3]

Authority in the order of representations such as these was indissolubly tied to a bold and precarious project of modern world mastery in which modern subjects in their alleged freedom throve on the controlled distance to a world of objects out there. The distance was important because it allowed the modern agent of "trafficke and travell" (to use John Lyly's phrase) to be free, and even to celebrate a new inwardness and spirituality, while doing business with the hardness of profitable things. Here, Max Weber's phrase "worldly asceticism" points to the Protestant ethic as part of a larger culture of early modern appropriation in which the possession of objects could reward the spirituality of subjects. It was a large view (or picture) of a world with room for both the material and the spiritual.

However, the new discipline of inwardness—the rigorous concern with a self-sustained, energetic type of interiority—was more than a cunning strategy for acquisitive action in a fallen world. Behind it, there was an intense and quite revolutionary principle of legitimation, in which the dualism of subject and object was religiously, ethically, and philosophically sanctioned. There was a new authority at work in these Protestant representations that deserves to be read literally (and in relation to a culture marked by literacy) as a scriptural mode of legitimation authorizing certain masterful uses of writing, reading, and interpretation. Again, the new inwardness was powerful: the discipline (and emancipation) of the middle class and the conquest of the world went hand in hand.

The biblical text and its diligent reception and interpretation provided the ultimate source of an authority informing both the world and those who read, prospered, and believed in it. But "the over-riding authority of the Bible," the "battle-ground of several ideologies," was, as Christopher Hill notes, a divisive tool, "a sword to divide" as well as one that "facilitated . . . double-talk."[4] In mainstream Protestant discourse, this authority was inseparable from an authorship of the spirit. It was the major impulse behind a scriptural mode of authorization that, as John Guillory has shown so well, sustained the writing of epic poetry between the end of inspiration and the nascent Protestant imagination in Spenser and Milton.[5]

The European Reformation and the various Protestantisms emerging from it provided the most intense site on which early modern uses of authority were radically redefined. If this is so, cannot sixteenth-century prose narrative, even where its outlook is quite remote from Protestant doctrine, be read in conjunction with the new mode of authority and authorization? This question cannot be answered with a simple yes or no; it points to the need for an approach according to which early modern fictional narrative can be viewed as the most experimental, least prescribed cultural space for unfolding (and retracting) self-sustained images and meaningful imaginings of a *subiectum* in a new mode of representation.

The space for fiction, more than that for any political, philosophical, or juridical type of discourse, is indicative of what, in measuring the objective, can imaginatively be appropriated for and through the subject in the picture. Early modern uses of fiction set out to draw on whatever self-contained cogency textualized images and imaginings could attain. Even where, as in Rabelais, Fischart, and Nashe, the oral art of the storyteller remained incalculably strong, there was—as there was in Protestant discourse—a readiness to construct, and a need to receive, self-authorized representations and interpretations (even when, in early modern fiction, these were located at an entirely secu-

3

lar point of intersection between ancient pleasure and reorienting knowledge). As Vassilis Lambropoulos notes in his remarkable study *The Rise of Eurocentrism: Anatomy of Interpretation*, the strength and availability, through print and literacy, of textual forms provide a secular "mimesis of redemption: the redemption of the world through representation, the communion of the word." But even when the encompassing, re-creative trajectory of such self-fashioned representations hovered over the no man's land "twixt divinity and poetry" (Nashe's dilemma), people of literacy "might not be enticed to accept . . . the gift of an (evangelized) present moment of unmediatedness, if it were not for a promise of freedom, of personal (specifically, spiritual) liberation from subservience to every (other) worldly authority, from worldliness itself, so that humans can now begin doing things with, or even to, this world. Interpretation promised emancipation: acceptance and independence in the civic society."[6]

At this point, when the production of spiritual and imaginative meanings became more important than any institutionalized order and matter, Protestantism and early modern fiction engaged in an alliance for a previously unauthorized type of representation. In this precarious alliance, the 'interpretive imperative' served as an invisible link between the diverse promises of emancipation associated with Protestant piety and the 'redemptive' uses of secular writing and reading respectively. In both directions, a new construction of the self emerged through the interiorization and privatization of meaning. What the inward, scriptural location of authority presupposed and helped bring about was not simply an emancipation of knowledge from the coercion of outside authority, but a state of affairs in which knowledge could achieve a kind of "autonomy by judiciously governing (and guarding) itself, by scrupulously observing the rules that it has itself chosen to follow. The law of immanence which rules the secular order—'the perfect law, the law of liberty' (James 1.25)—is the régime of truth that characterizes modernity."[7]

The resulting textualization of faith and truth constituted a noncoercive space for both dissension and verifiability—a space henceforth assured of the legitimacy of finding, asserting, and debating meaning. Hence, early modern discourse in both religion and literature was inseparable from those conditions of cultural practice that necessarily involved debate and contestation, the clash between diverse authorities engaging in rivalry for the more persuasive image, logic, truth, and form of saying things. What was implicated in these terms was a meaningful and powerful, though rarely violent, relocation of authority and authorization. The new regime of validity could interlock with the groundwork of early modern representation itself, with its parameters of referentiality, its proliferation of signs, and its strong constructs of subjectivity. All the while, traditional locations of premodern authority persisted in both the politics of secular fiction and the ecclesiastical hold over religious writings. But the claims on God-given legitimacy of secular and ecclesiastical institutions, and the centuries-old hallowed order of fealty and lineage, were irretrievably undermined. They could not withstand a different, more deeply divisive register of legitimation, one residing in the strength of personal beliefs and convictions, in the differentiating uses of knowledge, discussion, and a busier exchange of signs and meanings.

In several fields of early modern culture, this shift in the grounding of validity culminated in a new sense of the relations of authority and representation. Because authority, including the authorization of discourse itself, was no longer given, as it were, before the writing and reading began, the act of representation was turned into a site on which authority could be negotiated, disputed, or reconstituted. Modern authority, rather than preceding its inscription, rather than being given as a prescribed premise of utterances, became a product of writing, speaking, and reading, a result rather than primarily a constituent of representation.

As this provisional model (here schematically oversimplified) is traced and examined, its flaws and built-in contradictions will become obvious. This definition of early modern authority in and of representation is problematic insofar as it is read in terms of any linear notion of emancipation or any absolute opposition between spiritual and material locations of authority. Even so, this construct cannot be dismissed as a purely logocentric fiction. Ever since the Reformation, this paradigm was followed in an increasing variety of writings. At its culmination during the Enlightenment, it had an impact on relations of power and the use of language that can be neither disputed nor erased. Since this model informed not only textual production and reception but also the circumstances of authorization, intellectual and material, under which written texts were published and circulated, the paradigm cannot simply be dismissed as yet another *grand récit*. Based on ideational as well as institutional practices, this model, delimiting and differentiating the uses of power and thereby historicizing an early modern shift in its material and intellectual locations, has too sharp a focus on undetermined sociocultural struggle to be reducible to the level of any teleology of progress.

Power and Representation: Then and Now

To make these qualifications is not to disregard the conjunctural dimension of my own approach. The momentous events in the recent history of central and Eastern Europe may already appear to cry out for revisiting (and testing) the narrative of an opposition between power and the intellect, between the politics of power and the authority of representations.[8] There is good reason to suspect that these events, and their political and cultural repercussions, may indeed have to be read as a profoundly significant chapter in the history of modernity. But for all its undoubted impact this conjunctural moment needs to be viewed in perspective, not at short range. The outcome of events in central and Eastern Europe appears to contradict a good many premises on which the critical intellect sought to overcome the bastions of petrified power. Besides, analogies between then and now carry perils; the establishment of similitude invites at best self-projection, at worst self-congratulation. Even though the early modern history of relations between *Geist* and *Macht*, between intellectual and powerful locations of authority, appeared to be confirmed and revitalized in 1989, the whole binary scheme of things requires a skeptical response: today to reconstruct it is to deconstruct it.

Again, this is not to say that an important constellation in early modern discourse may not be read in terms of a conflict: as my 1987 essay phrased it, "the authority of signs versus the signs of authority." But for reasons to which I shall return, the authority of (external) power cannot ultimately be set against the power of an internal or inscribed authority, even when their opposition has over the past three centuries often enough been accepted as a matter of course.

My refusal to subscribe unwittingly to what is a mighty subtext of modern representations, reaching deep into both my own text and my biography, arises in response to yet another and quite different mode of correlating past significance and present experience. The Reformation and the late Renaissance in central and northwestern Europe, although never more easily available through research and documentation, persistently retreat from us and today appear further removed from what appears authentic and (the qualification is telling) *relatively valid* in our own world. For many in the profession, the early modern world of "trafficke and travell" is no longer a world of Burckhardtian promise or nostalgia, but one whose utterances have become strangely indeterminate and unreliable. As the distance between then and now increases, there emerges an ever widening gap between what these texts say and what actually, as we decipher them, they can be made to mean. The "discourse of modernism" and what Timothy Reiss calls its "exemplary formal statement *cogito-ergo-sum*" can now be discussed as if they belonged to another world. This was a world whose principal metaphors used to be the telescope ("eye—instrument—world") and the voyage of discovery ("self-possessed port of departure—sea journey—country claimed as legitimate possession of the discoverer")[9]—a world that, although it made ours possible, is light-years removed from the uses of power (and its opposite) in the age of electronic information.

However, even as the gap widens, the past language of modern legitimation and "possession" is one that harbors discursive and nondiscursive practices whose implications extend right to our own doorstep. For many (post)modern critics, sixteenth-century culture presents itself as a language ruptured by divisions, a language whose configurations need to be read against the grain of early modern meanings. There is an irresistible (some critics would say ethical) urge to look at the Renaissance rhetoric of aggrandizement as a discourse of impoverishment, to read the fame of exploration as infamous news of colonization, the triumphs of self-liberation as testimony to social fission, the pride in appropriation as a condoning of vast expropriations.

7

Introduction

If the early modern world appears distant from today's concerns, it nevertheless went a long way toward anticipating the presuppositions of some of our own anxieties. To an extent that an earlier generation of critics never dreamed of, sixteenth-century culture appears deeply divided. Individualism jostles with the norms of collectivity, traffic and mobility undermine the "married calm of states" (*Troilus and Cressida* 1.3.100), the perception of mutability more often than not is born of the apprehension that "everything includes itself in power, / Power into will, will into appetite," that self-devouring "universal wolf" (119–21). This division is one that explodes assumptions of any univocal articulation of authority as a given, unitary court of appeal. But as a profound fissure in authority was unprecedentedly manifested in the Reformation, traditional forms and functions of fictional representation, such as those associated with psychomachian allegory and chivalric romance, were themselves jeopardized. As these dominant forms of late-medieval discourse receded, the range of representational practices broadened immeasurably.[10] There is a link (which, I suspect, is of unique cultural potency) between the decline of given, unitary locations of authority and an unprecedented expansion of representational discourses.

It was at this point that modern cultural consciousness came to be locked up in a good many premises of late-Renaissance uses of language. The latter first brought to the fore a previously unknown element of vulnerability in the assertion and appropriation of authority, even in the authorization of writing itself. This vulnerability appeared (and continues to appear) inseparable from the proliferation of, and ever increasing differentiation in the uses of, signs. To the present generation of critics, early modern culture is especially captivating because of the contestatory quality of a good many of its discourses; it is in reference to their particularly divisive potential for signification that such contemporary critical concepts as 'negotiation,' 'transgression,' 'contestation,' and even 'rehearsal' have largely, though not exclusively, been developed. We still have, and will continue to have, a lot to do with this remote past, in which Shakespeare's plays existed side by side with the discourse of Protestantism, and, for that matter, the discursive and nondiscursive practices of colonialism.

8

Since it has become impossible to view early modern culture whole, there is good reason to do more than simply marvel at the boldness (and ideological blindness) of those great and serious scholars of the past who pronounced on the one "pattern" or "world-picture" of Elizabethan culture. Behind the contemporary reluctance to search for unity is a growing sense of doubt about fundamental premises of validity and legitimation in the writing of literary and cultural history. This doubt, which reflects a considerable loss of authority in the business of contemporary criticism, has many (institutionalized) sources and symptoms. The decline in the authority of our own profession ultimately is linked with what first emerged as a widely felt dilemma in early modern culture. Even then the temporary and sometimes quite unhappy alliance among humanists and political rulers tended to displace the gaps (and thereby to jeopardize potential links) between intellectual (written) and material (powerful) practices of appropriation.[11]

There is at least one area of discursive practice in which, I suggest, today's crisis in critical authority is directly and forcibly adumbrated in early modern developments. Although I can touch only briefly on the discourse in question, recent Western anthropology has "cast radical doubt on the procedures by which alien human groups can be represented." If, as James Clifford notes, "the activity of cross-cultural representation is now more than usually in question," the reason has to do with the "current crisis—or better, dispersion of ethnographic authority." But insofar as even today it seems vital "to break up monophonic authority" or any other "controlling mode of authority," the modern anthropologist needs to cope with the centuries-old "imposition of coherence on an unruly textual process."[12] This process goes back to an early colonial type of discourse, easily available to Shakespeare's contemporaries in, for example, the writings of Thomas Hariot or the collections of Richard Hakluyt. Here we have what Stephen Greenblatt calls "the self-validating, totalizing character" of an ethnographic discourse whose validity, in our own day, has become unthinkable in terms of such ethnocentrism.[13] Whatever the degree of subtlety and complicity in the relation of orthodoxy and subversion in Hariot's *Brief and True Report of the New Found Land of Virginia*

(1588), his (or any other sixteenth-century colonizer's) ethnocentrism is an investment in a type of authority that has irretrievably failed.

Colonial discourse (in which Shakespeare most intriguingly engages in *The Tempest*) deserves to be mentioned here at least in passing, because it is precisely in this type of discourse that the conjunctural moment in today's approach to early modern culture finds its most pronounced potential for discontinuity in legitimation. As Jacques Derrida suggests in the "Exergue" to *Of Grammatology*, ethnocentrism is at the heart of logocentrism in that "the metaphysics of phonetic writing" is "nothing but the most original and powerful" form by which the West has succeeded in "imposing itself upon the world," controlling not simply a concept of writing as phoneticized but, in conjunction with that, a "project of science" ("the scientificity of science") centrally determined by logic and representationalism.[14] In view of such wide-ranging implications, the crisis in ethnographic writing and tradition may arguably be used, as Robert Young suggests, as testimony to a more comprehensive need to scrutinize critically the issue of, and claim on, authority in those "forms of European thought" that, in the first place, stand for "the concept" and "assumed primacy" of a particular (modern and early modern) phase of Western culture.[15] If ethnocentrism finds itself in an ugly kind of complicity with logocentrism, then the writing of early modern cultural history involves a project that cannot be indifferent to "the traditional perspectives, norms and assumptions which form the basis of Western thought."[16]

My reference to ethnographic discourse underlines the "instability and instrumentality" of early modern representations, but it does not seek to minimize the potency of their contribution to the construction of a rapidly changing world. Representations, as Louis Montrose has noted, "are engaged in shaping the modalities of social reality and in accommodating their writers, performers, readers, and audiences to multiple and shifting subject positions with the world that they themselves both constitute and inhabit."[17] The world in which the Protestant reformers, as well as Erasmus, Rabelais, Sidney, Nashe, and Lyly, wrote was one that had to cope not only with the wider horizon of international traffic and exchange but also with a largely unsanctioned diffusion of signifying activities. These were correlated with both the technological revolution that brought about the printing press and the Reformation explosion of religious "discord." In England, early modern uses of representation were unthinkable without the growth in Protestant debate and interpretation; they went hand in hand with the gradual spread of literacy, nourished by the increased circulation of printed vernacular texts. Under these conditions, sixteenth-century English society witnessed the beginnings of a new mode of discourse that—suspending, exhausting, and finally breaking with the order of similitude—culminated in the disparate set of relations between language and existence that created the need for, and at the same time made possible the unfixed simultaneous workings of, several contradictory registers of authority and authorization.

Authority and Authorization

These early modern changes in the uses of representation connect with a complex shifting of credentials in writing and reading. The late-Renaissance constellation of authority was one of profound differentiation and division. As the traditional system of lineage relations, with their family loyalties and fealty, and the universal order of the old church gave way, centuries-old sources of validity came into disarray. Among the divisive forces in discursive action, the sixteenth-century European Reformation looms largest; here, the problem of authority appears especially acute where the old church was defied and where the resulting schism was directly as well as indirectly confronted with an explosion of largely unauthorized and partially uncontrollable tracts, printed sermons, and preachings. In view of what, at least in midcentury England, must have been virtually uncensorable discursive practices, there was the danger (as a conservative churchman perceived it) that these would "slip the anchor-hold of authority, and come to a loose disputation."[18] Such "loose disputation" stood for, and resulted in, an unbound, self-assumed type of authorization in the circulation and reception of discourses. It was this crucial link between the Reformation upheaval in the distribution of authority and the bifurcation in the authorization process that provided an unprecedented springboard for cultural change in and through diverse representational forms and practices.

11

Introduction

Between Shakespeare (who uses the word *authority* more than sixty times) and Thomas Hobbes, sociocultural and juridical links between authority and authorization emerged in a bewildering variety of ways; many of them crystallized in the semantic and semiotic space of representation. Chapter 16 of *Leviathan* (published in 1651) sets out by focusing on a "Representer" ("or *Representative*, a *Lieutenant*, a *Vicar*, an *Attorney*, a *Deputy*, a *Procurator*, an *Actor*, and the like"), defined as a person who is "considered as representing the words and actions of an other." No matter whether he does so "truly or by fiction," this person is called a "*Feigned* or *Artificial person*." Of these "persons artificial," "some have their words and actions *Owned* by those whom they represent. And then the Person is the *Actor*: and he that owneth his words and actions is the AUTHOR: in which case the Actor acteth by Authority."[19] The premises of authority, obliterating traditional grounds of legitimation marked by lineage relations, are reconstructed purely in terms of ownership and contractual considerations. It is in these terms that authority's presuppositions are examined; an entirely new type of representation is needed. Representing the words and actions of another presupposes an arrangement in which "the actor acteth by authority": in other words, the business of delegation and authorization, in this particular economic and judicial frame of reified relations and references, constitutes the act of representation itself.

Significantly, Hobbes's text as a matter of course brings together "any representer of speech and action, as well in tribunals, as theatres."[20] The philosopher of unrelenting "motion" (for him, the one universal cause) and of "contract" (the antidote for it) is concerned first and foremost with the politics of authorizing representative action, "as if every man should say to every other man, I authorize and give up my right of governing myself, to this man, or to this assembly of men, on this condition, that thou give up thy right to him, and authorize all his actions in like manner."[21] As the *Oxford English Dictionary* records it, the word *authorize* (with two exceptions—of which, characteristically, Wyclif is the earlier) derives from fifteenth- and sixteenth-century usage. Hobbes here uses it in the sense of marking a legally valid political decision, conferring, through formal contract and warrant, legality on the self-motivated act of surrendering the right of representation to another or a group of others. In this mid-seventeenth-century language of personal "right," the subject of authorization is the self-limiting individual joining others in subscribing to a contract. (In contrast to the ideas of Hobbes, the unformulated assumptions of Tudor prelates and politicians continue to presuppose a given corporate framework, which by implication happens to be one of prescribed unity and obedience among Christian authors and readers.)

This is not the place to address the vast panorama of sociocultural and political developments against which, in the period in question, the major shifts in the uses of 'authority' need to be seen. Suffice it to note that studies in Elizabethan parliamentary history have drawn attention to a growing sense of members' "accountability" aspiring to authority in parliamentary proceedings, these members came "to regard themselves as 'representing' their constituencies in a much wider sense than before."[22] Since the days of J. E. Neale there has not been the slightest doubt that Elizabethan parliaments were primarily not so much authorizing as authorized; they furnished a site for "communication between the central government and the governors of the localities."[23] Yet that is not the whole story. Even when Parliament's major role was in the first place a legislative one, there was a "decisive shift from medieval concepts of the relationship between God, the law and the state to more modern, secular rationales," culminating in Bacon's historicizing redefinition of authority.[24]

The dominant political discourse of the period reveals few premonitions of the change that was to lead to Hobbes's reappraisal of the links between authority and representation. However, the drama of the period, like the continuing post-Reformation debate, which included Bancroft's cogent assessment of the state of the controversy, is an entirely different matter. Here I need only refer to the important work of British cultural materialists, among them such distinguished critics as Jonathan Dollimore, John Drakakis, Malcolm Evans, and Graham Holderness, to suggest that what we are dealing with is a highly divisive and rapidly expanding discursive field. But although many of the divisions and contradictions in question have been traced in the relations of transgressive discourse and political or ideological

13

inscriptions of power, I propose in this study to examine a bifurcation, even a potential fissure, of authority *within the circumstances of discursive practice itself*. What I have in mind is an equivalent, in both early modern narrative and drama, of what Shakespeare's Troilus describes as "bifold authority," a dichotomy informing the forms and formations, the process, the semiotics, the semantics, and the uses of representation itself.

The first requisite for this approach is to acknowledge that early modern manifestations of authority found themselves in a state not only of differentiation but of flux and relocation. As my readings of Luther and Calvin will suggest, the Protestant Reformation provided an efficacious impetus to internalize authority, "to shift the basis of its verification from external and public modes to internal and private ones."[25] Although this shift was only beginning in the period considered here, it was powerful enough to affect and, partially at least, to assimilate the gesture of appropriation to the internal workings of textual production and reception. There, appropriation was turned into an intrinsic operation by which the author-function was no longer given, as it were, prior to the act of writing itself. Correspondingly, traditional relations between writing and its sources (and *their* authority) could readily be suspended within the very process of their adaptation and reception. The point is not that thereby the author's subjectivity achieved any autonomous status of self-determined creation (it clearly did not); rather, the author-function, by falling in with a larger political economy of acquisition and appropriation, could communicate its drive for assimilation, for making things its own, to the very order of (re)reading and (re)writing the text in the world. The political economy of the early modern market was, so to speak, intercepted or mentally anticipated in a discursive practice that felt *authorized* by itself to reorder its own procedure, its aims and strategies. Thus, in certain forms of early modern fiction, the politics of "trafficke and travell" was made to engage the configuration of ambition and desire that is processed through the author-function, the theme, the imagery, and the fictional discourse of artificial persons.

As a brief illustration of the Renaissance assimilation of traditional generic conventions of romance, Philip Sidney's *Arcadia* may perhaps best serve. Here, the "choice, and working," of the author-function are no longer given, as by and large they were for Thomas Malory; the author-function certainly is not circumscribed or, literally, prein-scribed by what Malory's source, "the Frensshe booke," says. In chival-ric romance, as well as in a heroic epic such as *Beowulf*, authority is tied to the range and vividness of the memory, the reproduction and (re)writing, even translation, of the story, with its names and deeds revitalized. For premodern writers and performers of narrative, au-thority was not a function of their own inventions, the originality (and contingency) of their appropriations. But early modern writers no longer took for granted, or sought to subscribe to, the validity of the efforts of their predecessors; they did not accept as part of their own authority the labor and competence already invested in the invention of a great story with publicly known events and characters. That is why these writers went out of their way to treat the text as their pos-session, something that they had made their own.

Thus, the process of appropriation was conveyed through a new sense of ownership, even when the underlying market relations were at best concealed by metaphors of procreation. For Sidney, for in-stance, the sheets of the *Arcadia* were "this child, which I am loath to father";[26] similarly, Cervantes looked on *Don Quijote* as "hijo del en-tendimiento,"[27] the "son" of his "understanding." Although the pro-creative stance may easily be deconstructed, it effectively serves as a metaphor of authorization, by which a new type of authority in the writing of fictional narrative was emphatically vindicated. The avail-able body of discursive choices and conventions could more freely be reconstituted when the given "schemata" of narration so began to lose the force of their restraint that the modifying thrust of early modern rewriting or "correction" (to use Wolfgang Iser's phrase) gained new potency.[28]

At this point, improvised projections of authority emerged in sig-nificant relocations. For Malory, authority was inseparable from the proper mediation of a literary matter already authorized. (In con-cluding book 21 of *Le Morte Darthur*, he uses the same word: "I fynde no more wrytten bokis that bene auctorysed.") But this whole frame of reference would soon be discarded. For Sidney, for instance, a more modern, novelistic type of authority was hinged precisely on dispensing with, even explicitly renouncing, the traditional repertoire of heroic norms and choices. Thus, Pyrocles and Musidorus set out "in unknowne order to see more of the world . . . thinking it not so worthy, to be brought to heroycall efects by fortune, or necessitie (like *Ulysses* and *Aeneas*) as by ones owne choice, and working."[29] Note how the location of authority in fictional prose narrative shifted away from the 'known order' inscribed in the classics to an unknown, and yet to be assimilated, space of self-authorized "choice, and working." Without tracing further ramifications of this remarkable passage, I will confine myself here to observing how the author-function redefines the site of narrative authority on an intrinsic level of emplotment: rejecting a traditionally given pattern of authorizing heroic action à la "*Ulysses* and *Aeneas*," this writing relocates the uses of authority on the level of its investment in the very order of rewriting the fictional text itself.

However, in circumstances marked by what Michael McKeon has called "the destabilization of generic categories,"[30] there was no source of validity external to the writing of the text that could provide a recognized set of principles conducive to an as yet unformulated poetics of fictional narrative. In this situation, the time-honored issue of authority in writing must have assumed a new and special urgency. Since generic authority found itself in a state of disarray, there must have been a strongly felt need to sanction each essay in narrative fiction and especially to validate the experimental uses to which it was put.[31] This is why the question of authority proved less crucial and was much less often raised in those forms of prose fiction that rehearsed traditional or Renaissance forms of courtly pastoral, Greek epic, or popular chivalric romance.[32] But wherever the usable repertoire of generic norms and formal choices proved to be less securely established, authority in fictional representation became an issue that must have cried out for certification on more than one level. In the absence of any given "booke" or tradition of narration, authority now had to be achieved, or so it must have appeared, through appropriation of an "unknowne order" of writing, "by ones owne choice, and working."

Under these circumstances, the circulation of authority tended to be channeled into two directions. On the one hand, the author-function acquired a new space for self-fashioned variation, invention, composition, and emplotment. The location of authority thereby was moved from any court of appeal given prior to the act of writing (and listening or reading) to what "in unknowne order" emerged, and was to be responded to, in the processing of discursive practice itself. Here, authority could unfold on the level of what was representing and performing. Now validity accrued to the text in the making, but it could only be certified in public (and this is the second, contradictory direction) by its success on the level of transaction and circulation. At this juncture, in the theater but also, as I shall suggest, through a new mode of reading, the spectator's or reader's entitlement was affirmed. His or her cooperation, and his or her own discursive competence, began to be sought after as an unprecedentedly public court of appeal, one that was able by itself to offer certification in an emerging market for cultural goods.

Paradoxically, this public mode of authorization, geared as it was to the political economy of exchange, appeared to be linked to a countervailing investment of validity in what, on an intrinsic level, was represented. The contradiction in question was, at least on the surface, displaced rather than resolved. A good deal of the discursive energy, imagination, and invention that went into the author-function was designed to conceal, even to suppress, whatever politics resided in the public mode of transaction, especially in the performer's practice and intervention. In the drama, Hamlet's strictures on the (now) unauthorized privilege of clownish performers are a case in point; the players are to "speak no more than is set down for them" (3.2.38). In early modern fiction, even though Rabelais and Nashe continued to inscribe traditional, distinctly oral voices of performance and presentation, their future was strictly limited. In the theater as well as in narrative, the future belonged to the order of representation pure and, as far as possible, uncontaminated. Even by the time of Cervantes (there are important intimations in George Gascoigne, Philip Sidney, Jörg Wickram, Mateo Alemán, and Spanish picaresque fiction), relations of authority that would further unfold in the eighteenth-century

17

novel began to be anticipated. Here we have, as John Bender has shown, "the convention of representational neutrality" as a latent site of authority: "novelistic conventions of transparency, completeness, and representational reliability (perhaps especially where the perceptions represented are themselves unreliable) subsume an assent to regularized authority."[33]

In early modern narrative, the convention of neutrality, linked as it was to a surge of referentiality, did not of course predominate. Even so, a new type of interplay developed that correlated with what existed in the drama, between an increased range of thought and matter being represented *and* a growth in authorizing practice and function. The broadening space (and depth) of what was represented appeared to thrive on such redistribution of authority as, simultaneously, benefited the sovereignty, the privilege and materiality, of what and who was representing. Although in the theater the bifurcation in authorization between written and materially performed (oral or corporeal) uses of signs implicates a vitally important complicating factor, there is in each case a more or less overt tension and engagement between diverse and partially (in)compatible locations of authority.

In both genres, then, the representation of authority (in images of royalty, dignity, privilege, ceremony, degree, and order) intersects with a new type of authority in representation whenever the author-function gains in volume and stature, attaining a position of its "owne choice, and working." In both genres, this intersection involves interaction as well as friction, continuity as well as discontinuity. But, again, in the early modern period the representation *of* authority was not a site of perfect closure; authority *in* representation (and performance) was not a site of unending rupture. The space in question was one of contradiction, even though the two poles did not entertain a binary or purely oppositional relationship. Rather, as representation and existence came to engage one another more searchingly, there resulted an intense circulation, allowing for mutual interrogation among diverse locations, of authority. In the drama as well as in narrative, the historiographic and the "phantasticall,"[34] the poetics of *fabula* and that of *historia*, engaged in the endless work of their mutual contamination. That, exactly, is the point where representation and

18

existence established a modern kind of intercourse in which aperture and closure came to entangle one another in quick succession and unpremeditated motion.

Preaching, Paging, Playing

In his *Acts and Monuments* John Foxe records a letter written by Stephen Gardiner, the conservative bishop of Winchester, in which he points to three areas of "uncertainty" in contemporary uses of discourse. These were marked by the activities of "printers, players, and preachers" who made "a wonderment, as though we knew not yet how to be justified."[35] The question for them, it seemed, was how to be authorized when in the wake of the Reformation momentous issues of authority appeared to be open for redefinition. From Gardiner's point of view, there was a connection between the crisis in ecclesiastical and political authority and certain areas of unsanctioned and partially uncensorable discursive practices involving the Protestant pulpit, the printing press, and the common stages.

Although the bracketing of these discursive institutions may sound strange to modern ears, the phrase can serve to remind us of a potent alignment of cultural activities in early modern England that transcended canonized and generic as well as any strictly literary boundaries. What, from Gardiner's point of view, preaching, printing, and playing had in common was the dangerous ability to "slip the anchorhold of authority, and come to a loose disputation." These public agencies shared a multifaceted sociocultural space where, through collision or alliance, discursive practice and political power as a matter of course were bound to engage with one another. Again, such an engagement—involving representations in an unfathomed nexus of cultural interchange and productivity—cannot simply be read in terms of the eighteenth-century opposition between repressive power and progressive knowledge. Rather, this engagement marked a site of cultural conflict and dislocation, even when, in sixteenth-century Europe, the circulation of legitimacy and validity continued to move in relatively fixed channels: it was impossible to appropriate and represent new sites of authority without at least threatening to expropriate the old ones. To disturb the traditional flow of authority—from top to bottom—was to threaten disorder. The resulting confusion was disturbing and, in Gardiner's phrase, "noisome to any realm. And where every man will be master, there must needs be uncertainty."[36]

In attempting to realign such early modern fields of discursive practice, this study can focus on only a limited number of significant texts and circumstances. Even so, there is no better way to marshal submerged relations and connections in the cultural landscape of sixteenth-century authorization and representation. First, there was "preaching," here used as a synecdoche for those religious (and, by implication, political) discourses that rapidly spread in the wake of the European Reformation, as that huge upheaval ushered in a series of profound crises in both traditional concepts of authority and modes of authorization. Second, there was the new medium of print, far-reaching in its consequences, not only for the Reformation but also for secular authors who could avail themselves of an as yet immature marketplace for printed matter as an alternative or a supplement to the declining institution of patronage. In part 2 of this book, the idea is not simply to trace the changing locations of authority between premodern and early modern representations, but, more importantly, to study their implications and correlatives in fictional narrative. In this connection, the unusual "paging" points to the vocabulary of Thomas Nashe, "gosling of the Printing-house," as he projects his hero, the page Jack Wilton, onto the "pages of his misfortunes." The conjuncture, first explored by Jonathan Crewe, is remarkable: it is one of socializing a fiction through circulating its medium, in both the narrative and the technological sense of the word.[37] Authority for the art of inventing an artificial person and authority for its dissemination through the mechanical arts of print go together: the "King of Pages" unfolds, in his own fiction, a counterfeit existence that is inseparable from what irony and parody can authorize this "grand printed Capitano," as he is "entombed" in a "stationer's stall." In this freewheeling location, Nashe's own author-function may well stand for those of Rabelais and Cervantes and the modes of appropriation that marked early modern fictions in general. The author's vulnerable property rights in a textual representation could be complemented by the reader's purchase of its printed form; but intellectual authority, as distinct from juridical ownership, presupposed a second appropriation. What pleasure and knowledge the text could be made to give was unthinkable without investing "imaginary puissance" (*Henry V* prol. 1, 25) in its reading, page by page.

Insofar as such "puissance" was available both to readers and to spectators, the Elizabethan playhouse had a special stake in its own kind of "loose disputation." As distinct from preachers, author-narrators, and printers, players and their playwrights were in a special position: they could negotiate the issue of authority in and through performance-games with textual representations. They could do so in direct address to their audience, where it seemed possible momentarily "to slip the anchor-hold of authority," to "digest the abuse of distance" and to appropriate so remote and "so great an object" as the fortunes of royalty (ibid.). Here (but that is a different book altogether),[38] to cope with the "distance" between "so great an object" in political historiography and its treatment on "these unworthy scaffolds" was, literally, as the prologue goes on to say, "to force a play."

The theatrical appropriation and representation of "so great an object" would, then, inevitably juxtapose two locations of authority, one residing in the 'worthy matter' of historiography, the other in its dramatic rewriting, production, and performance. "Bifold authority" (*Troilus and Cressida* 5.2.144), so deeply implicated in Protestant and fictional representation, would in the playhouse be foregrounded as a site where, vulnerably, the signs of power could come to life through the "imaginary puissance" of the signs themselves, those on stage and those in the grappling "minds" of the audience.

The drama is a special case in that the act of performance, the representing process in the theater, achieved a unique degree of visibility and materiality as sanctioned by whatever authority the cultural institution and the immediate response of audiences themselves possessed. But in this direction, in self-authorizing their work through the strength of their media, printers, preachers, interpreters, and author-narrators followed close behind. There was comparable growth in the performative register of their representations. As the area of contingency and (in)determinacy between representation and existence expanded, early modern discourse charted a space in which language and institution, the puissance of signs and the signs of power, became both hopelessly entangled and significant in their own right. This entanglement, which adumbrated (and yet concealed) writing's future claim on autonomy, provided what may well be the ultimate matrix of early modern cultural productivity. In late-Renaissance prose fiction but also, partially at least, in Reformation discourse, the engagement that is most vital (and that criticism has most consistently underprivileged) is that between represented signs and their representational function. It is the point of discord and interaction between world-picturing representations *in* the text and that text's cultural uses in the circumstantial world of actually achieved cultural transactions and appropriations.

I

Reformation Discord
in Authority

In sixteenth-century northern and central Europe, the Reformation brought with it profound and far-reaching changes in the conditions of discursive practice, realigning the relations, in the cultural history of reading and writing, between diverging and at least partially irreconcilable locations of authority. As Thomas Docherty notes, there emerged "a conflict between one mode of authority whose source is external, 'other-directed,' . . . and another mode which claims internal, self-directed authority"; and while the former based itself on "a power, sanctioned by tradition, to which one submitted," the latter implied "a power of instigation or innovation on the part of an individual capable of choice."[1] Such a reallocation of diverging types of authority must not of course be conceived of schematically; it is not reducible to a binary pattern of opposition between outward power and inward spirituality. However, the Reformation did bring to the fore vast and previously unknown contradictions between the enforceable authority of an ecclesiastical (and state) institution and such different types of authority as accrued to faith, conviction, knowledge, and the competent uses of interpretation, discourse, and scripture. These contradictions involved unprecedented gaps (as well as new links) between church and belief, institution and text, political rule and discursive practice.

The Reformation cannot be detached from social, political, and economic changes in sixteenth-century Europe. These formed a context of momentous cultural and technological transformations within which the rise of early modern conditions of authorizing discourse must be studied. In England, the various forces of change were particularly interactive. But to a remarkable extent, their interaction went hand in hand with new and unprecedented divisions in interest, power, and discursive practice. Indeed, the Reformation constituted, in the words of the British historian Joel Hurstfield, "in the profoundest sense a crisis of authority";[2] it served as a catalyst for a veritable explosion of "debate and discord."[3] Stimulating an unparalleled host of discursive activities, the Reformation helped vitalize a culture in which Protestantism and humanism entertained close and often fruitful ties. But unlike the received canon of Renaissance discourses and neoclassical doctrines, Protestantism in England was both more deeply divided in itself and a cause for division in ecclesiastical and political matters.

Even in its early decades, the English Reformation was anything but a unitary movement. The vexed and still unresolved question of whether the Reformation was primarily a popular movement or an act of state policy is symptomatic of its own historical ambivalence. What this question does address is an uncommonly large area of discontinuity between these two never quite congruous affiliations in the growth of English Protestantism. But whatever the answer, the indisputable sites of tension and division themselves are important in that they help constitute an unsuspected space for conflict and difference, a previously unreflected repertoire of diverging norms and contestatory choices in writing and thinking, reading and listening. Part of this diversity resulted from the spread of such discursive skills as made political, religious, and cultural issues accessible to an unprecedentedly large number of people. Sixteenth-century English culture, including the part of it that made possible the Elizabethan theater, was profoundly affected by this proliferation of "debate and discord." At its center was the issue of authority, which implied not simply a friction between various locations of legitimacy but the question of what, scripturally and for performance on stage and in the pulpit, could legitimately be authorized.[4]

At this point, the question of authorization addresses the power not only to relay or bring forth certain discourses but also to sanction, endorse, and justify their interpretation and dissemination. In the Reformation context, however, authorization itself was at issue. There was no longer a firmly fixed and officially sanctioned circuit in which texts were penned and distributed when important factors in the legitimation of discursive practice itself had become controversial. In these circumstances—and the Reformation multiplied them—the juxtaposition of "external, 'other-directed'" and "internal, self-directed" sites of authority, although undoubtedly useful, must be qualified. The dichotomy needs to be adapted to the untidy traffic between discourse and power and to a complex circulation of divergent locations of personal faith and cultural energy, intellectual puissance, and interpretive claims for validity. When preachers and biblical exegetes could avail themselves of the printing press, religious ideas and convictions were propelled into material forms that defied the great contingency in the flow of personal memory and oral tradition. Internalized faith, with the help of such external extensions of signs and contacts, might well be experienced as "self-directed" in its claims on validity. As a result, the hardly controllable assimilation of a "loose" but fervidly held semantic space must have created an unprecedented dynamic of its own.

This was especially the case when Protestantism in its radical form intervened in some of the more urgent issues emerging from the uneasy balance between the formation of a Tudor polity and the absence of unity and uniformity in the doctrinal and ecclesiastical platform of the post-Reformation church. Here, the burning questions asked among representatives of the church would engender a wide spectrum of engrossed responses among laypersons, even among those who stood or sat in the public theaters. Under these conditions, traditional boundaries among discourses would not prevent Protestant positions on authority from being inscribed and negotiated in contemporary poetry, drama, and fiction. To take the most obvious example, it must have been difficult for Shakespeare and his possible collaborator in *Henry VIII* not to address and assimilate conflicting moral, emotional, and political stances that could be found (and were surely articulated) outside the gates of the theater. As a result, the acknowledgment of more than one authority in argument and belief must have helped dramatically to negotiate the fall of Cardinal Wolsey, as in the dialogue between Katherine and Griffith (4.2.31–68). Similarly, the dramatic representation of a leading figure in the English Reformation, Cranmer, profited from being exposed to a twofold authority, as (in the language of a modern historian) he was led down "opposite paths by his dual loyalty to the supreme truth of Scripture and the supreme public authority of the monarch."[5]

Some of the previously unsuspected links between preaching and playing have only recently come to be recognized. As critics have suggested, throughout the 1560s the dramatic representation of Protestant positions "was sponsored and protected by all the traditional organizations responsible for producing drama"; what is more, the Royal Proclamation of 1559 ironically "may have helped to protect Protestant drama promoting national religious policy," since, according to Harold Gardiner, "the establishment of the law was an easy method by which authority could apparently disown an activity which it was in reality favouring."[6] As David Bevington has shown, this was part and parcel of a tradition reaching back to and beyond "the formative midcentury years," when "religious politics was virtually the whole substance of drama."[7] Nor was the theater's active involvement in religious and political affairs limited to the midcentury situation. Julia Gasper notes in her recent study of Thomas Dekker's plays that such involvement "was of course illegal, but it was also characteristic of the age"[8]—or at least of such drama as continued to be informed by a decidedly Protestant perspective. As the work of Margot Heinemann, Martin Butler, and Donna B. Hamilton suggests, it will no longer do to dismiss religious and political circumstances as only marginally relevant to English Renaissance theater.[9] On the contrary, as Paul W. White argues in *Theatre and Reformation*, there was, at least before the breakup of "the pro-drama consensus," an unorganized type of "alliance between the drama and Protestantism." Until around 1580, when commercial orientation became central, this alliance could draw on "a nationwide system of Protestant patronage" to the effect that the drama, "involved in the dissemination of Protestantism," did not merely convey but (to an extent that needs to be examined) "shape[d] Protestant beliefs, attitudes, and modes of thought in Tudor England."[10]

The language of Protestantism has recently come to be documented in Elizabethan and Jacobean drama; it seems only consistent to look for a similar space of interaction between Protestant discourse and early modern prose fiction. Again, the point here is not to argue for some sort of influence but to explore what stimulating grounds there were for an alliance between representation and the "redemption of the world" through interpretation. The question here is not what impact the Protestant redefinition of authority had on contemporary fiction but, rather, how the redistribution of authority and its expanding circulation among writing, reading, and interpreting changed fundamental premises in both types of discourse. If there was an "interpretive imperative" (Lambropoulos's phrase) in both discourses, then the issue is what common ground there was for circulating authority beyond the preordained space for traditionally sanctioned questions and answers. The expansion of the area of a self-directed type of validating activity must in each case have been conducive to a reallocation of means and sources of such intellectual and emotional empowerment as would help authorize untapped uses of language and imagination.[11]

According to this approach, recent revisions in the relationship between drama and Protestantism are of signal importance, especially where they have produced evidence of Shakespeare "incorporating the idioms of Protestant polemical discourse in his plays."[12] As Thomas Nashe's *Unfortunate Traveller* witnesses, the same incorporation can be traced in Elizabethan fiction. Here too we have an unfolding alliance for representation and interpretation that, for printers, players, and preachers, just as for author-narrators, presupposes the loosening of the "anchor-hold" of traditional authority and, simultaneously, a redistribution of self-fashioned competence and capacity for unsanctioned uses of signs and meanings. Early modern fiction, like Reformation discourse, greatly contributed to the project. In doing so, language and institution, textual authority and performative agency, engaged in a new, more deeply divided and dynamic interaction, one that greatly stimulated the unique cultural productivity of the time. Not fortuitously, early modern England produced a vital and articulate setting within which traditional versions of authority could be intercepted by or subjected to the "imaginary puissance" (and empowerment) of the writer's, reader's, and interpreter's conscience.

The Reformation context, then, is one in which issues of spiritual "truth," political power, and imaginary "puissance" consistently interlock and interfere with one another. These areas of mutual interrogation are at the heart of the formation of an early modern culture in large parts of Europe. To attempt to view together the divergent locations of authority, the emerging functions of authorship, and the authorization (or censorship) of public uses of discourse is a formidable undertaking—especially when the context cannot be defined as an exclusively national one. As A. G. Dickens has noted, "nothing could be much more international in character than the foundations of the English Reformation."[13] As the Reformation spread from Germany to Geneva and throughout northern and northwestern Europe, the most hallowed and central locations of authority were first challenged, not in England, but in Wittenberg, Zurich, and Geneva. What the Continental reformers almost unanimously rejected was the traditional claim of the old church to the authorization of the biblical text in its administration, interpretation, and reception. Radically redefining the relation of church and Scripture, Luther, Zwingli, and Calvin all argued for a church that found its true function in serving the knowledge of Scripture rather than vice versa—that the biblical text should be a function of the church (in the sense that its meaning was to be determined and administered by an allegedly infallible council or papacy). As Protestant divines and laypersons began to dispute previously unquestioned ways of administering grace and truth and of wielding power; as the formerly infallible institution of the papacy and the rule of cardinals, bishops, and priests began to totter; and as the immense power of the confessional began to crumble, the most basic levels of religious legitimation shifted away from the collective bodies and the institutionalized rituals of the church. Throughout Protestant Europe, an altogether new emphasis fell on the reading and reception of Scripture, on the translation and interpretation of the biblical text as the supreme locus of the highest spiritual authority.

1

A Protestant Author-Function
Luther

Martin Luther's early-Reformation pamphlet, *To the Christian Nobility of the German Nation* (1520), reveals the new Protestant author-function almost at its inception. Here, a distinctly self-authorized activity manifests itself in terms of a proud, if precarious, performative mingled with a strangely groping rhetoric of something akin to embarrassment and apology. Although Luther, even before his appearance at the Worms parliament, was to publish ninety-one titles in some seven hundred editions,[1] he felt compelled, only a year before Worms, to associate his own pamphlet with the newly perceived need to open up public discussion and textual communication. As the opening sentence of the preface suggests, "the time for silence is past, and the time to speak [die Zeit zureden] has come" (44:123).[2] With the rapid increase in the public reception of printed texts on the one hand and his feverish literary productivity on the other, Luther could identify the uses of his own authorship in reference to a public demand for an end to silence and the nascent discussion of matters of great consequence, ecclesiastical as well as secular. The rapidly changing conditions, at the beginning of the Reformation, in political action and textual communication were so inscribed in Luther's writing that his own discursive practice may be seen as propelled by its consonance with a public demand for articulation.

At this stage, Luther's idea of his own author-function was not yet definitely divorced from his previous position as a cleric of the Roman church. This is why his appeal, in the vernacular, to a secular, national audience involved, as he understood it, the articulation of a submerged conflict between social propriety and political necessity. The most important question now, he says, is whether "God may help His church through the laity, since the clergy, to whom this task more properly belongs, have grown quite indifferent" (44:123). In other words, the Roman church, having failed to reform itself from within, must surrender its previously held monopoly on the authorization of reform activity in ecclesiastical affairs. It is noteworthy that Luther, an ordinary cleric and professor of theology, felt called upon to delegate authority for spiritual and political action to forces that, in matters of ecclesiastical polity, had never been publicly authorized to act against the highest religious office and council in Christendom. But Luther, in providing evangelical legitimation for secular action in the church's affairs, at the same time undertook a self-authorization of his authorship when he claimed that "all Christians are of truly spiritual estate, and there is no difference among them except that of office" [alle Christen sein warhafftig geistichs stands unnd ist unter ihn kein unterscheid denn des amts halben allein] (44:127; 6:407). Since every Christian layperson is in close and direct contact with divinity, the institutionalized monopoly of the church on the reading and understanding of Scripture was radically put into question. Positively speaking, every Christian, every layperson, every ordinary cleric thenceforth might feel authorized to address "such high and great estates" as the Christian nobility of the German nation in order to offer good advice in affairs of great moment (44:123).

Thus the Reformation crisis of ecclesiastical authority had already begun to affect the presuppositions on which writing as an officially uncontrolled act of public communication could base itself. In challenging the sacred authority of the almighty papal church, Luther's new mode of legitimation was all the more consequential in that he acted on his own initiative, without having been commissioned by any authority other than that residing in his conscience. Defying the major institutionalized source of clerical authority, Luther had to look elsewhere for friends and allies. But in the crucial year 1520, the rejection of papal authority had not yet been followed by the commissioning of any new secular authority; furthermore, assurances of support, on the part of the German nobility, involved yet another act of defiance against the imperial crown of the Habsburgs. In this situation, the pressure on Luther's self-authorized performance in writing must have been enormous. Indeed, as he half-addresses and half-creates his audience, the burden of his newly assumed representativity is so great,[3] the unconfirmed authority so precarious, that it tangibly affects his performance, making his utterance sound tentative, self-conscious, and defensive, as perhaps never before or after:

> I know full well that I shall not escape the charge of presumption because I, a despised and inferior person [ich vorachter, begebner mensch (6:404)], ventured to address such high and great estates on such weighty matters, as if there were nobody else in the world except Doctor Luther to take up the cause of the Christian estate [der sich des Christlichen stands annehme (6:404)] and give advice to such high-ranking people. (44:123)

What follows is both an apology for and an assertion of pride in this new author-function, a function that clearly transcends all traditional norms of legitimating the production and circulation of printed texts in the vernacular. But as the defiant assumption of the writer's authority involves a break with the norms of both clerical and secular subordination, the twofold burden on Luther's pen becomes so heavy that the author, son of generations of peasants, takes refuge in a remarkable figure: he uses the persona of the fool, with its pagan relics of coxcomb and motley, so as to be able to persist, through what he portrays as his foolish arrogance, in overreaching his social station:

> Perhaps I owe my God and the world another work of folly. I intend to pay my debt honestly. And if I succeed, I shall for the time being become a court jester [unnd auch ein mal hoffnar werden (6:404)]. And if I fail, I still have one advantage—no one need buy me a cap or put the bells on me. I must fulfill the proverb, "Whatever the world does, a monk must be in the picture, even if he has to be painted in." More than once a fool has spoken wisely, and wise men have often been arrant fools. Paul says, "He who wishes to be wise must become a fool" (1 Cor. 3:18). Moreover since I am not only a fool, but also a sworn doctor of

Holy Scripture [dieweyl ich nit allein ein narr, sondern auch ein geschworner Doctor der heyligenn schrifft (6:404)], I am glad for the opportunity to fulfill my doctor's oath, even in the guise of a fool. (44:123–24)

Few other figures of speech could have conveyed the same strange mixture of license and fear, defiance and self-consciousness, that went into the self-understanding of this new author-function. In his use of the fool topos, Luther projects into the text an outsider's position in society, an intellectual station of precarious independence from at least some of the dominant secular and clerical forms of institutionalized power.

Here, indeed, we may watch what Stephen Greenblatt has called "the fashioning of the Protestant discourse of self out of conflicting impulses: rage against authority and identification with authority, hatred of the father and an ardent longing for union with the father, confidence in oneself and an anxious sense of weakness and sinfulness, justification and guilt."[4] Luther's inherently antiauthoritarian stance is fortified by recourse to divergent types of authority—here, for example, those of St. Paul and of the common proverb. The proverb, as Natalie Z. Davis has shown, may be assumed to be close to an oral tradition of popular utterance, especially when there is reason to assume a theatrical context.[5] Hence, there is a wide gap between the institutionalized sources of authority—which Luther defied—and the ones on which his vernacular writing throve. For one thing, both the imagery of the fool, with its playful signs of irresponsibility, and his proverbial language were related to a more common mode of authorization located outside the ken of clerical learning and tradition.

Thus, at an early stage in Reformation writing, the ways of legitimation through representation had changed. The Protestant effect of legitimation no longer drew its strength from representation as a delegated act of institutionalized power and homogeneity, where authority was affirmed as something given even before the particular acts of writing, thinking, or reading began. Rather than following predetermined functions of representativity, such as those in the discursive practice of papal annunciations or the cardinals' council of the Roman church, the reformer's mode of authorizing a text, especially in the early phases of the Reformation, involved a different strategy, one that involved elements of indeterminacy, as well as incertitude, between the signifying and the signified levels of representation. It is in filling this distance with a type of discursive activity that was not preordained that Luther's use of the topos of the fool is so revealing: the figure of the fool in sixteenth-century writing, so conspicuous in Brant, Erasmus, Rabelais, Fischart, and Shakespeare, becomes important precisely because this topos was useful in figuring forth the vulnerability of the process of representation itself. And although in later years Luther's own reentry into orthodoxy at least in part attempted to cope with contiguous areas of indeterminacy, the uncertainty could be dispelled only marginally.

The manifestations of this vulnerability in the representational uses of language were not confined to the incidental use of the figure of the fool; rather, Luther's experimental and innovative use of a vernacular whose received written standard he substantially helped to bring forth was a correlative of the attempt to cope with a larger crisis in the traditional order of things. What was central to the issue of authority in Luther's early-Reformation texts was the ambivalence in his treatment of what the reformer called *selige Aufruhr*—the soul's "spiritual rebellion."[6] This Protestant idea of the compatibility of political subordination and spiritual freedom is fundamental to the Lutheran (though not entirely to the Calvinistic) position. Subordination to the state and freedom of the soul go together to such an extent that the hardness of things political is either ignored or compensated for by a new kind of *Innerlichkeit*, or interiority, according to which "a man is abundantly and sufficiently justified by faith inwardly" (31:358). As Luther asserts in *The Freedom of a Christian*, it is through faith that "we are all equally priests" [wir wol alle gleych priester seyn] (31:356; 7:28). And again: "we are also priests forever, which is far more excellent than being kings" (31:355). He who believes, and has faith within his soul, "is through his kingdom capable of all things, through his priesthood he is powerful in God" [durch seyn künigreych ist er aller ding mechtig, durch sein priesterthum ist er gottis mechtig] (31:355; 7:28]).

In the sixteenth century, however, the emergence of such an interiorized intellectual mode of self-justification was relatively new, and it is surely not fortuitous that, only three years later, Luther felt called upon to publish his *Temporal Authority: To What Extent It Should Be Obeyed*. Starting from the observation that his previous advice to the nobility remained largely unheeded, he noted, "I must change my tactics and write them, this time, what they should omit and not do" (45:83). In other words, by qualifying the grounds of secular authority, Luther now proposed more positively to assert the new evangelical "freedom of a Christian" to which the spiritual sources of his own authority, tied as they were to the revealed word and will of God, were indissolubly linked. Because the mighty nobility "will continue to be princes and never become Christians" (45:83) and since, even worse, "they are . . . presumptuously . . . lording it over men's consciences and faith, and schooling the Holy Spirit according to their own crackbrained ideas" (45:84), and also because "it has gone so far that the rulers have begun ordering the people to get rid of certain [that is, Luther's] books," Luther announced his determination "to resist them, at least with words" (45:85).

Although Luther remained quite unambiguous in his proposition that "we must provide a sound basis for the civil law and sword" (45:85), "the limits of temporal authority" [wie fern welltlich gewallt sich streckt] (45:118; 11:271) now emerged more clearly. According to Scripture, "perfection and imperfection do not consist in works, and do not establish any distinct external order among Christians. They exist in the heart, in faith and love" [steht ym hertzen, ym glawben und liebe] (45:88; 11:249). And no matter "how violently they [princes and bishops] rage," "the heart they cannot compel" [das hertz mügen sie ja nicht zwingen] (45:108; 11:264). No man-made law, then, may be imposed upon the spirit; there is no secular authority that "shall or can command the soul" (45:106). Because "every man runs his own risk in believing as he does," and because "how he believes or disbelieves is a matter for the conscience of each individual" [weyl es denn eym iglichen auff seym gewissen ligt, wie er glewbt odder nicht glewbt] (45:108; 11:264), the nature of spiritual authority is projected inward. And because "it is futile and impossible to command or compel anyone by force to believe this or that" (45:107), the autonomy of the individual conscience tends to limit the authority of "force" and power. Although "the governing authority [der oberkeyt] must not be resisted by force, but only by confession [bekentnis] of the truth," the limits of temporal authority (*welltlich gewallt*) are to be found at the point where authority of force gives way to "the assertion of truth" [bekentnis der warheyt] (45:124; 11:277). Even more crucially, authorities both secular and spiritual are expected to submit to the same test of "truth" that, even when it is inner-directed, does not preclude empirical verification. In the words of Luther, "we cannot conceive how an authority could or should act in a situation except where it can see, know, judge, condemn, change and modify" (45:107).

At this point, the semantic contours of *oberkeit* or *welltlich gewallt* (worldly power) begin to be drawn more sharply through their differential relation to *erkentnisz* and *vorhor*—knowledge and judgment—and "the heart." The concomitant complications in the semantic field of authority, however, are never actually formulated; at best they are adumbrated in the altogether binary and largely oppositional notions of the two kingdoms and the two regiments. This doctrine of the *Zwei Reiche* goes back to the strong element of dualism in Luther's theology, according to which every Christian has two natures, resulting from two relationships: he or she exists in a spiritual relationship to God through Christ and, during his or her lifetime, as a temporal creature in the flesh, in relation to other people. In these two rival natures or kingdoms, the *regnum dei* and the *regnum mundi*, Luther distinguishes two divine orders of government that God has instituted for mankind: the kingdom of heaven (and the order of the Word), and the temporal order in which men and women live out their earthly existence.[7]

Although the uses of secular power—or, as Luther tends to call it, "the sword"—are clearly of this world (which, as *regnum diaboli*, is a fallen one), they are also of divine institution. Since the two kingdoms are radically distinct but also parallel manifestations of one heavenly design, the corresponding locations of authority, although different, overlap. As a matter of course there is only one ultimate authority, the Word as revealed in Scripture, but there are also various forms of secular authority. Insofar as these—in line with Luther's own intensely worldly experience in Wittenberg, Worms, and the Wartburg—tend to be inscribed together with his own author-function, the nascent differentiation emerges as latent where a secular context intervenes in the Protestant uses of the Word. But such interception of Scripture in *regnum mundi* is of little consequence for any differentiation among secular locations of authority: although Luther, by using *gewallt* in the sense of *potestas* (as force, or even violence), does emphasize the more external uses of power, including its punitive and repressive functions, these for him would remain perfectly reconcilable with his notion of governing or administrative authority (or those *in* authority), for which in most cases the German term *Oberkeit* or *die Oberen* is used.

It is the absence of any effective distinction between *potestas* and *auctoritas*, then, that marks the semantic space into which a new dimension of communicative energy is unleashed by the reformer: to say "the heart they cannot compel," and to postulate that "the assertion of truth" is impervious to the constraint of either *gewallt* or *oberkeit*, points to a remarkable complication and differentiation in the signification of authority on the threshold of the two rival kingdoms. Here, the semantic structure of *auctoritas* begins to engage, and even to qualify, certain connotations of *potestas*. True enough, the latter must not be resisted; but the use of this power by any particular institution is measured by parameters that are inseparable from the Lutheran sense of justification by faith through the interiorized knowledge of the Word. Luther's emphasis on the capacity to "see, know, judge, condemn, change and modify" remains a measure of discursive action that neither secular authorities nor the evangelical church could entirely do without.

There was one major area of his activities where "authority," including the authorization of his own writing, had become particularly indivisible from judgment, study, and knowledge. In his letter on translation (*Sendbrief vom Dolmetschen*, 1530), Luther's sense of his own authorship appears remarkably assured; having in the meantime reaped abundant public acknowledgment as the greatest Protestant authority on the translation of the Bible, Luther's own triumphant sense of self-legitimation is obvious on every page. Here we find a self-confident voice that, far from having scruples about its own legitimacy, challenges the "useless braying" [unnütze geplerre] of his Catholic critics: "Luther will have it so, and says that he is a doctor above all the doctors of the whole papacy" (35:187; 30.2:635–36). Self-consciousness is almost turned into arrogance; if his metaphors of triumph sound deeper than that, it is because his imagery retains the sensuous, open-air quality of hard, physical *work*: "The plowing goes well when the field is cleared. But rooting out the woods and stumps, and getting the field ready—this is a job nobody wants" (35:188). The newly assured sense of direction is based on the self-made authority of a successfully accomplished piece of work. "I have learned by experience [das hab ich wol erfaren] what an art and what a task translating is. Therefore I will tolerate no papal ass or mule to be my judge or critic, for they have never tried it" (35:193; 30.2:639).

The new authority clearly has a lot to do with the writer's self-legitimating ability to "see, know, judge, condemn, change and modify." When we consider the points of intersection between the spiritual and the purely intellectual (not to mention political) aspects of authority involved in the production and circulation of biblical readings in the vernacular, the cultural impact of this self-legitimation appears highly significant as well as complex. Even more than his previous acts of self-justification, the words of Luther the translator appear to set a pattern of legitimizing public discourses in early modern history. The Roman church's fervently upheld monopoly on the authorization of biblical exegesis is replaced by Luther's "faith," exercising the power of its own "liberty" and sovereignty in the translatable letter and the evangelical spirit of Scripture.

This Protestant mode of self-authorization involved radically different standards of "knowledge of the truth." For all its emphasis on faith and inwardness, it inevitably brought forth an increased amount of discussion and debate. This discursive practice resulted from the newly sanctioned circulation and reception of the Protestant Bible, which after its translation into the vernacular called for a mode of reading that presupposed and at the same time promoted a more subjective range of understanding. In the crucial years around 1525, which marked the climax of the German peasant revolt, the previous monopoly of the church on the exegesis of Scripture exploded into every Protestant's freedom to write, read, and think about the Bible. The new evangelical sources of spiritual authority were dissociated from office, ritual, and confessional. They were planted "in the heart, in faith and love": Protestant access to the biblical text was inseparable from new and interactive levels of emotional, intellectual, and political activity.

While the new availability of this text vastly increased both the number of its readers and the spectrum of its interpretations, the new concept of authority, residing in the spirit and the letter of the text itself, was associated not with inspiration, nor with the sectarian cause of enthusiasm, but with the deepest intellectual grasp of biblical meaning.[8] Luther's own words, written in his pamphlet of 1520, anticipate a major element in the future uses of intellectual authority: "Moreover, many times have I offered my writing to stand for knowledge and interrogation" [Auch hab ich mein schreyben viel mal auff erkentnisz und vorhor erbotten] (my translation [cf. 44:217]; 6:469). His statement points to the semantic range of *authority* as comprising knowledge and interrogation, through which writing comes to authorize itself as a public agency of intellectual activity and self-projection.

This still says little about the multiple uses of the new authority in representation. Luther's language may provide us with some tentative clues, however. The self-conscious use of the fool topos and the metaphors of labor point in the direction of a new and larger space for the inscription of spiritual, emotional, and cultural activities hitherto unrepresented in vernacular writings. Equally crucially, the representation of such activities appears to go hand in hand with new and dynamic uses of difference in the language of the Protestant conscience. Unlike the hierarchy of Thomistic thought, where the temporal world was a preliminary and preparatory stage to the heavenly order of divinity, the two worlds represent for Luther not so much a sequence as a ubiquitous parallel or even a site of permanent struggle and irretrievable bifurcation. For the German reformer there is friction as well as potential confusion between the two kingdoms, and the *confusio regnorum* between them always and everywhere threatens chaos.

Thus, the Protestant world from its inception was one of tension, division, and dualism. There was significant discord between what men and women were surrounded by and what, through discipline, conscience, and appropriation, they could hope to achieve. To cross the invisible threshold and go beyond the *regnum mundi et diaboli* was to assimilate and appropriate the true Christian meaning of the Word. For this, pious listening and reading and faithful interpretation were essential components of the indefatigable endeavor to make the sacred text one's own.

It was through such an endeavor, rather than through ordination, that Luther (to be followed by Calvin and other early reformers) felt authorized to speak out. But despite the extraordinary achievements of the reformers, their success was marked by an element of contingency and unpredictability. The grounds of authority in their representations remained more vulnerable than anything in the old church. One way for Luther to cope with the discordant state of his newly achieved authority was to convey the strength of his faith through an uncommon energy informing the semiology of appropriation and (self-)authorization. As distinct from medieval and humanist uses of Latin, Luther's language—retaining an oral dimension of performance and delivery—achieves an articulateness that is inseparable from an early modern capacity for both widening and bridging the gulf between representation and existence.

2

The Spirit betwixt Polity and Scripture

Calvin

Protestantism in Jean Calvin's Geneva presents us with a context different from Luther's for the changing conditions of writing and reading in the Reformation. Here the relationship between "internal" and "external" locations of power, justice, and legitimacy appeared far more dynamic and interactive; the Lutheran gulf between ecclesiastical doctrine and secular polity was narrowed remarkably. There was a sense of interconnection, unknown to the German Reformation, between political and religious practices. In contrast to Luther's remoteness from the centers of feudal and imperial power in Germany, the cause of the Reformation in Geneva was inseparable from that of the safety and viability of the *chose publique*. Here, the affirmed line of distinction between church and state involved cooperation rather than indifference or hostility.[1] Although "Christ's spiritual Kingdom and the civil jurisdiction are things completely distinct . . . we must know that they are not at variance" (1486–87). This confirms the need for "a public manifestation of religion . . . among Christians" (1488). Hence, the magistrates as legates are not called upon to "lay aside their authority and return to private life, but submit to Christ the power with which they have been invested" (1490).[2]

The ministers of the Genevan church, although strictly organized, formed no elaborate hierarchy: like the magistrates, they were all officeholders. The elective manner of their appointment did not reflect any sovereignty on the part of the electors, but rather their common subordination to God. Neither political nor ecclesiastical authority was thus highly personalized. The reformed pastor was expected to excel in his conduct, his knowledge, his capacity for preaching, and his ability to inspire devotion in others. Sharing with his fellows in their corporate guardianship of the ways of the faithful, the pastor followed the consistory of six ministers and twelve elders, who recognized no need for a bishop. But any resistance to the authority of the consistory was simultaneously a resistance to the authority of the government. Calvinism was the creed of the state; to challenge it was to defy the law and to incur the charge of treasonable conduct. Calvin's writings from at least 1542 onward reveal an attempt to establish some degree of "homology between the order of ecclesiastical and of civil polity"; in fact, the "apex" of his idea of a Christian commonwealth was "the twofold regime of magistrates and ministers."[3]

In these circumstances, it must come as a surprise that Calvin's language of authority only partially reflects the situation of the foremost Protestant regime at the time. Although deeply immersed in humanist studies, the reformer at first sight seems close to Luther when, in his use of Latin and French, there is a distinctly traditional, medieval refusal to differentiate between *potestas* and *auctoritas*. In the last chapter of his main work, for instance, *potestas* stands not for imperial might and authority, but for that of the church, while "civil government" is rendered as *administratio*.[4] There is an undifferentiated connotation of legitimacy in his uses of both *potestas* and *autoritas* (*sic*), as well as in his signification of *imperium* or even *dominatio*. In this, the final Latin version of 1559 anticipates the equally authentic French version of 1560, which, for all the discrepancies between them, likewise fails properly to differentiate the semantic field marked by *puissance* and *authorité* as well as, again, by *domination*.[5] Calvin's language, like Luther's, in its lexical order clearly precedes (even while it helps bring about) modern differentiations among sociocultural locations of authority.

However, if Calvin's vocabulary is deceptive in not mapping out the expanding semantic space of "authority," the structure of his argument is decidedly unambiguous. Even though he follows Luther in emphasizing the right of governors to expect obedience, citing familiar biblical precedents (above all, Rom. 13), the conceptualization of authority in its publicly verifiable and visible implications is spread out wide on the lexical coordinates of civil order, such as *civitas, magistratus,* and *administratio,* and related terms such as *ordinatio, gubernatio,* and *respublica.* Again, these by and large correspond to Calvin's uses of *chose publique, république,* and *ordonnance.*[6] But while neither contemporary French nor German had any word to render adequately the semantic contours of the nascent nation-state, owing to its Latin roots Calvin's language confronted less severe impediments than did Luther's vernacular in coming to terms with the ongoing differentiations among the traditional locations of authority.

It would thus have been unthinkable for Luther to develop a concept that, in Calvin's approach to authority, came almost as a matter of course: for the Frenchman to think of a Protestant Christian 'polity' was possible, once such *politia* or *civitas* could be conceived of as structured by a twofold type of officeholding authority, embracing the ministry of both political magistrates and evangelical pastors. Once church and state could be viewed as equally deriving their ultimate legitimacy from a divine instance identical with God, the claims of the old church could be exposed in their arrogance. According to Calvin, no church was exempt from the derivative quality of the authority of *civitas* (or *administratio*) and *ecclesia* alike. For Calvin, the secular magistrate no less than the religious pastor was a lieutenant, in the full sense of "placeholder." These *vicari* were to serve and fulfill their duty to God either through church or through commonwealth. Hence, a Calvinist keyword like *ministerium* was, in its connotations of office qua authority, considerably more encompassing and less divided than anything Luther, with his duality of sword and soul, had at his disposal.

There is little doubt that Calvin sought to intertwine *ecclesia* and *politia* in terms of their respective locations of authority. As Harro Höpfl notes in his magisterial study *The Christian Polity of John Calvin*, the reformer's "very choice of language . . . points to the conclusion that he recognized himself as engaged in a labour of diminishing the distance between the office of magistracy and the minds and hearts of the godly."[7] In fact, it is possible to say that he sought "to resacralize the magistracy by investing it with a dignity commensurate with so elevated a position in the divine economy." Thus, he chose the term *administratio* so as "to exploit the connotation of 'ministry' implicitly in the term"; he referred to the magistracy as a *sacrum ministerium*. Simultaneously, he went out of his way to associate the pastors of the church with the language of secular authority, employing a terminology originally used "to designate the relationship between a Roman emperor and his agents": the subordination of ministers to their "Sovereign" was conveyed by reference to their *mandatum*, by which, acting as delegates (*legatione fungantur*), they represented God's person and *imperium*.[8]

Since the Lutheran chasm between *spiritus* and *politia* was unknown in Geneva, the Calvinistic comprehension of authority stood a much greater chance of success in a controlled politicization of its Reformation project. Here Protestant notions of relations of power, Scripture, and legitimacy were relieved of some of their more insidious antinomies—only to confront a potentially even more massive contradiction in the mediation of authority itself. For if the Genevan administrators were considered "the vicars of God," and their judgments were "appointed an instrument of divine truth" (1491), how were they to relate to the vicarious claims of the ecclesiastical sphere as put forth by Calvin himself?

This was not a purely theoretical question. In the late 1530s, "the evangelical ministers of Geneva . . . were little more than civil servants" themselves; their positions—Pierre Viret's, Guillaume Farel's, and also Calvin's—could be described as "exceptionally vulnerable to shifts in political alliances within the city."[9] As Farel's and Calvin's expulsion from the city in 1538 would confirm, it was the city council that controlled religious affairs in Geneva. Calvin's return in 1541 was far from an unmitigated triumph; in the late 1540s the council again became quite hostile to him, and at least until the mid-1550s he did not receive any decisive support within the power structure of the city.

Since issues of political power themselves were a formative element in the Genevan Reformation, the question of authority had to be searchingly renegotiated between the city-state and the reformed church. As long as both sides subscribed to the Word of God as the ultimate source of authority, it was out of the question for any secular authority to be thought of (as Luther conceived of the German feudal overlords) as categorically distinct from the true source of faith and Christian righteousness. Narrowing the Lutheran division between worldly power and heavenly truth, Calvin nevertheless considered the Genevan city-state an independent institution. He was careful not to seek any office in it; in fact, he did not even become a citizen of Geneva until 1559.[10]

Calvin's attempt to reconcile political and ecclesiastical locations of authority took as its point of departure the notion that any purely "external" authority by itself was untenable, and that both state and church had to accommodate themselves to this condition. The only true and lasting authority was scriptural, and not—as the Romanists had it—ecclesiastical. The Word of God was traceable in the Bible only; because the visible, readable text of Scripture itself contained the ultimate answer to the question of authority, the role of the church must be a subservient (though crucial) one.

On this issue, Calvin's conviction was expressed in no uncertain terms. In the title of chapter 7 of book 1, the reader is told that "Scripture [and] its authority (may) be established as certain [ut certa constet eius authoritas]; and it is a wicked falsehood that its credibility depends on the judgement of the Church [impium esse commentum, fidem eius pendere ab Ecclesiae iudicio]" (74; 3:65). This polemical emphasis is sustained throughout the *Institutes*; it is explained at some length not only in book 1 but even more fully in book 4 (especially in chapter 8). Taking as his premise the idea that "the church is itself grounded upon Scripture" (74),[11] Calvin proceeds to trace the handing down of scriptural authority to "the prophets and apostles."

He condemns the "wranglers" who question the divine authenticity of the received canon by arguing "that Scripture has only so much weight as is conceded to it by the consent of the church." But here Calvin refers to the word of St. Paul himself:

> He testifies that the church is "built upon the foundation of the prophets and apostles" [Eph. 2.20]. If the teaching of the prophets and apostles is the foundation, this must have had authority before the church began to exist. Groundless, too, is their [the wranglers'] subtle objection that, although the church took its beginning here, the writings to be attributed to the prophets and apostles nevertheless remain in doubt until decided by the church. For if the Christian church was from the beginning founded upon the writings of the prophets and the preaching of the apostles, wherever this doctrine is found, the acceptance of it—without which the church itself would never have existed—must certainly have preceded the church. It is utterly vain, then, to pretend that the power of judging Scripture so lies with the church that its certainty depends upon churchly assent. [Vanissimum est igitur commentum, Scripturae iudicandae potestam esse penes Ecclesiam: ut ab huius nutu illius certitudo pendere intelligatur] (75–76; 3:66)

Again, the church is close to and resembles the state in the derivative nature of whatever authority each in its different provinces possesses; neither can possess the more decisive authority for judging the authenticity (*certitudo*) of Scripture. But if the church does not have such "Scripturae iudicandae potestam," where does such authority (or *potestas*) reside? What instance can authorize the mediating and determining link between authority's external locations in political and ecclesiastical institutions and its definitive source in the divinely revealed Word?

At this juncture, Calvin committed himself to a finished revelation in its necessarily textualized form. To all intents and purposes there was an unambiguous fountain of divine truth which, issuing from "the writing of the prophets and the preaching of the apostles," must "certainly have preceded the church." But the prophets and apostles in their turn had submitted to the external circumstances of their "writing" and their "preaching." They were inspired mouthpieces or, as Calvin (in his sober manner) wrote, "reliable and authentic amanuenses of the Holy Spirit" [certi et authentici Spiritus sancti amenuenses] (5:141). Their knowledge, at any rate, was derived from a deeper source of truth that was even at this late date accessible as an "inward" instance of guidance. "Those whom the Holy Spirit has inwardly taught truly rest upon Scripture [quos Spiritus sanctus intus docuit, solide acquiescere in Scripturae (3:70)], and that Scripture indeed is self-authenticated; hence it is not right to subject it to proof and reasoning" (80). If the "credibility" of doctrine is not established until we are persuaded beyond doubt that "God is its Author" (78), the prophets and apostles can, with the help of the Spirit, be believed. But at this point Calvin seems unable to make up his mind: on the one hand, there is the inward guidance, the inspiration and certification of the Spirit; on the other hand, scriptural truth as such is self-evident: "Indeed, Scripture exhibits fully as clear evidence of its own truth [veritatis suae sensum ultro Scripturae prae se fert (3:66)] as white and black things do of their color, or sweet and bitter things do of their taste" (76).

Understandably, Calvin is not content to leave the question of mediation at the level of such metaphoric intimations. In order to "see manifest signs of God speaking in Scripture," Calvin addresses and revises the nature of Protestant faith by qualifying (and, to a certain extent, externalizing) Luther's own somewhat unspecified vessel of mediation, that of each Christian believer's "soul." In *Freedom of a Christian*, Luther repeatedly referred to the "soul" and the "heart" as perfectly legitimate, self-authenticating receptacles of divine grace, valid locations for the genuine faith and belief in Scripture. But in Geneva in the 1540s and 1550s, every officeholder must have known that this had come close to the strategy of the Anabaptists: discarding the idea of a finished revelation and resorting to each believer's soul as the unquestioned organ of unending self-authorization. Calvin could not ignore the dire consequences of this strategy. Rather than trusting some such (all too readily available) purely internal medium of legitimation, he put forward, as the supreme criterion of divine truth, a much less accessible "secret" testimony, that of the Holy Spirit.

Calvin's doctrine of the Holy Spirit as guarantor of the truth of Scripture is one of the most resolute, if desperate, attempts to come to terms with the issue of authority in the Reformation. It is highly significant in that it culminates in the endeavor to close the gaps in authority between letter and spirit, external institution and internal truth.

Calvin confronts the issue most squarely in book 4, chapter 8, sections 3–4, in direct reference to "the doctrinal authority of the prophets [and] the apostles." Here he finally commits himself to the "Scriptural foundation of the Word of God" and its incarnation in Jesus Christ through whom "the Word became flesh" (1153–54). Emphasizing the "unity and multiplicity of revelation," Calvin is careful to disown it, after the advent of Christ, as an ongoing source of authority:

> For Paul means, in fact, openly declares, that God will not speak hereafter as he did before, intermittently through some and through others; nor will he add prophecies to prophecies, revelations to revelations. Rather, he has so fulfilled all functions of teaching in his Son that we must regard this as the final and eternal testimony from him [ut hoc ultimum aeternumque ab eo habendum sit testimonium (5:139)] (1154–55)

Hereafter, then, "the mouths of all men should be closed when once he has spoken" (1155). The closure of revelation affects all claims of doctrinal infallibility apart from the Word: "not even the apostles were free to go beyond the Word, much less their successors" (1156). Thus the church, far from being infallible, cannot by itself sanction doctrine, not even through an appeal to the presence of Christ.

Calvin here fights a battle on two fronts, against the old church and against those who uphold revelation as unfinished. Carefully differentiating between "true and false councils," he is skeptical of the Romish authority of conciliar decisions, since most of these departed from Scripture (1166–71). Yet he is no less severe about the practice of "fanatics, abandoning Scripture and flying over to Revelation." His impatience with the latter is understandable, because these men "wrongly appeal to the Holy Spirit" (93)—that is, to that most sanctioned medium of divine authority, to which Calvin himself had appealed. For the Genevan reformer to appeal to the Holy Spirit was to make the Spirit's "testimony" serve as the firm link connecting the absolute authority of the Word and the contingent circumstances of its reception.

With the help of this fine differentiation, the Spirit is to be "both 'seal' and 'guarantee' (2 Cor. 1:22)" (80): it bears the "seal" against unauthorized appropriations of the Word of divinity and therewith serves as a "guarantee" of its authoritative reception, "sealing" the reproduction of the Word in this world. The Spirit, so understood, was on the lips of the prophets and in the pens of the apostles and, in our own time, must again be present so as to "penetrate into our hearts":

> The testimony of the Spirit is more excellent than all reason. For as God alone is a fit witness of himself in his Word, so also the Word will not find acceptance in men's hearts before it is sealed by the inward testimony of the Spirit [ita etiam non ante fidem reperiet sermo in hominem cordibus quam interiore spiritus testimonio obsignetur (3:70)]. The same Spirit, therefore, who has spoken through the mouths of the prophets must penetrate into our hearts to persuade us that they faithfully proclaimed what had been divinely commanded. (79)

As supreme intermediary, the Spirit serves as both aperture and closure of revelation, sealing the faithful reception and "acceptance in men's hearts" of divine authority. This, then, does not—as Luther's own soul did—constitute a site of fearful struggle and awesome questioning; rather, the Spirit is to be conceived as bringing together the sublime past of the sacred text and the respect for, and recovery of, its authentic meaning in the present. The Spirit "has not the task of inventing new and unheard of revelations, or of forging a new kind of doctrine . . . , but of sealing our minds with that very doctrine which is commended by the gospel" (94). It is difficult not to read the imagery of the seal as an oddly composite vehicle of both closure and certification ("et sigillum, et arrha" [3:70]). In Calvin's text such a metaphor was to serve as an antidote against self-authorized license in the religious, social, and sexual practice of "certain giddy men . . . who, with great haughtiness exalting the teaching office of the Spirit, despise all reading and laugh at the simplicity of those who, as they express it, still follow the dead and killing letter" (93).[12]

It is at this juncture that the text's admirable balance of guidance and reproof is upset, and that Calvin's brilliant *clarté* leaves something to be desired. Perhaps the burden of a twofold polemic turned out to be too heavy; perhaps the weight of the gruesome images of Münster as a slaughterhouse of German Anabaptists was fresh in his mind. In any event, Calvin here turns his attention to "these miserable folk" who

> willingly prefer to wander to their doom, while they seek the Spirit from themselves rather than from him. Yet, indeed, they contend that it is not worthy of the Spirit of God, to whom all things ought to be subject, himself to be subject to Scripture. As if, indeed, this were ignominy for the Holy Spirit to be everywhere equal and in conformity with himself, to agree with himself in all things, and to vary in nothing! To be sure, if the Spirit were judged by the rule of men, or of angels, or of anything else, then one would have to regard him as degraded, or if you like, reduced to bondage; but when he is compared with himself, when he is considered in himself, who will on this account say that injustice is done him? Nevertheless, he is thus put to a test, I confess, but a test by which it pleased him to establish his majesty among us. He ought to be sufficient for us as soon as he penetrates into us. But lest under his sign the spirit of Satan should creep in, he would have us recognize him in his own image, which he has stamped upon the Scriptures. He is the Author of the Scriptures: he cannot vary and differ from himself. (94)

Calvin, with his humanist background, would not follow those he viewed as semiliterate, men who were determined to "despise all reading." Rejecting the dualism of Luther's antinomies between the freedom of the soul and the subservience of the flesh, between spiritual defiance and political submission, Calvin paradoxically projected a Holy Spirit whose identity, in bridging two radically different worlds, must be resolutely fixed; when all is said and done such fixture ("to be everywhere equal and in conformity with himself, to agree with himself in all things, and to vary in nothing!") is that of the meaning of Scripture itself.

The paradox is that Calvin here came close to echoing—even as he was voicing his objections to—the language of contemporary mysticism. For Calvin, the "test" of the Spirit is that "he penetrates into us" and yet does so "in conformity with himself": as both authority and

"Author of the Scriptures" he is supposed "to vary in nothing." The argument, advancing in a spiral curve, collapses into a vicious circle. The Spirit authorizing the Protestant appropriation of Scripture needs to bring forth his own legitimation: "quam authoritatem habebit apud nos Spiritus, nisi certissima nota discernatur?" (3:83). The enormous energy in this spiritualized lecture of the sacred text was supposed to be released as an appropriating force, and yet was supposed to be appropriately harnessed in the potential of its meaning. The difficulty could not be solved. And even though Calvin's structure of authority and authentication turned out to be more solid and substantial than that of Luther, this brave new language of Protestant authorization signally failed in the attempt to relocate authority through strengthening the relations of institution and inspiration, state and church, Spirit and Scripture.

3

Discord and Identity
Religion "Politized"

U nlike Continental Protestantism, the Reformation in England presents us with a hybrid and sometimes ambiguous
picture in which secular power and religious reform become
intertwined. Whereas German reformers, with the exception of
Thomas Müntzer, conceived of spiritual authority as aloof from secular rule, and whereas Calvin in Geneva attempted to realign church
and polity, in England the relations of worldly and spiritual authorities turned out to be intricate, changeful, and paradoxical, especially
when the history of post-Reformation Puritanism is taken into account. Here, as Henry noted in his last parliament, the Reformation
led to an unprecedented groundswell of "debate and discord."

This groundswell, however, proved to be an element not only of
dissension but also of revitalization in cultural and political, as well
as national, affairs. Debate and discord were inseparable from the rich-
ness and diversity of early modern English vernacular culture. They
were intricately connected with the idea of a twofold sovereignty by
which the Tudors appropriated almost absolute authority in matters
both secular and ecclesiastical. But absolutism in England, with its
stake in both Protestantism and commerce, sealed the decline of feu-
dalism. The Tudors, in their opportunistic alliance with the forces of
both trade and stability, stood for larger than local figurations of iden-

tity through which, especially after 1588, the idea of God in his preference for the English was made to assist in the formation of a distinctly Protestant nation. Thus, in its later impact, the English Reformation may be said to have been Janus-faced: it divided the nation in its uses of authority, but also, as Patrick Collinson notes, "extended and intensified the religious sense of English nationhood."[1]

At its very inception, then, the English Reformation was marked by an assembly of discordant interests. It took a commoner and faithful servant of the Crown, Thomas Cromwell, to embrace the discrepancies with which such a situation was fraught: in view of these diverse interests, it was his endeavor to devise an encompassing and at least partially unifying platform of authority. The early modern nation-state, a new concept, was defined as a space for sovereign imperial authority, with absolute rule by the "one supreme hedde," yet in conjunction with the whole nation personified in the king-in-parliament.[2]

This concept of sovereignty came in response to a whole set of changes that "crowded together so thickly and so deliberately that only the term 'revolution' can describe what happened."[3] Whether or not the notion of a Tudor revolution in government is justified or can by itself account for this density of change, the basic premises of early modern authority emerged in England in conjunction with the Reformation. These premises were positively linked with a process of social, economic, and cultural transformation that opened up unprecedented means and strategies (as well as technologies) for authorizing diverse uses of language and for assimilating differing sites of intellectual authority.[4] The theme of authority, in fact, became an absorbing topic in the course of the later sixteenth century, when the absence of unity in its foundations was most acutely felt.[5]

As Christopher Hill has suggested, these transformations must be seen as preparations for the peculiar strength of the ties between the sixteenth-century Reformation and the seventeenth-century revolution.[6] As John N. King notes, "the seeds of Elizabethan disunity and of the violent controversies of the seventeenth century lay in the factional disputes of the English Reformation of the mid–sixteenth century. Lines of conflict had been drawn that were to develop into the Puritan Revolution."[7]

This is not the place to discuss these vast issues in mid-sixteenth-century English history, except to regard them as part of a context in which the sense of "disunity," the dispersal and distraction of authorities, was already acutely perceived. But at this stage, the perception of discord went hand in hand with a search for new levels of identity. In view of the need for clarification, experienced by an ever-broadening section of a society marked by increasing literacy, representations began to obtain a role unheard of in pre-Reformation Europe. In particular, the awareness of incertitude between the sense of discord and an anxiety about identity helped propel sixteenth-century uses of representation toward a new aperture and variability. In opposing the firmly anchored privileges and obligations of a society tied to lineage and fealty, the forces of mobility dislodged not only the symbolism of ancient status, but also the cultural fixtures and fittings of social identity. In the wake of the Reformation, loyalty toward a person, family, or dynasty, formerly accepted as a duty, came to be adapted to a newly abstract, contractual or pragmatic mode of legitimation.

The need for further clarification through representation throve on an increasing volatility in the uses of signs and on the more contested uses of ideas through discourse. Discourse as a vehicle of ideas used for self-identification became particularly important as a divisive force in political thought and action. Again, it is the middle of the century that marks, as Wallace MacCaffrey calls it, "a fundamental turning-point," a "profound transformation in the whole nature of English politics," which in the end was connected with the "intrusion of religious ideology into politics."[8] Whereas traditionally developed relations of fealty had previously determined most people's thinking and behavior, now ideas, convictions, abstract principles—all conveyed through more flexible and accessible uses of discourse—stimulated new gaps (and allowed for new links) among individuals and groups of people. While constituting both a stronger impulse and a larger space for representations, these gaps and these links accompanied more flexible, contingent uses of language. These in their turn allowed for a new space for (in)determinacy in the correlations of signs and meanings. Concealing or displaying ideological discord as well as new areas of identity and identification in the communicative process, such representations had a "self-fashioned" order of authority, or at least one that was not altogether given prior to the representing, the reading, or the interpreting. As Frank Whigham writes in regard to Renaissance courtesy literature, it "uncouples the existing order from transcendent authority and refounds it on the sheerly formal, learnable, vendible skills of persuasion."[9] Such dissociation of discursive activities from traditional locations of authority was to be of great consequence not only for the literature of courtesy.

With the emergence of Protestantism, significant numbers of ordinary people were motivated to enter into discussions on the subject of their religion. These people were confronted with divergent claims on their loyalty, with the need for a choice between conflicting authorities. In previous centuries, such a choice had been the prerogative mainly of those in power. Now, however, with increasing literacy and the beginnings of a market for the printing press, more and more people found themselves involved in deliberations based on their responses to argumentative discourse. They were forced to make decisions not only about religious but also about political and cultural questions pertaining to their own lives. These were situations in which the representation of meaning in textual documents (the Bible in the vernacular, sermons, pamphlets, and so forth), far from being given, constituted itself in the face of a growing spectrum of responses that allowed much greater scope for diverging views. As never before, ordinary people were in the position of having to judge for themselves what was true and false, the 'correct' and the 'incorrect' meaning of Scripture. And they had to do so in the absence of the overriding, largely unexamined authority to which they had long been accustomed.

This disruption of a largely accepted system of authority coincided with a surge in population growth and a wave of rising prices and heavier burdens on the shoulders of the peasant classes. These changes are by now well documented: estate owners raised rents to meet their own rising costs; they drove out tenants from the land they had long cultivated and enclosed huge areas, transforming them into pasture to produce and sell profitable wool. Social unrest, especially in the southwest and east, assumed unprecedented dimensions as this accumulation of capital coincided with the reformation of the church.[10]

The resulting divisions in status, welfare, and outlook led to diverging concepts of self-identification between various positions and interests. In the ensuing rebellions, the leaders appeared "more self-conscious than ever before, and to some extent articulate."[11] The underlying matrix of social discontent was primarily economic. But the political self-definition of these rebellions and the symbols by which they were represented were marked by contingency and discontinuity. The ideological representations of social unrest were such that the ways of legitimizing these actions in one area were diametrically opposed to those of the other. The peasants in East Anglia hoisted their flags under the sign of radical Protestantism, while those in Cornwall and Devon did so under the sign of restorative Catholicism. But in both risings, as a historian of these revolts writes, "it was as though in breaking with Rome and implementing radical changes in the structure of the Church, Henry VIII had, however unwittingly, unloosed a host of disruptive forces whose existence was not realised."[12]

Thus the participants in the wave of social unrest that stirred the country in 1549 were ambivalent in their search for alternative signs of authority. The revolt, which developed into a massive threat to Somerset's Protectorate, should be viewed as complementary to, rather than isolated from, the process of cultural revolution culminating in these years. As had happened in the Pilgrimage of Grace (1536), tens of thousands rose up against the authority of those in power. Commoners armed themselves against a governing class that appeared to have lost its traditional claim to legitimacy since the dissolution of monasteries and the imposition of enclosures and exorbitant rents. But, whereas in the 1530s the members of the landed gentry were still wavering, and conservative elements of the aristocracy seemed prepared to enter the field against Thomas Cromwell and his Protestant faction at court, a decade later the situation had drastically changed. In Cornwall in 1549 only two gentlemen joined the protest; in East Anglia a wealthy Protestant farmer named Robert Kett headed a movement against those gentry who were supporting enclosures. Kett's followers were prepared to turn the cultural upheaval of the Reformation into a kind of social revolution: their claims contained a distant echo of the Ten Articles of German peasants.[13]

57

Following the defeat of Kett in the valley of Dusinberre and the bloody rout of the uprising in the southwest, neither the old faith nor the radical wing of Protestantism had triumphed. As the turbulent years, first under the Protectorate and then under Mary, came to an end, the country at large must have found itself in a state of indecision, its cultural bearings uncertain. And although under Elizabeth the supremacy of the Crown as head of the church finally seemed assured, and the images of royal and civic authority more firmly installed than before, the crisis of authority in church matters was at best shelved. Though the Tudor integration of political and ecclesiastical power had broadened the range of its national and religious representations, the regime was never really in a position to establish uniformity. The broadened range of these representations concealed an increasingly heterogeneous set of voices and interests.

To a certain extent, then, the course taken by the English Reformation, with its many irresolutions, compromises, and reversals, tended to dilute its effects on society at large. Again, this is not the place to rehearse the controversial issue of whether the English Reformation drew its strength from a popular movement with an unofficial rate of conversion and Protestantization (as A. G. Dickens, Patrick Collinson, and others maintain), or whether it owed almost everything to official coercion from above (as Christopher Haigh, J. J. Scarisbrick, and others argue).[14] In view of the inconclusive nature of the evidence, it seems safest to conclude, with Robert Whiting, that in those regions where Catholic enthusiasm declined before the Reformation, "the Dickens/Elton model has a measure of validity," but where traditional patterns of devotion remained strong, as was generally the case in the rest of England, "it is the Haigh/Scarisbrick model that seems the more applicable."[15] This is not to overestimate—as the revisionists tend to do—the resilience of the old religion; the evidence does make it clear "that traditionalist commitment collapsed dramatically in the Reformation decades." What we have, then, is "less a transition from Catholicism to Protestantism than a decline from religious commitment into nonconformism or indifference."[16]

Once we conceive of the post-Reformation political and cultural landscape as containing extensive areas of uncommitted territory, the coexistence of diametrically opposed positions (like those of Gardiner and Cranmer in Shakespeare's *Henry VIII*) becomes more understandable. But there as elsewhere, the Henrician Reformation and the Protectorate pointed the way: the issue of authority in contemporary religion continued to be in a state of flux. The various forces in the unfolding of the English Reformation could only add to and prolong the indecision in the uses of authority.

Hence it seems safe to suggest that, precisely because of its divisive affiliations and its uneven course, the Reformation in England must have had a particularly unsettling effect on deep-seated assumptions about authority's sanctions. For one thing, as Ralph Houlbrooke has shown, the church was never able to recover the "moral authority lost during the Reformation and the Elizabethan years of neglect," especially because the ecclesiastical courts emerged from the Reformation "gravely weakened" and with the scope of their jurisdiction restricted.[17] More importantly, in the daily lives of a great number of English people, especially in the north, the Edwardian Reformation had proved to be "almost entirely destructive; the old Church was damaged but Protestantism was not enforced."[18] As Joel Hurstfield notes, a child born—as Elizabeth was—in 1533, "had, if his family was conformist, subscribed to five different versions of the Christian religion by the time that he was twenty-six."[19]

Small wonder, then, that English Protestantism was associated with a wave of anticlericalism that swelled massively in the course of the sixteenth century. The Essex ecclesiastical court archives made available by F. G. Emmison, like other transcripts, probably represent only a fraction of the actual number of incidents in one county alone.[20] The servants of the church had changed their faith too often; they were considered corrupt, lazy, and self-interested, and were subject to slander and derision. "What is more houted at, scoffed and scorned in Englande now then a religious man in his wede?" asked Thomas Stapleton in 1565.[21] "The people . . . have conceived an heathenish contempt of Religion, and a disdaynefull loathing of the ministers thereof," wrote Bishop Cooper.[22] The English Reformation, as far as it was decreed from above, was devoid of that fervor which had found its most sustained source in the spiritualization of faith associated with the Lollard movement.

It was no coincidence that Protestantism succeeded in putting down roots in the economically advanced east and southeast of the country, where the Lollards had already quietly done the groundwork. Hence it was, as A. G. Dickens has suggested, that a "gradual merging of the new Protestant faction with the old Lollard cause" so helped institutionalize the "ambivalence" of the English Reformation that the contradiction between the "State Reformation" and the "popular Reformation" became a constituent element in the overall issue. Henceforth, the inherent gulf between institutionalized power and unauthorized discourse remained always potentially deep. Protestantization at the heels of the popular Reformation followed the scenario of state rule only to a limited extent and so remained relatively unaffected by the curbing of the reformatory process by Mary and by Elizabeth's Archbishop Whitgift.[23] This does not mean that there were no important links between state or church policy and popular Protestantism. We need only recall Thomas Cromwell's placing of the vernacular version of the Bible in English parish churches (1539); the abolition of the chantries for their connections with the Catholic cult of saints and the requiem mass (1549); or Thomas Cranmer's *Catechism* of 1549, soon followed by Martin Bucer's second *Book of Common Prayer* (1552).

These were irreversible measures; but it seems difficult not to connect them, at least indirectly, with openings between the two poles in the English Reformation that helped release discursive activities in different directions. Along with the bifurcations between (post-)Lollard spirituality and state-controlled episcopacy, the emerging positions on authority seemed to affect Protestant discourse on more than one level: they served as a source of discord but also as the potential for a new mode of realignment. The forced, inconsistent, and often indifferent cohabitation of church and state under one supreme head had, as we shall see, its limits. The combined grounds for authorizing (and censoring) religious and political writings could, even before

Martin Marprelate, be scandalously undermined. In the long run, the blanket of control was rarely effective enough; the centralizing location of supremacy could hardly serve as a practicable arrangement by which vast sociocultural changes were to be assimilated to, and represented in terms of, one valid and encompassing position of authority. The government could contain neither the Lollard-Protestant undercurrent nor the anticlericalism of the time. On the contrary, a state of affairs by which the clergy had become "a sort of civil service for religious matters"[24] must have proved counterproductive to the institutionalized endeavor in favor of uniformity. All along, the centrifugal (and largely antiprelatic) forces of debate and discord were situated at the very frontiers of the Reformation's division between official polity and self-authorized exegesis of Scripture. Such divisiveness came to a head during the time of the Protectors, of which it may well be said that "the events of 1547 to 1553 had unleashed forces which should never again be wholly brought under control."[25]

When, therefore, the duke of Somerset was faced with a rising tide of religious, political, and social divisions, he was confronted first of all with the problematic legacy that the late Tudor had bequeathed to his heirs in governing the country. Although Henry had destroyed his own servant (when Cromwell, his purported tool, turned out to have a mind too much his own), he could not undo the consequences of what the latter had undertaken to perform in the name of his master. In his last parliament (1545–46), the sick and aging king looked back and tried to size up the full extent of "debate and discord" in the country. Bearing witness to an unprecedented crisis in the authorization of discourses, Henry's speech allows us to study the colossal impact of the Reformation, *in statu nascendi* as it were, on modes of discursive practice. As recorded by the Tudor historian Edward Hall, the king expresses his concern in no uncertain terms about one particular matter, which "surely is amisse, and farre out of ordre," and which he expects "with all his fervor" will be rectified: instead of harmony and benevolence, "discord and dissencion, beareth rule in every place."[26] As a result of the outburst of conflicting interests (and meanings) within Reformation discourse, and the loss of an unquestioned authority in spiritual matters, one side—as the king complains—begins

to curse the other as "Hereticke and Anabaptist," while the other side
in its turn derides its opposers as "Papist, Ypocrite, and Pharisey." A
"wound" is inflicted on the state by the mishandling of clerical authority: first it is appropriated in unheard-of ways, and then attacked,
and, as a result, expropriated:

> I se and here daily that you of the Clergy preache one against another,
> teache one contrary to another, inveigh one against another without
> Charity or discrecion. Some be to styff in their old Mumpsimus, other
> be to busy and curious, in their newe Sumpsimus. Thus all men almoste
> be in variety and discord . . . alas how can the pore soules live in con-
> cord when you preachers sow emonges them in your sermons, debate
> and discord. (865)

Discourse is here depicted, in the final phase of the Henrician Reformation, as continually in conflict between sharply diverging positions.
The language of the sermon has become the language of argument;
the priests themselves are charged with sowing the seeds of the
dissension that now dominates writing and thinking. Ultimately, the
Reformation appears to have changed religious discourse itself: once
a vessel of Catholic order, it has become a medium of evangelical "variety."

At this point in his address, the king's use of language in his attempt to promote an ecclesiastical conciliation is revealing. The contradiction between "Sumpsimus" and "Mumpsimus" conveys the
sense of an absence of unity by means of a binary use of onomatopoeia.
Both these words—the earliest recorded use of which, according to
the *Oxford English Dictionary*, dates from 1517—stem from the mouth
of an illiterate priest of the old faith, who in the following words justified uttering gibberish while celebrating Mass: "I will not change
my old mumpsimus [my mumbling] for your new sumpsimus [a perfect indicative form of sumere = to take]."[27] "Mumpsimus" has ever
since been acknowledged as denoting the attitude of a "bigoted op-
ponent of reform," as a symbol for a position that "obstinately adheres
to old ways, in spite of the clearest evidence that they are wrong."

While Henry directs the "Lordes spiritual to preach honestly and
truly the word of God" (that is, to base their discourse on the authority of the Bible), his admonition to the secular lords seems equally re-

vealing. Instead of "rayling" on clerics, lords are to bring any well-founded complaint about an instance of "perverse" religious teaching to the attention of the Privy Council or to the king himself, because only he could act as God's lieutenant:

> And bee not Judges your selfes, of your awne phantasticall opinions, and vain exposicions, for in suche high causes ye maie lightly erre. And although you be permitted to reade holy scripture, and to have the word of God in your mother tongue, you must understande that it is licensed you so to do, onely to informe your awne conscience, and to instruct your children and famely, and not to dispute and make scripture, a rayling and a tauntyng stocke, against Priestes and Preachers (as many light persones do). (865)

Plainly, Henry's effort to resolve the new contradictions among power, authority, and religious discourse by referring to the "true" Word was an attempt to fight the symptoms of the disease with its own causes. Just as the demand for "truth" sidestepped the criteria of evangelical exegesis, the restriction to the private sphere ("your awne conscience") overlooked the political consequences of setting individual expression to work. Instead of using a polemical voice—an inevitable product of the Reformation—members of the church were unanimously to sing the praises of royal supremacy. Henry's version of "truth" is grounded in *political* authority—that of the Privy Council and that of his role as king. In the passage above he reasserts, with such words as "permitted" and "licensed," his own authority to restrict the reading of Scripture. But such a reassertion must have been of little consequence when the authority of Protestant exegesis was ever more widely being appropriated by the public. Thus, Henry lay an impossible expectation before Parliament in the hope that inflammatory material in public places might be defused:

> I am very sory to knowe and here, how unreverently that moste precious juel the worde of God is disputed, rymed, sung and jangeled in every Alehouse and Taverne, contrary to the true meaninge and doctrine of the same. And yet I am even as much sory, that the readers of the same, folowe it in doynge so fayntlye and coldly: for of thys I am sure, that Charitie was never so faint emongest you, and verteous and Godly

63

livyng was never lesse used, nor God him self emongest Christians, was never lesse reverenced, honored or served. (866)

What Henry here describes is a rarely documented effect of the Reformation—its impact on the growth of popular discursive activities. Protestantism appears as an arena in which a good many common uses of language are stimulated: the Word is debated, rhymed, sung, and distorted in alehouses and taverns. "That moste precious juel the worde of God" (that is, the highest authority) thus loses its claim to a single true meaning and interpretation; the "true meaninge" of the gospel must, according to Henry, be lost if the word of God is exposed to the scoffs and jests of the street. As the king explains it, the new popular space for interpreting the Bible in English has been turned into a site of irreverence, whereas belief in the "doctrine" of the Word lives on "fayntlye and coldly."

Henry could not have expressed more cogently the uneasy relations among the vernacular reception of the Bible, the loss of church authority, the spread of discursive activity, and the growing variety in representational strategies. He presents a surprisingly comprehensive picture of the expanding frontiers of discourse, noting "debate and discord" among the reformed clergy, "phantasticall opinions, and vain exposicions" among the aristocracy, and irreverence among the ordinary people. Henry implicitly identified a legacy of discord that was to last well beyond Shakespeare's time: as both the prerogative and the dynamite of the Reformation, this legacy was linked to the need to negotiate vital interests ideologically, to shift the medium through which power was appropriated from that of violence and tradition to that of discourse and argument.

There was a new sense, then, that the "politizing" uses of religion were positively interfering with traditional modes of social and individual identity. This is what, decades later, Christopher Sutton must have had in mind when he coined the profound dictum "Religion is become nothing lesse than Religion, to wit, a matter of meere talk: such politizing is there on all parts, as a man cannot tell, who is who."[28] The question of identity here was raised in response to a discursive practice marked by "debate and discord." And while ultimately conducive to new and highly complex means of identification, such a practice blurred many of the traditional lines of demarcation. The answer to the question "who is who" had become abstract; it was no longer given by the preordained implications of hierarchy, fealty, and lineage, but was now founded on a more contingent spectrum of norms and choices, including personal responses to the question of meaning. In this sense, religion implicated a discursive type of endeavor for the attainment of the highest, most passionately felt truth for which, as a contemporary put it, radical Protestants felt a need to "Search, examine, trie and seek." This indeed was "a matter of meere talk" but clearly not an innocent one. It involved intangibles: convictions and ideas with an inevitable political underside. Such "politizing," by complicating the uses of discourse and the question of identity, transformed matters of faith into ideology, identity into discourse, and religion into "nothing lesse than Religion."

Sutton's observation was not confined to a Protestant context. Many voices of the time indicate that the whole complex groundswell of change could be seen to culminate in newly interactive and precarious relations between language and existence. Since the traditional coordinates of signs and status appeared to be in a state of flux, the theater, more than any other medium of signification, could assimilate a vital area of interchange between playful word and worldly meaning. Long before Shakespeare's theater chose the Globe metaphor for its signature, the new element of contingency was inscribed as a semiotic complication in the playful definition of theatrical identity. At the opening of Henry Medwall's *Fulgens and Lucrece*, the actor "B," disguising himself as a spectator, denies that he is "a player." The actor denoted as "A" responds:

> There is so much nyce aray
> Among these galandis now a day
> That a man shall not lightly
> Know a player from another man.[29]

Ironically, the playful denial of an existential kind of identity provokes an opening. Here, the gap between actor and role provides a welcome site where an element of confusion between signification and identity can be played out. Signifiers have ceased to be trustworthy; whether in the uses of costume and apparel or those of language, the link between what they seem to say and what they actually do is precarious. Again, the question of "who is who" has no reliable answer.

The representation of identity, whether in the theater or outside it, had no predetermined authority to follow. This was especially the case at the precarious point where the private appropriation of religion, the divided uses of discourse, and the political economy of the market would constitute powerful disruptions of unity and identity. Take, for example, Thomas Adams's sermon, "The White Devil; or, The Hypocrite Uncased" (1612), where the language of Protestantism and the discourse of commerce entered into a strange symbiosis: "marry, we are Protestants, and protest away our souls: there is no other way to put off bad wares, and put up good moneys."[30] To "protest away our souls" was another way of dissolving identity into "a matter of meere talk." Adams seems to illustrate the concomitant metamorphoses with some relish:

> To say truth, most of our professions (thanks to ill professors) are so confounded with sins, as if there went but a pair of shears between them; nay, they can scarce be distinguished: you shall not easily discern between a hot, furious professor and a hypocrite, between a covetous man and a thief, between a courtier and an aspirer, between a gallant and a swearer, between an officer and a bribe-taker, between a servitor and a parasite, between farmers and poor-grinders, between gentlemen and pleasure-lovers, between great men and madmen, between a tradesman and a fraudsman, between a moneyed man and a usurer, between a usurer and the devil. (276)

When the rise of internal authority coincided with conditions of social mobility, the self-authorized, unlimited uses of discourse must indeed have made it difficult to "tell, who is who." "Social mobility," as Jean-Christophe Agnew reminds us, "implied social disfigurement, a donning of masks."[31]

This had far-reaching consequences for representation. There was a new complexity of links and gaps between what human beings actually desired or *did* and what they *represented* by their speech; hence the undetermined, unpreordained element in political and fictional representation that emerged. Unlike the tangible, comprehensive dependency relationships of the past, the new relationships in line with modern political representation united elements of self-determination and heteronomy, embracing areas marked by both the concurrence and the diversity of interests.

As the barriers between religion and ideology were lowered, discourse achieved a far greater potential for representing heterogeneous interests outside as well as inside the church—in pamphlets, in songs and ballads, and in the theater. It was above all the unlicensed appropriation of the word that the press, the stage, and the Protestant pulpit had in common. And it was this conjunction that was attacked by the conservative position on the authorization of discourse, as for instance represented by Stephen Gardiner, who questioned the grounds on which "to be justified."[32] How to be "justified"—authorized—was the most "politizing" question of the time; for certain "printers, players, and preachers," this question was now, more than ever, an open one.

An irreversible process of change had begun, one that implicated the uses of representation at their most vulnerable level: it was through the representational function of discourse that legitimacy, identity, and "character" had to be established. From now on, the authority to do so had to be negotiated; it was no longer available as simply predetermined by traditional relations of power and meaning. Authority now constituted itself not so much at the beginning of discourse, where traditional sources might be cited as valid by consensus, but rather in the perception of meaning as *process*. Tyndale spoke of the conjunction between the finding of "meaning" and the perception of "process" in direct reference to the ultimate matrix of Protestant authority. He had undertaken to translate the Bible "because [he] had perceived by experience how that it was impossible to establish the lay people in any truth except the Scripture were plainly laid before their eyes in their mother tongue, that they might see the process, order and meaning of the text."[33] Increasingly, authority and identity obtained—if at all—at the end of the text as a product of perception and reception: available to those who, in Luther's words, were prepared to "see, know, judge, condemn, change, and modify."

4

Breach in Authorization
Gardiner to Bancroft

Although the Tudor debate over the rightful sanctions of sovereignty continued almost undiminished until the end of Elizabeth's reign, the issue of authority *in* representation, the authorization of discursive activities, turned out to be pregnant with far-reaching consequences. Somewhat surprisingly, it is this aspect to which recent studies in the Protestant tradition have paid least attention. But because this question is seminal in any reconsideration of sixteenth-century uses of representation, there is compelling reason here to look more closely at this facet of Tudor "debate and discord." From the days of Tyndale and More to the years of Shakespeare's presence in London, there was, I suggest, an ongoing concern with the problem of the authorization of discourse within and without the boundaries of an officially sanctioned orbit of representation.

The first of the great Tudor debates on this issue was that between William Tyndale and Thomas More. Tyndale in his translation of the New Testament followed as a matter of course in Luther's footsteps. In both his theoretical and his practical work, he strengthened a discursive practice according to which every Christian reader, to the best of his or her understanding, was called upon to arbitrate problems of textual meaning. Readers of the vernacular text were expected to receive evangelical truth on the basis of scriptural authority, piously guarded by the believer's conscience. There was a feeling, which was shared by Cranmer and later Protestant divines, that the translated English text of the Bible would take care of its own interpretation. Once it was assumed that the Bible explicated itself, all that was needed was homiletic guidance to inspire as well as to supplement unrestricted Bible reading by the laity. This was Tyndale's position, based on the Protestant emphasis on personal faith as the one reliable medium of Christian understanding. True, there were bound to be limits to the layperson's exegesis; but for all that, it seemed enough for the Protestant theologian to set up a signpost of warning for the faithful reader, who was advised, in the words of Cranmer, to "expound it no further, th[a]n you can plainly understand it."[1]

Although the early debate between Tyndale and More had brought out a good many irreconcilable positions in their respective modes of authorization, the line of division was to become more blurred than the hostile opposition between Protestantism and the old church might lead one to assume.[2] As soon as the issue of authority was viewed in relation to conflicting strategies of representation, there emerged a more complex awareness of the divergent uses of signs, images, and symbols. This at least was the case in the letters exchanged, in the spring and early summer of 1547, between the Lord Protector Edward Seymour, duke of Somerset, and Stephen Gardiner, then bishop of Winchester. At that time Gardiner, already under suspicion for his Catholic leanings, must have been cautious about airing his views too freely. But looking back at the undisturbed days of his bishopric ("as it was when I was in some little authority"),[3] he went out of his way to recall how graciously the late sovereign tolerated him when "I stooped not, and was stubborn" (36).

Gardiner's appeal to the past was part of his policy of resistance to any further changes in church and state. As he bluntly put it, "I can admit no innovations" (42). Thus he admonished Somerset "to keep and follow such laws and orders in religion as our late sovereign lord [Henry VIII] left with us" and not, during Edward's minority, "to call any one thing in doubt . . . whereby to impair the strength of the accord established" (40). Based on that platform, Gardiner's position on the unsanctioned uses of Protestant discourse remained quite inflexible. Above all, he was anxious "not to suffer . . . to slip the anchor-hold of authority, and come to a loose disputation" (41). For the conservative bishop, "authority," far from being the *result* of discussion and clarification, appeared to *precede* "disputation." It was important to him to avoid the loose, uncontrolled uses of public discourse, especially about what he saw as the given meaning of Scripture. Hence, the "authority" once and for all to fix such meaning was "the anchor" to hold the "accord" that refused further innovation. Such authority was "to make for stay of such errors as were then by ignorant preachers sparkled among the people" (41). Although, as Gardiner admits, "the ministration of the letter, which is writing and speaking, . . . hath been from the beginning delivered, through man's hand," he held "the setting out of the authority of the Scripture" (40) to be a matter of institutionalized privilege, not to be meddled with by any curious preacher or layperson.

While this could in no way obviate the conflict over authorization, Gardiner's reformulation of the familiar contradiction was noteworthy in more than one respect. First, he was concerned with what he called the "setting out of the authority of the Scripture" not only in religious but also in other types of discourse. In fact, by listing preachers along with printers and players, Gardiner faced the problem of how to cope with a wider constellation of unauthorized discursive activities. What he objected to in these discourses was that the "setting out" of the inscribed agent of authority, the act of authorization itself, was uncontrolled and thus left subject to definition and appropriation:

> Certain printers, players, and preachers, make a wonderment, as though we knew not yet how to be justified, nor what sacraments we should have. And if the agreement in religion made in the time of our late sovereign lord be of no force in their judgment, what establishment could any new agreement have? and every uncertainty is noisome to any realm. And where every man will be master, there must needs be uncertainty. And one thing is marvellous, that at the same time it is taught that all men be liars, at the selfsame time almost every man would be believed; and amongst them Bale, when his untruth appeareth evidently in setting forth the examination of Anne Askew, which is utterly misreported. (31)

The context of this passage leaves no doubt that the setting out of authority in writing is here linked to both the question of power ("where every man will be master") and the issue of representation in cultural history. On the one hand, there are "books written without authority, as by Master Bale" (30). But the element of "uncertainty" implies greater complications than the absence of authority. What seems so "marvellous" (and contradictory) has to do with what is viewed, on the other hand, as some sort of flaw in the uses of representation: although quite unreliable ("all men be liars"), these uses "at the self-same time" set forth claims on truth ("every man would be believed").

It is tempting here to trace the barely concealed tension between the general reference to "all" and "every" and the sharper thrust toward those unsanctioned representations that are used as vehicles of power and "untruth." Obviously, it is the self-authorized uses of language that especially combine an "enterprise to subvert religion, and the state of the world" with that strange incongruity between "untruth" in discourse and the desire to "be believed." What is telling in his attack on dissident writers such as John Bale is the underlying assumption that authority in truly authorized uses of language involves a stable or even fixed relation between signs and their meanings. This much at least appears to be confirmed by a letter written in the same month against iconoclastic "innovation" in the town of Portsmouth, "where the images of Christ and his saints have been most contemptuously pulled down" (26). In his response to this incident, Gardiner puts forward what may well be called a semiotics of political and cultural stability:

> For the destruction of images containeth an enterprise to subvert religion, and the state of the world with it, and especially the nobility, who, by images, set forth and spread abroad, to be read of all people, their lineage and parentage, with remembrance of their state and acts; and the poursuivant carrieth not on his breast the king's name, written with such letters as few can spell, but such as all can read be they never so rude, being great known letters in images of three lions, and three fleurs-de-lice, and other beasts holding those arms. And he that cannot read the scripture written about the king's great seal, yet he can read St. George on horseback on the one side, and the king sitting in his

majesty on the other side; and readeth so much written in those images, as, if he be an honest man, he will put off his cap. And although, if the seal were broken by chance, he would and might make a candle of it, yet he would not be noted to have broken the seal for that purpose, or to call it a piece of wax only, whilst it continueth whole. (27)

For Gardiner, "the destruction of images" involves, on the level where signs and politics interact, an unforgivable heresy. In terms of its semiotic structure, such heresy occurs when the continuity between material signifiers and social signification is, in his view, illicitly disrupted. Social stability and linguistic continuity are perceived as strong when religious icons and their transcendent symbolism appear indivisible; such stability is guaranteed by the inseparability of social status symbols and the message of subordination (as when the illiterate churl "readeth so much written in those images, as . . . he will put off his cap"). In dealing with the "king's great seal," an honest subject would, as long as "it continueth whole," make no distinction between the signifier (the piece of wax) and what it signifies: he would not call the wax "a piece of wax only," even though its use-value (as a candle) is so self-evident. The "wholeness" of the sign involves complete continuity—or rather, the ignoring of discontinuity— between what materially signifies and what is spiritually signified by it. The "whole" nature of social symbols, in this semiotics of political order, presupposes closure in representation; stability in their political and cultural functions appears linked to stable relations in their semiotic structure.

Gardiner is here concerned with the threat that derives from a rupture taking place in unauthorized representations. Writing against the Lollard-Protestant distinction between the material of "stocks and stones, in which matter images be graven" and their (internal) spiritual meaning, he points out how absurd would be a similar differentiation between the meaning of "writing" and its signifiers "comprised in clouts and pitch."[4] Again, the lesson is one of social subordination, suggesting, in the face of the "Lollards' idolatry," the need for royal ceremony and social symbols: "If this opinion should proceed, when the king's majesty hereafter should show his person, his lively image, the honour due by God's law among such might continue; but as for the king's standards, his banners, his arms, they should hardly continue in their due reverence for fear of Lollards' idolatry, which they gather upon Scripture beastly—not only untruly" (27).

Gardiner's text, taken as a whole, reads like a report on an early modern crisis in representation. Such crises occur when a preconceived continuity in the representational use of signs is challenged by those who either seek the "destruction of images" or do not know "yet how to be justified" in accepting the sign as denoting the real thing. Behind the challenge in either case is the self-authorized stance of an intense subjectivity in reading and interpretation. In alliance with what Max Weber has termed an "inner-worldly asceticism," this self-authorized critique of the identity of seeming and meaning is especially vigorous in iconoclasm. Iconoclasts, as Victor Turner and Edith Turner have written, "do not recognize any *necessary* linkage between signifier and signified," emphasizing as they do "the constitutive value of internal factors (belief, conscience)."[5]

Gardiner attacks the Lollard-Protestant position, but behind this position there is a cultural poetics of much wider significance, pointing well beyond any direct impact of the Reformation. To make some obvious analogies: in Shakespeare a disruption of this linkage occurs when Lear sheds his "lendings," when Henry V questions the use-value of "ceremony," when Juliet asks, "What's in a name?" and when Hamlet makes a distinction between what "seems"—that is, the signs of mourning—and his truly felt experience "within."[6] These gestures convey a probing doubt about "how to be justified" in assuming the validity of a linkage as simply given (though the desire to reauthorize meaning in the "order" of each "process" of representational closure must not be read as indicating a Protestant conscience).

Even in Gardiner's own critique of contemporary iconoclasm, the subversion of representational order cannot be defined in terms of doctrinal differences between Catholic and Protestant positions. Although Gardiner finds fault with Bale's Protestant writing, there is a good deal of closure and stability in the latter's representations, while the most forceful energies of disruption obtained where the eye of orthodoxy may never have looked for them. For instance, among Bale's dramatic representations, it is the Vice "Idolatry" who most disrupts stability, including any stable language of identity. And while in Bale's *Three Laws* Natural Law's sincerity "had dictated that character, appearance, and name were one," identity becomes altogether fluid when through the use of disguise the grotesque figure of Vice shifts his gender. In his amazement, Infidelity cries: "sometime thou wert an he!" Replies Idolatry: "Yea, but now Ich am a she, / And a good midwife, perde!"[7] As this excursion suggests, Gardiner's linkage between the lack of orthodox authority and a crisis in representational closure has considerable implications for the cultural history of Tudor drama. His insistence on stable relations between signs and meanings buttressed the distinction between "true" and "false" representation, between authoritative uses of "images and ceremonies" (58) and mere "idolatry": "so hath 'idolum' been likewise appropriate to signify a false representation, and a false image" (59).

As their correspondence showed, however, the bishop's poetics of stability and suppression did not sit well with the Protestant inclinations of the duke of Somerset. Urged by Gardiner to "command books to be bought" (43) only with authority, the Lord Protector responded with an unambiguous rebuff. His letters indicate that he chose to follow an altogether different notion of how to authorize discourses. Rather than dividing discourses on the basis of a given authority into "false" and sanctioned ones, Somerset took a considerably more relaxed and less coercive position:

> There be some so ticklish, and so fearful one way, and so tender stomached, that they can abide no old abuses to be reformed, but think every reformation to be a capital enterprise against all religion and good order; as there be on the contrary side some too rash, who, having no consideration what is to be done, headlong will set upon every thing. The magistrate's duty is betwixt these, so in a mean to sit and provide, that old doting should not take further or deeper rust in the commonwealth, neither ancient error overcome the seen and tried truth, nor long abuse, for the age and space of time only, still be suffered; and yet all these with quietness and gentleness, and without all contention, if it were possible, to be reformed. (30)

Concerned with the "good and politic order of the commonwealth" (30), Somerset appears to follow the Tudor strategy of via media:

"quiet," he writes, "may as well be broken with jealousy as negligence, with too much fear or too much patience: no ways worse, than when one is over light-eared the one way, and deaf on the other side" (35–36). To a certain extent, this recalls Henry VIII's position. In both Somerset and Gardiner there is the repeated (almost nostalgic) turn to the days of the earlier king as a time of glory, a continuing source of legitimation.[8] In the present context, however, Somerset, in arguing for a more balanced response, addresses himself to a new distinction between the authority of power and that other form of authority that derives from authorship and writing. On the one hand, there is the authority of "magistrates"; on the other, the unsanctioned uses of printing, playing, and preaching referred to by Gardiner:

> The world never was so quiet or so united, but that privily or openly *those three which you write of, printers, players, and preachers, would set forth somewhat of their own heads, which the magistrates were unawares of.* And they which already be banished and have forsaken the realm, as suffering the last punishment, be boldest to set forth their mind; and dare use their extreme license or liberty of speaking, as out of the hands or rule of correction, either because they be gone, or because they be hid. . . . In the most exact cruelty and tyranny of the bishop of Rome, yet Pasquill (as we hear say) writeth his mind, and many times against the bishop's tyranny, and sometimes toucheth other great princes; which thing, for the most part, he doth safely: not that the bishop alloweth Pasquill's rhymes and verses—especially against himself; but because he cannot punish the author, whom either he knoweth not, or hath not. In the late king's days of famous memory, who was both a learned, wise, and politic prince, and a diligent executer of his laws—and when your lordship was most diligent in the same—yet, as your lordship yourself writeth, and it is too manifest to be unknown, there were that wrote such lewd rhymes and plays as you speak of, and some against the king's proceedings, who were yet unpunished, because they were unknown or ungotten. (34–35; emphasis added)

Although the Lord Protector objects to Gardiner's lumping together "goodly sermons" and "Jack of Lent's lewd ballad" ("which be evil in your letters joined together"), he takes no exception to a common mode of authorization on the part of all those discourses that "dare use their extreme license or liberty of speaking." Note how close the "license" of lewd ballads and the "liberty" of godly sermons remain, for all their obvious generic and functional differences. What they do have in common is that they are "out of the hands or rule of correction." In the face of the authority of "rule," the author of discourses such as these, as Somerset puts it, "writeth his mind." The authorization of the "license or liberty of speaking" was one thing; the "rule of correction," the authority of the "diligent executer of . . . laws," was quite another. From now on, their incongruity was to be reckoned with (34–35).

For Somerset not only to make a distinction of such consequence but also to accept it as practically inevitable was an indication of the post-Reformation direction of things. Already the medieval emphasis on the wholeness of the hierarchical order must have appeared untenable. After the Great Schism, the grand scheme of universal harmony and unity implicit in the Roman concept of Christendom tended to be superseded by "dissencion." As Somerset put it, "the world" simply did not appear "so quiet or so united" that, amid the noise and strife, one type of authority could hold sway. In the absence of unity, those unified uses of representation that Gardiner continued to advocate could find no place. Rejecting as "evil" a view in which all the different forms of unruly language were "joined together," Somerset reformulated a vision of varied discursive activities. But by returning to Gardiner's outlets for unauthorized discourse ("printers, players, and preachers"), he did not have in mind a suppression of the elements of nonconformity among them. Rather, he was making an early (possibly the earliest known) attempt to come to terms with that nascent differentiation of discourses which may well be said to be constitutive of modernity.

Clearly, this early emphasis on diversity was incompatible with a unifying approach to the uses of signifier and signified. In correcting the bishop in his "reading" of the king's great seal, the duke of Somerset reconsiders the meaning of signs: "your lordship (as appeareth) hath not truly read a most true and a most common image" (29). Correcting Gardiner's confusion of St. George with the image of royalty—an error often made by "the rude and ignorant people"—Somerset refers to the validity of the seal's inscription: "as the inscription testifieth, the king's image is on both the sides." He reminds Gardiner that "not . . . what is commonly called so, is always truest" (29). Emphasizing such difficulties with the "true" uses of representation (though not relinquishing the notion of their possibility), Somerset rejects altogether a black-and-white approach to signification:

> What you mean by true images and false images, it is not so easy to perceive. If they be only false images, which have nothing that they represent, as St. Paul writeth, "An idol is nothing," (because there is no such god,) and therefore the cross can be no false image, because it is true that Christ suffered upon it: then the images of the sun and the moon were no idols, for such things there be as the sun and the moon, and they were in the image then so represented, as painting and carving doth represent them. (29)

In this view, the charge of idolatry cannot be proven on the basis of the representational content of an image. Indeed, according to a strictly Protestant poetics and semiotics, mimesis cannot serve as a reliable register of "true" meaning. "True" and "false" thus emerge as highly problematic categories in pictorial art and language. What this remarkable piece of theorizing suggests is that the meaning of representations is not a question of epistemology. Such meaning cannot be gauged by the extent to which what is represented corresponds to what exists prior to the act of representation. The "meaning" of representations, here, is not a matter of "true images and false images."

It is worth noting that the positions taken by the writer of this letter are considerably more subtle and balanced than those of its editor, John Foxe. Even so, Foxe returns to the uses of unauthorized discourses, presumably with an eye to directing their shattering impact on the archenemy, the pope. Keeping in mind the limits of Foxe's reliability as a chronicler,[9] we should not be surprised to find him attempting to unify the various types and sources of self-authorized discourse under the exclusive rubric of their antipapal slant. Thus he all too easily accounts for the idea that Gardiner "thwarteth, also, and wrangleth much against players, printers, preachers. And no marvel why: for he seeth these three things to be set up of God, as a triple bulwark against the triple crown of the pope, to bring him down; as, God be praised, they have done meetly well already" (57).

Despite this inevitable bias, *Acts and Monuments* documents the two dominant positions in the mid-Tudor debate on authority with admirable clarity. To use John King's convenient phrase, this debate was over "the relative merits of internal and external authority."[10] Whereas the latter appeared to be established on traditionally institutionalized grounds, the former, as Christopher Hill notes, was "an internal authority, whose validity he [the believer] can test in discussion with other believers." And he adds: "That distinction is what the Reformation had been about."[11]

This central debate continued well into the seventeenth-century political revolution, culminating in Thomas Hobbes's paradoxical solution whereby the absolute natural rights of individuals necessitate the constraining authority of the sovereign.[12] But even at the height of the Elizabethan settlement, when the threat of anarchy arising out of the self-authorizing Protestant conscience must have appeared not quite so alarming, the controversy continued unabated. This was the case especially with those writers who zealously responded to what they perceived as dangerous parallels between the revolutionary fringe of the German Reformation and the potential (or actual) insubordination among English Puritans.[13] For an illustration, we have only to glance at Richard Cosin's *Conspiracie for Pretended Reformation: viz. Presbyteriall Discipline* ("Published now by authoritie," 1592) or at Oliver Ormerod's *Picture of a Puritane* (enlarged edition, 1605). Cosin's lengthy subtitle asserted the "resemblance" between Puritan dissent and what "happened heretofore in Germanie"; Ormerod's advertised "A Relation of the opinions, qualities, and practices of the Anabaptists in Germanie, and of the Puritanes in England," and claimed in his pamphlet "that the Puritanes resemble the Anabaptists, in above four score several things."

It was in this context that the clash between internal and external positions of authority became most pronounced. The antagonism between the two positions was turned into a sensational theme through the implication that behind this antagonism sinister patterns of contamination were at play. When, for instance, Ormerod attacked those who "are become scalding hot in desire of innovation" (repeating the very same phrase Cosin had used),[14] he made it plain that the revolutionary "opinion of equality of authority and dignitie," as Cosin described Thomas Müntzer's position,[15] involved internal questions of conscience as well as external considerations of power. Addressing himself to the English Puritans, Ormerod argues that they desire "this equalitie . . . because you condemne and disdaine to be ruled, and to be in subjection. Indeed your meaning is . . . to rule and not to be ruled, to do what you list in your several cures, without controlement of Prince, Bishoppe, or any other. And therefore pretending equalitie, most disorderly you seek Dominion" (25). The emphasis on "rule" was unambiguous enough. Those in power, as Ormerod warned, were being challenged at the level of a common appropriation of spiritual authority: "are all Prophets? are all teachers? . . . do all interpret?" (70). The dangers resulting from this must have appeared obvious when the self-authorized claim to read and "interpret" was aimed at a "meaning" in which questions of textual exegesis and the issue of political power were inextricably entwined.

While these pamphlets were more concerned with wild denunciations of the specter of Anabaptist anarchy than with any balanced assessment of the actual state of the crisis in authority, there is at least one high-Elizabethan text that provides a truly remarkable epitome of post-Reformation divisions on the issue of authority. This is Richard Bancroft's *Sermon Preached at Paul's Cross* (1588). At the time of its publication (the sermon was preached earlier that same year), Bancroft was chaplain to Sir Christopher Hatton, Lord Chancellor of England; he soon was to become bishop of London, and before taking over England's highest ecclesiastical office, he served as the right hand and closest confidant of Archbishop Whitgift. The *Sermon* may well be read as a strategic statement made by one of the most promising high-ranking representatives of the Elizabethan settlement.

To say that Bancroft's utterance had strategic significance is no exaggeration; on the highest levels of church and state, the issue of authority tended to be treated pragmatically rather than theoretically. But while the uses of authority (except in Richard Hooker's *Laws*) were usually considered in negative reference to both the Catholic church and the Puritan movement, Bancroft, from his high-Elizabethan post, went one step further. Attempting to define the grounds for what was to become the Anglican position on authority, he provided a carefully worked out, coherent context to the left and right of his own orthodox via media position. In his concern not simply with authority as such, but with diverse modes of authorizing discourse, Bancroft rejected any facile caricature of positions hostile to the state church. Whereas Cosin had reduced both the old-church and the Puritan concepts of authority to a theological justification of diverging aspirations to power, in his *Sermon* Bancroft sees the opposition between the two as constituting a wider cultural and political pattern of antagonistic discourses. He distinguishes two unacceptable positions. On the one side are the "false prophets" of Rome:

> The Popish false prophet will suffer the people to trie nothing, but do teach them wholie to depende upon them. . . . First they forbid them the reading of the scriptures. And the better to be obeied therin, they will not permit the scriptures to be translated into their vulgar toong. . . . The second shift which these false prophets of the Romish church do use, is this: Now that they perceive the scriptures to be translated into the language almost of every nation; and that the bookes are now so common in every mans hands, as that with their former devise they are no longer able to cover their nakednes: they labor with all their might to bind us to the fathers, to the councels, and to the church of Rome, protesting verie deeply, that we must admit of no other sence of place of the scriptures, than the Romish church shall be pleased to deliver unto us. . . . If a man have the exposition of the church of Rome touching any place of scripture, although he neither know nor understand, whether and how it agreeth with the words of the scripture, yet he hath the very word of God.[16]

Once again the old-church authority is located prior to the "order" and the "process" of exegesis: the meaning of discourse, the Biblical "sence," is delivered by and through the religious institution. Diametrically opposed to this is the extreme stance of Protestant self-authorization:

> Another sort of prophets there are, (you may in mine opinion call them false prophets) who would have the people to be alwaies seeking and searching: and those men (as well themselves as their followers) can never finde wherupon to rest. Now they are caried hither, now thither. They are alwaies learning (as the apostle saith) but do never attaine to the truth. . . . They wring and wrest the Scriptures according as they fansie. It would pittie a mans hart considering what paines they

will take in quoting of places, to see how perversly they will apply them. . . . To represse therefore this boldnes, first I say with *Tertullian* . . . that it hath ever been noted as a right property of heretikes and schismatikes, alwaies to be beating this into their followers heads: *Search, examine, trie and seeke*: bringing them thereby into a great uncertainty. (38–39; last emphasis added)

The radical Protestant position is taken to task on opposite grounds: inscribed authority is not given, but needs to be appropriated by the reader. "Meaning," in this view, is not nearly so determined as in the case of preordained authority. Rather, the biblical text is "searched," "examined," and "tried" for what it truly says. As a result, Christian doctrine itself is tried "by private men, and privately." This "trial of doctrine" has grave dangers, for "if authoritie and libertie of judging shall be left to private men, there will never be any certaintie set downe, but rather all religion will whollie become doubtfull."[17]

The point is for Bancroft to reject both procedures in favor of a more balanced position. Authority as inscribed in the biblical text is neither preordained nor "delivered" ready-made by the councils or by the church, nor can it be sought freely by "private men." Instead, Bancroft attempts to sanction the via media position of the state church through rejecting both extreme modes of authorization: "The meane therfore betwixt both these extremities of trieng nothing and curious trieng of all things, I hold to be best" (41). The irony of this position was not that it recommended a sort of hermeneutical halfway house (as when he advised his listeners, "Read the Scriptures, but with sobrietie" [42]), but that in repudiating "unlawful authoritie" (79) on the part of both popes and heretics, Bancroft would do so on behalf of and "according to the lawful authoritie which is united unto hir [Elizabeth's] crowne" (80).

This was a necessary strategy of legitimation in these circumstances, and Bancroft seemed to know as much. Wherever he looked, debate and discord had not diminished in the wake of the Reformation. In much the same way as Henry VIII had been before him,[18] Bancroft was confronted by the "laie factious" and "the clergie factious" (23). "I warrant you," the high-Elizabethan divine noted, "they are not toong-tied on their own behalfe" (25). Not "toong-tied," that is, by external authority when their own self-fashioned purpose required articulation. Shakespeare, having arrived in London about the time of the preaching of the sermon, might have remembered the phrase. In the post-Reformation context, outside the theater, there were few places (Paul's Cross was one of them) in which it was possible to attempt to sound the gulf dividing the uses of authority in discourse. Richard Hooker had first cited a telling biblical metaphor in his *Laws*, and he was to use it again in his *Two Sermons upon Part of S. Judes Epistle*: "Thy breach is great like the sea: who can heale thee?"[19] he wrote, applying the words of the prophet Jeremiah to the conflict-ridden state of the kingdom. Bancroft, from his own position, contented himself with a fainter echo: "who . . . would ever have dreamed of such division?"[20]

5

"Bifold Authority"
Law versus Conscience

R ichard Bancroft's sermon was preached at Paul's Cross. As
Millar Maclure has shown, the wooden pulpit in the church-
yard of St. Paul's Cathedral was a traditional site for outdoor
preaching to congregations as mixed as the audiences in Shakespeare's
theater.[1] Combining the learned and the vulgar, aristocrats and peasants, dwellers in the city, court, and country alike, the social topography of Paul's Cross had for some time made it a highly effective site
for public instruction. Bancroft used this social space and religious occasion to chart the precarious trajectory between Puritan Scylla and
Catholic Charybdis that delineated the official Elizabethan policy on
authorization. His sermon was designed to appeal to a great diversity
of religious and political shades of opinion by assuming a via media
position that, if it did not bridge "these extremities of trieng nothing
and curious trieng of all things," could nevertheless address various
types of discursive response and activity. The occasion provided an
outlet through which an authoritative pronouncement on ecclesiastical polity could intervene in the debates among Puritan preachers and
laypersons as well as among what Bacon called "schools, academies,
colleges" and "the arts." In other words, here was a public platform
on which the dominant positions in church and state could be made

to respond to and perhaps intercept diverse religious and cultural discourses.

However, for Bancroft, to address on this broad platform divergent locations of authority was to project a divisive (as well as, ultimately, a divided) position. Even as he spoke he appeared to mediate between the authority of power and the authority residing in the most competent uses of rhetoric, argument, faith, and conviction. But this apparently neat mediation was deeply flawed: while Bancroft offered cogent interpretations of "unlawful authoritie," he had behind him, as its "lawful" alternative, the unquestioned use of force, including an alert apparatus of censorship and suppression.

Annabel Patterson has defined the intriguing constellation in which the uses of interpretation can be contaminated (as well as supplemented) by censorship.[2] To this context should be added that of Jacques Derrida in his reading of Walter Benjamin's *Critique of Violence*: "The law is a power with which one has complied, which one has authorized, an endorsed, justifiable power, a power that is justified by its application, even when this application itself is unjust or cannot be justified."[3] While involving the criterion of the "lawful" in his own interpretive reading of contradictory forms of authority, Bancroft sought to undo the ugly symbiosis of correct interpretation and justified censorship (for which he stood). He thus posited criteria of validity that would themselves endorse the link between the external power of censorship and the internal forces of intellectual conviction, energy, and persuasion. As a Protestant who served as a high-ranking dignitary in the Elizabethan Settlement—a settlement marked by sociopolitical compromise and a studied avoidance of extremes—Bancroft could not but aim at a reconciliation of these differing locations of authority. What was at risk under these circumstances was a strategic alliance, of existential importance to the regime, between post-Reformation Protestantism and the absolutism of the state.

Bancroft's speech was part of the conservative reaction that, having set in with the appointment of John Whitgift as archbishop of Canterbury (1583), led to a marked decline of the more radical Protestant polity in the 1590s. In the long run, however, the via media position was far from secure. Its ultimate failure was adumbrated by James himself at the end of the Hampton Court conference, when he summed up the impasse in the words "No bishop, no king." The reasons for this failure are far too complex to be entered into here. What is of more immediate interest in the present context is the concomitant differentiation among sites of authority in late-Elizabethan discourses—together with the growing incapacity to communicate across the boundaries of hostile convictions and interests.

Although only a generation earlier it had been possible for Foxe to lump together the contexts of preaching, playing, and printing (as, presumably, the unsanctioned fountainhead of all sorts of unauthorized utterances), by the end of the century such an extraordinary alliance could scarcely be taken for granted; the picture had become much more complicated. Even as the scandalous voice of Martin Marprelate found its clandestine way into print, the space for authorization itself was beset by increasingly distinct (and articulate) claims. Censorship, although only marginally able to meddle with performance texts, emerged as a tool of differentiation. The distinction between "matters of state and the arts," unknown in this sharp form to mid-sixteenth-century writers, was now unavoidable. But the "distinction"—as, for instance, developed by Francis Bacon—reflected a blurring of boundaries between the respective power of discourses and the institutionalized discourse of power.

> But surely there is a great distinction between matters of state and the arts, for the danger from new motion and from new light is not the same. In matters of state a change even for the better is distrusted, because it unsettles what is established; these things resting on authority, consent, fame and opinion, not on demonstration. But arts and sciences should be like mines, where the noise of new works and further advances is heard on every side.[4]

What Bacon had in mind was not a reformation of the episcopal church but a reform of the institutions that impeded the "progress of science." It was in this context that he saw a need for tolerating, even encouraging, "the noise of new works," including the work of the "innovator":

> In the customs and institutions of schools, academies, colleges, and similar bodies destined for the abode of learned men and the cultivation of

learning, everything is found adverse to the progress of science. For the lectures and exercises there are so ordered that to think or speculate on anything out of the common way can hardly occur to any man. And if one or two have the boldness to use any liberty of judgement, they must undertake the task all by themselves; they can have no advantage from the company of others. . . . For the studies of men in these places are confined and as it were imprisoned in the writings of certain authors, from whom if any man dissent he is straightway arraigned as a turbulent person and an innovator. (64)

There were political constraints on dealing with "matters of state," and traditional restrictions of "anything out of the common way" in scholarly discourse, but "poesy," as Bacon noted in *Of the Advancement of Learning*, was kept in no such prison. On the contrary, its alliance with "the Imagination" (which "may . . . make unlawful matches and divorces of things") resulted in something "extremely licensed."[5] (Bacon might have added that the performance of poetic texts in the theater was even less "confined and as it were imprisoned in the writings of certain authors." If, on common stages, actors availed themselves of "any liberty of judgement," they did have "advantage from the company of others." Discourse in the theater was not averse to "the danger from new motion"; on the contrary, as Lyly had noted, "trafficke and travell" was its lifeblood. Nor was it shackled to a canon or a poetics that was determined by a veneration for antiquity.)

In Bacon's reading, the basic measure of difference was functional, even in the sense that only through this differentiation was it possible for "innovation" in the arts to be vindicated, because in politics "a change even for the better is distrusted." But this was not to be taken as an endorsement of "loose disputation"; Bacon's voice was not to be "arraigned" as that of "a turbulent person" who might endorse writing and speaking as acts of self-authorized license. His differentiation among discourses allowed for a sense of order among fine distinctions in the respective locations of authority.

It was not simply the temporary setback of Protestant debate and dissension in the 1590s and shortly thereafter that made it possible for Bacon, by keeping aloof from post-Reformation issues of authority, to plead for lawful disjunctions in "liberty of judgement." But in this pleading, the ultimate arbiter of lawfulness was radically redefined. True enough, there was no intention to endorse the self-centered license of authors; whatever "truth" individual writers could procure was not defined as a product of their self-authorized endeavor, and certainly owed nothing to the "authority" of their reputation. "And with regard to authority, it shows a feeble mind to grant so much to authors and yet deny time his rights, who is the author of authors, nay, rather of all authority. For rightly is truth called the daughter of time, not of authority."[6]

Bacon's attempt to historicize "authority" is very different from Bancroft's effort at legitimation. But is it conceivable that it was precisely in view of the growing gaps among sociocultural uses of discourse that the issue of authority could be redefined in the language of temporal contingency? If "time" itself was here posited as a source of "truth" and, at least by implication, as the most potent force behind the given space for authorization, Bacon reconfirmed the rejection of prescribed authority—what Shakespeare's Berowne called that "base authority from others' books" (*Love's Labour's Lost* 1.1.87). The weight, the force, the efficacy of authority had to be found elsewhere, in circumstances in which "truth" was not permanently fixed. But the representation of that truth in language must have been marked by "demonstration" and innovation as well as by instability. In a contingent world, the uses of authorship within contemporary discourses varied greatly. To Bacon's eyes (as well as to Shakespeare's), the conditions of authorization themselves must have appeared mutable, to such an extent that Iago could actually speak of "corrigible authority" (*Othello* 1.3.320).

In the years following 1588, the radical Protestant offensive was effectively halted—so much so that, in the words of Diarmaid Mac-Culloch, there resulted a "Puritan debacle"[7]—but the deep divisions over authority had by no means been overcome. Even when, as a recent historian of the Hampton Court conference suggests, "the Puritans had lost their duel with the bishops," the abandonment of an active political program did not mean the end of competing concepts of church government.[8] Nor was Bancroft's emphasis on "lawful authoritie" widely accepted among Protestant dissidents. Despite the post-Armada wave of unifying sentiment and patriotism that must have inundated many divisions in ideology, the officially sanctioned positions on the law continued to be challenged.[9] Even as the open polemic of Field, Cartwright, and Travers had given way to more introspective, private, and domestic concerns, the Protestant position kept on being fortified.

The Protestants responded to the intellectual and spiritual stalemate that followed the anti-Puritan parliamentary statute of 1593. As in earlier parliaments, the official position had failed to persuade the more radical Protestants of any substantial concurrence between the direction of parliamentary legislation and their own godly model of Christian behavior. In responding to the political defeats of Puritanism inside and outside Parliament, Protestant divines began to project "a theology of dissent that raised conscience over law."[10] Separating the juridical foundation of the Tudor state from that of their own vision of a Protestant church, these theologians would readily concur with William Perkins: "Men in making lawes are subject to ignorance and errour. . . . Therefore it is against reason, that humane lawes being subject to defects, faults, errours, and manifold imperfections, should truly bind conscience, as God lawes doe, which are the rule of righteousness."[11]

Such a differentiation among juridical and religious locations of authority, even when negotiated in strictly theological terms, inevitably articulated differences over the purpose of government and what ultimately authorizes "lawful authoritie" in a commonwealth. By the early seventeenth century, therefore, the theological legitimations of the body politic tended to be increasingly neglected; they were seen as being of little relevance in determining the nature of the law. The irony was that, on a political level, for radical Protestants there was less and less need to conform to any juridical codification of what was seen as the "defects, faults, errours, and manifold imperfections" of the law as a secular source of authority. "God lawes" were something quite different. Nor could "the rule of righteousness" be viewed as being represented by canon law. Instead, it was "conscience" that provided the divinely sanctioned key to the issue of authority.

It was along these lines that Perkins, in *The Whole Treatise of the*

Cases of Conscience (1606), set out to define and appropriate a space for conscience beyond the reach of secular interference. "Conscience" here is the supreme site of self-knowledge, an unfailing source of self-awareness:

> Therefore it [conscience] is nothing els but a part of the understanding, whereby a man knowes what he thinkes, what he wills, and desires, as also in what manner he knoweth, thinketh, or willeth, either good or evil. . . . The natural condition or propertie of every man's conscience is this; that in regard of authoritie and power, it is placed in the middle betweene man and God so as it is under God and yet above man. . . . Upon this it followeth, that no mans commandement or Law can of it self, and by it [*sic*] owne sovereign power bind conscience, but doth it onely by the authoritie and vertue of the written word of God, or some part thereof.[12]

Taking "conscience" as an almost epistemological organ of negotiation between secular and spiritual authority, Perkins emphasizes its independence of "mans commandement." As a catalyst of moral choice, "it signifieth a knowledge ioyned with a knowledge" (44). Knowledge so inspired and, as it were, scripturally fortified cannot abide by the "defects, faults, errours" that underlie the authority of the "Law" of the times and the practice of jurisdiction. "Subjection," he continues, "is indeed to be performed to civill authoritie . . . but not for conscience of the said authoritie or lawes properly and directly, but for conscience of Gods commandements, which appointeth both Magistracie and the authoritie thereof" (45). In other words, "conscience" is an authoritative vessel, a sensitive register through which to appropriate a personal conviction of one's righteousness; at the same time, it is an appropriate instance of expropriating any "civill authoritie." Ultimately, the true location of sublunary authority is inseparable from "the rule of righteousness." Only a generation later, it began to dawn on Perkins's followers that "the rule of righteousness" could only be achieved in the rule of the righteous.

6

Reformation "For Ever After"

The juridical debate about the roots of law, sparked by English Protestantism, could not at its deepest level circumvent the question of an alternative order in the legitimation of ecclesiastical rule. From the point of view of Elizabeth and Whitgift, there was a longstanding wariness of "innovation." But at the height of the Elizabethan regime, in the form of its greatest popular scandal, the issue again came to the fore: Martin Marprelate—"disciple both of Calvin and Dick Tarlton"—had spoken out as "a kind of dramatist in exile."[1] Through his clandestine outlet, he sought to turn the tables on the issue of what constituted the "lawful" grounds of authority. In the *Epistle*, his first attack on John Bridges, "doctor of Divillity," Martin claimed "that our Prelates usurpe their authoritie. They usurpe their authoritie who violently and unlawfully retain those under government that both would and ought (if they might) to shake of that yoke where with they are kept under."[2]

Episcopal rule was unlawful and allegedly usurped authority because it disregarded the desire of those who would "shake of that yoke" and, presumably, replace it with a more representative delegation of authority in church matters. Surprisingly, the envisioned alternative foundation of ecclesiastical authority sought to legitimize itself in reference to its own representativity, conceived of as some more or less contractual form of presbyterian "government." At the same time, this remarkable attack on prelatic authority went hand in hand with a counteractive gesture toward reforming the very grounds of authorizing discourse. Martin's text was authorized in reference to "circumstances" and the presumed needs of its readers who "could not be gotten to read anything" about the issue of the true authority:

> I saw the cause of Christ's government and of the bishops' antichristian dealing to be hidden. The most part of men could not be gotten to read anything written in the defence of the one and against the other. I bethought me therefore of a way whereby men might be drawn to do both, perceiving the humors of men in these times (especially of those that are in any place) to be given mirth. I took that course. I might lawfully do it. Aye, for jesting is lawful by circumstances, even in the greatest matters. The circumstances of time, place and persons urged me thereunto. (14)

Iterating the uses of "lawful," Martin—possibly recalling Luther's fool topos—facetiously linked his own discursive self-empowerment to the clownish privileges of a jester. But on a more serious level, this stance in its turn was legitimated through recourse to the "circumstances of time, place and persons." Martin did not, as Bacon put it, call "truth . . . the daughter of time"; nevertheless he thus specified the grounds of his own authorization. Here was someone in hiding, fashioning the legitimation of his own unsanctioned writing in print—a defiant author-function, in the very teeth of censorship and threatening violence, quite prepared in playful provocation to discuss its own contingent conditions of authorization.

This defiance drew its strength from the debate and discord that followed in the wake of the Reformation, and it anticipated a pattern of radical division. Even before the turn of the century, the conflict over the lawful foundations of authority led to a hardening of official policy, which found justification—in contemporary pamphlets and narratives—for its own increasing apprehensions concerning the spectral image of Anabaptism and its call for unlimited reform.

Soon after her coronation, Elizabeth had attempted to stabilize the effects of the state Reformation, mainly by resisting any uncontrollable move toward further Protestantization. For several years it must have appeared to many that the concentration of all political and religious authority in one absolute office could once and for all unite the nation. Hoping to secure as much unity as was possible under the circumstances, the queen in fact attempted to enforce a modicum of uniformity. But she could do so only by stringently curbing what Gardiner had called "loose disputation" and its Protestant authorization.

The limits of uniformity being what they were, Elizabeth's dilemma emerged early in her reign. It had been an easy enough gesture to arrange to prohibit plays and interludes from dealing with religious matters or with "the governaunce of the estate of the common weale";[3] she now sought to impose limitations on preaching. Here she attempted to make use of potential areas of friction between state-appointed church dignitaries and nonconformist preachers on the radical wing of the Reformation. Under John Field, their indefatigable organizer, and Thomas Cartwright, their leading theologian in Cambridge, these preachers had joined forces under the battle cry of "a further Reformation."[4] Unsanctioned preaching had provided a doctrinal matrix into which the Puritans had introduced a Presbyterian form of religious self-guidance, the classis; as early as 1572 they had gone to Parliament with two "Admonitions." Thus, radical Protestantism, pursuing what Hooker called "the strategem of Reformation for ever after,"[5] was creating its first institutional apparatus outside the officially controlled state church. These evangelists, professing the free interpretation of the gospel, apparently followed the principle of seeking truth by "meere talke." As Richard Cosin portrayed it, they were "scalding hotte in desire for innovation, which they falsely call reformation."[6]

To the queen and all those who upheld the status quo, the call for "further Reformation" must have appeared menacing. The "desire for innovation" stood for a self-justified claim to authorize criticism of the episcopal system and the dissemination of practical counterproposals for its reform. Thus, the phrase "innovation" connoted a radical infringement on the authority of the status quo endorsed by the queen herself. This is the way Cosin used the phrase; it was repeated verbatim by Ormerod. At an early date, Bishop Gardiner had squarely confronted the stratagem of renewal "for ever after" when he declared, "I can admit of no innovations." But to no avail; at the height of the Elizabethan Settlement, Nashe still had innovators at home in mind when, in his portrayal of the Anabaptists, he recorded *their* "owne desires of revenge and innovation."[7] The "false glittering glasse of Innovation" (2:236) referred to by Nashe was a mirror of the encroachments threatening the authority of the Crown.

Faced with the prospect of self-authorized debate and dissension (soon to culminate in Martin Marprelate's subversive attack on the episcopacy), Elizabeth acted promptly. She charged Edmund Grindal, her archbishop, with the task of restricting the preaching of the Word of God. For each county three or four licensed preachers were considered adequate; the rest were to be told to keep quiet, and, above all, no layperson was to be allowed to speak publicly on matters of church or state. The authorized homilies would suffice as vehicles for religious instruction, and (much as Cranmer had designated them) as efficacious—in fact, binding—aids to laypersons' understanding of Scripture. The queen would be more than satisfied if these homilies were read on Sundays; the trumpets of social and religious unity would thus be blown every week for all to hear.[8]

Clearly, this was an intervention of state power in an effort to control the most basic Protestant uses of religious discourse. But the queen was entangled in the post-Reformation settlement and, for the first and only time, she found herself sharply contradicted by her archbishop. Basing his remarks on the authority of the Bible, the intrepid churchman dared to remind the queen that "the Gospel of Christ should be plentifully preached," and that not the sacraments but "the public and continual preaching of God's word" alone aided the salvation of the soul. This could not be achieved by the homilies. Grindal entreated the queen, when addressing matters of faith and religion, "not to pronounce so resolutely and peremptorily, *quasi ex auctoritate*, as ye may do in civil and extern matters."[9]

To resist Elizabeth's disapproval of "public and continual preaching" was a bold move by any standards. The archbishop was put under house arrest for months, but the queen learned her lesson; she ceased trying to implement a plan that, instead of solving the problem, might have produced a deeper crisis by driving a wedge between Crown and church. The outcome again was a compromise, in spite of the quiet suspension of the mild Grindal from his duties; Grindal was followed by the more resolute Whitgift. For the time being the Elizabethan alliance between political power and religious institution may have been strengthened, while the Crown at any rate hesitated to enforce a strict uniformity. But the state church was granted neither a constitution nor a definition of external form or inner structure.[10] In the words of a British historian: "It was not the interest or wish of Court, Council, or Commons to allow the Church they had 'amended' to develop its organisation or to gain a basis for independent action. Let it remain as amorphous, as vague, as harmless as possible, consistently with such decent conformity to the rules of State as any branch of civil service would demand."[11]

In the long run, the refusal to grant the church a constitution only served further to blur the line of demarcation between church and state, and thus failed to fortify the grounds of ecclesiastical authority in Reformation England. In fact, the area of uncertainty must have spread as the links between state church and grass-roots Protestantism tended to wither. The potentially dangerous extent of 'ambivalence' in the post-Reformation settlement only now began to emerge. No doubt the early hopes for integration on the part of the Protestant reformers were slow to die. Perhaps there continued to be some grounds for hope—as Cranmer had wished—"that an open Bible and free discussion would rapidly bring all men to the same conclusions."[12] Hence the surprising tenacity of the feeling that "the new system could be left in vagueness till a general conviction of true religion had come about."[13] As long as the merest illusion of a link between the monarchy's political interest in uniformity and the Protestants' hope for evangelical unity subsisted, the growing divisions in authority and the gaps in controlled authorization could at least partially be contained by the prevailing national sentiment.

Still, these gaps offered unprecedented scope to a host of discursive practices, from the sermon and the pamphlet to tales of travel, jestbooks, narrative fiction, and Elizabethan drama. Ignoring for the moment the popular theater, the most revealing inscription of Elizabethan divisions in authority may well be found in certain narrative representations of the collapse of secular authority under the impact of radical Protestantism. The crisis of authority itself became a scandalous theme when images of armed rebellion in Germany were represented, as in Richard Cosin's tract, as ominous warnings of a "Conspiracie" against the truce of the Tudors.[14]

The description of the Anabaptists in Thomas Nashe's *Unfortunate Traveller* is a *locus classicus* of this kind of account.[15] In this highly experimental prose narrative (to which I shall return in a later chapter), the concurrence of social change and radical Reformation is presented as a problem of the first order in political and spiritual authority. Two diametrically opposed forms of legitimation come into conflict: the ruling authority of state and church is challenged by a radically subversive, socioreligious polity marked by an apparently arbitrary, self-willed authorization of discourse. This challenge is rendered as a grotesque, strangely exaggerated, obsessive gesture of spiritual defiance, culminating in the vehement self-authorization of Protestant prayer. The "lawfulnes of the authoritie they [the Anabaptists] oppose themselves against is sufficiently proved" (2:236), writes Nashe (thereby associating his text with Bancroft's position), whereas its alternative, the challenge to this authority in the discourse of the radical Reformation, becomes the object of satire. The Anabaptists (among whom "John Leiden and all the crue of Cnipperdolings and Muncers" [239] are ranked) use "inspiration" as their battle cry; it is their sole basis for authority. These revolutionary plebeians, adds Nashe, believe that "they knew as much of Gods mind as richer men" (233). Thus their dialogue with God was a wild and passionate prayer "to his face" (239).

Nashe's description of the "violence of long babling praiers" (234) deserves special attention, because this "violence" is represented as informing a highly performative mode of worship in intimate contact with God. Traditional forms of political and spiritual authority are obliterated or displaced when the violence of this kind of discourse reaches its climax in the enthusiastic speech-act replacing all preordained forms of institutionalized mediation by a much more personal, emotional, and indeterminate dialogue with God.

In his attack on the Protestant discourse of self-authorized enthusiasm, Nashe is not far removed from the anti-Puritanical pamphlet; Cosin's *Conspiracie for Pretended Reformation*, for example, also portrays the authority of office as clashing with the (counter)authority of inspiration. And the crisis of authority in England is again negotiated in terms of a narrative of Continental Anabaptism:

> The Bishoppe of Munster demaunded of the King [John Leiden] by what authoritie he tooke upon him to rule in that Citie? Who asked the sayde Bishoppe again, by what authoritie he the sayd Bishoppe claymed any power there? When he answered, that he had it by meanes of election of the Chapter, and by the consent of the people, the King replying, sayde, that himselfe had this authoritie from God. (95)

"That the common people have an especiall authoritie in determining and establishing of Church causes" (96) was the most pugnacious position, because the unsanctioned discourse of Protestantism now took on an institutional form that, as Richard Hooker wrote, sought "farther to erect a popular authority of elders."[16] In England, this democratic authority was for the most part of Presbyterian provenance, but it was also said to apply to the German Anabaptists, stimulated by "Thomas Muncer," with his "opinion of equalitie of authoritie and dignitie" of all believers.[17]

Nashe's attack on self-authorized uses of enthusiasm in religious discourse falls into place in this context. The Anabaptists appeared to him entirely in alliance with those English "fanatical fantastiques, Schismatiques, heretiques, or malecontended treasonable conspirators" whose language was so incomprehensible, so unrestrained, and so violent because it refused to follow the traditional signs of authority in church and state. As Nashe could have read in Cosin, disrespect for these signs was erroneously justified by that self-determined "maner of praying" which made the authorization of religious discourse by bishops and priests superfluous. As a result, the authority of the church as the privileged site of mediation with divinity was undermined by more immediate sources of legitimation derived from "speaking to God face to face."[18] In the language of Cosin as well as in that of Nashe, an almost grudging perception of the power of the performative shines through the hostile description of prayer. "They pray, they howle, they expostulate with God . . . and use such unspeakable vehemence," says Nashe in depicting "their vehement outcries and clamours" (2:285, 289).

In contrast to these violent images of self-authorization, there is here as elsewhere a marked reticence in the portrayal of the ruling authority, a remarkable readiness to admit the limits of the idea of "lawful" authority as defined by the state church. In *An Admonition to the People of England* (1589), Bishop Thomas Cooper went out of his way to emphasize these limits in his discussion of the intensity of radical "inspiration." "These men," wrote the bishop, "in rebuking [worldly] ambition, reach at higher authoritie and power, then any bishop in England hath or will use."[19] The bishop knew the strength of an unmediated inspiration by the Word of God; he suspected the relative weakness of the opposed form of legitimation, which for the prelate arises from the mere power of his office in the state church—an office that had lost a good deal of its prestige and independence following the Reformation.[20]

As opposed to such vulnerability in the official authorization of supreme power, the force behind unsanctioned, internalized authority is evident even in the satirical language of a caricature such as that offered by Nashe. The imaginative assimilation of discursive spontaneity, "face to face" with divinity, drew on an untapped source of cultural energy. In the later and more refined form of devotional lyrics, this distinctively Protestant dynamic helped inspire what Barbara Lewalski calls "the various and vacillating spiritual conditions and emotions the soul experiences in meditation, prayer, and praise."[21] But although the Protestant lyric, harking back to the psalmist's anguished cries *de profundis*, embraced the written word as the incarnation of divine truth, the earlier tradition of "vehement outcries and clamours" was less literary and quite unbridled.

At this stage, the internalization of the Word served to appropriate an unprecedentedly deep range of conviction and sentiment, guarding it against external delegitimation. And this oral mode of discourse was often buttressed by printed texts, which made it possible for the individual reader to "go back over difficult passages, compare texts and glosses, and find one's own way about the scriptures."[22] Even so, the performative force of the word spoken in rapture helped transcend not a few frontiers of authorization. Seen in conjunction with the Protestant practice of diligent reading and homiletic listening, these discursive activities cannot be discounted as mere wild enthusiasms. Despite the ineluctable differentiation of discourses, the alliance of preaching and printing continued right into the years of the Civil War.

In the late sixteenth and early seventeenth centuries, the scope for the authorization and appropriation of new uses of knowledge and judgment was thus scarcely controllable. As long as Protestant preachers continued to have access to the pulpit, writers to the printing press, and dramatists to the public theater, it was possible for them to assimilate unacknowledged areas of meditation, signification, and performance. Throughout the period, the gaps between the exercise of power and the authorization of written and spoken language grew wider, and the use of channels of propagation and mediation became more flexible and effective. To recognize these gaps is important, especially where the process of differentiation led to what Bacon called "the noise of new works" and "the boldness" to use "liberty of judgement." But far from unfolding within a self-enclosed system of signs, the bold, silent work of new significations was inseparable from an external and internal process of socialization. Such "boldness" was particularly hard to resist when the gaps between power and writing could at least sometimes be bridged, even though they were not yet filled by, or assimilated to, new alliances between them. The process of this socialization was unsaturated and remained this side of closure, thus allowing for appropriations of insight, knowledge, and privilege, as well as for expropriation. All this had a historical and, more strictly speaking, a political underside, which censorship could not control.

It is in this context that Elizabethan divisions in authority were conducive to unprecedented representations. Historically, these have a lot to do with what the historian Joel Hurstfield called "the enormous gap" between the Elizabethan uses of language and the circumstances of contemporary history, including "the gap between the constitution and the political reality, between those who wielded authority and those who merely legalized its use, between the language of law and the facts of life."[23] More specifically, the "language of law" could be intercepted by such interiorized locations of authority as befitted the radical Protestant conscience. In the effort to ward off the letter of the law against the spirit of justice, the distance between Anabaptists and William Perkins—otherwise very considerable—shrank: there was a sense that "law can do no right," even that "law itself is perfect wrong" (*King John* 3.1.111, 115)—a sentiment culminating in Shakespeare's great indictment of "the great image of authority" where the difference between "the thief" and "the justice" was to be suspended in the burning pain of a suffering conscience that is "bound / Upon a wheel of fire" (*The Tragedy of King Lear* 4.6.39–40).

II

Sign and Authority
in Early Modern Fiction

The Protestant paradigm of self-authorization can provide no more than one distinct procedure in a complex spectrum of discursive practices constituting the new strategies of legitimation and representation in the early modern period. If, as John Lyly noted in the prologue to *Midas*, the "whole worlde" had become a "Hodge-podge," the sense of expanding "trafficke and travell"[1] could hardly be confined to the topography of the Reformation.

The sixteenth- and early-seventeenth-century prose narrative was a particularly prominent site for the tracking of these strategies. Throughout Europe, the breakdown of barriers between various literary traditions was accompanied by an explosion of experiments in fiction writing in which diverse types of author-function began to collide, coalesce, or interlock. Several of these narratives continued to draw on an older oral culture of communication; at the same time, most of them were subjected to the circumstances of an emerging market, and could ill afford to disregard popular demand.

This was especially the case wherever the declining institution of patronage came to be superseded, or complemented, by an as yet immature market for the products of the printing press—in Lyons, Paris, Antwerp, Frankfurt, Strassburg, and Madrid. The combined impact of print and commerce, together with increasing literacy, stimulated new patterns of authorizing and reading fictional narrative. It was in these thriving centers that a new type of authorship could come about by being able to exploit multiple cultural uses and conflicting expectations in the reception of texts in the vernacular. These were inscribed in and appeared to sustain whatever authority the new author-narrator was able to muster. For such writers as Rabelais, Fischart, Nashe, Cervantes, and the authors of picaresque fiction, such authority was no longer given by traditional standards; rather, the new prose fiction could almost teasingly be both traditional and scandalous in its respective levels of appeal, heavily stylized and at the same time down-to-earth, moving between topos and topicality, rhetoric and experience, in a newly self-conscious manner.

It is difficult to historicize and to define concisely the new author-function in the making because of its varieties and highly experimental points of departure. There were several traditional sites of authority from which this writing sought to distinguish its own rhetoric of legitimation, forms of fictional narrative that had previously been dominant but now found themselves in a state of crisis: these were, as my discussion of Erasmus, Rabelais, Nashe, and Cervantes will suggest, the allegorical mode and, especially, chivalric romance. The authority implicitly inscribed in these literary forms could polemically or through parody be engaged by the emerging author-function in early modern prose fiction.

7

Contexts of
Renaissance Humanism

In coming to terms with the issue of authority, the new fiction confronted the humanist attempt to reestablish classical grounds for the authorization of discursive practice in a variety of pedagogic, poetic, moral, and political domains. In England in particular, the humanist claim for writerly authority was virtually undisputed. According to Sir Philip Sidney, "the Lawrell Crown" was conferred "upon the Poets as victorious, not onely of the Historian, but over the Philosopher."[1] Since the latter was thought to hold forth "by precept," and the former "by example," poetry could be said to be "passing each of these in themselves" (3:13), in that it "coupleth the general notion with the particular example." But since "the Poet is indeed, the right popular Philosopher" (16), the more consequential distinction, well established in neoclassical doctrine, was made with admirable clarity: "Poesie," Sidney notes, "dealeth with . . . the universall consideration, and the Historie with . . . the particular." While the particularizing historian appeared to be "captivated to the trueth of a foolish world" and hence "bound to tell things as they were," the poet, according to high-Renaissance doctrine, was thought to be more philosophically concerned not with what was but with "the divine consideration of what may be and should be." Even to Sidney, the classical authority of a privileged "Vates" continued to be immense, when "our Poet" appeared as "the Monarch" (19), precisely because "the Application [was] divinely true, but the discourse itself fained" (2).

Writing that was in accord with neoclassical authority appeared to legitimize itself through its association with a specific idealizing mode of representation, especially that of the epic. The authorizing muses, as in Homer and Virgil, could be used as efficacious agents of invocation; in referring to them it was possible for the poet in Renaissance epic to justify the elevated level of his artful creation, "having all," as Sidney put it, "from Dante his heaven to his hell, under the authority of his pen" (17–18). The function of the poet in the epic could be fortified by association with the social role of the courtier or the virtuoso, as well as with a godlike vatic status. The author-function in the Renaissance epic was sustained by the providential powers of the poet, who felt called upon to assert an element of divinity in his life-giving creation.

It may be right to see in Western philosophy at this time what Hiram Haydn has called "the ultimate desertion of the universal for the particular";[2] indeed, the skeptical disintegration of providentialism was one aspect of this change. But we should not underestimate just how difficult it was, then and subsequently, even to attempt to make the particular signify independently of the universal. "The particular example" had for so long been reduced to a function of "the universall consideration" that any independent assertion of particularity had to be problematic, unsanctioned as it was by any universalizing context of validation. Because of this largely subsidiary relationship, the particular, far from simply being foregrounded by the destabilizing of the universal, was itself always in danger of destabilization. Participating in a supreme order of universality, the epic poet was perfectly authorized to particularize any truthful "application." But without such participation, the ultimate source of authority—the godlike access to truthful creation itself—was jeopardized. As Tasso put it, the poet of excellence "is called divine for no other reason than that, resembling the supreme Artificer in his operations, he comes to participate in His divinity" [il quale non per altro divino é detto, se non perché al supremo Artefice nelle sue operazioni assomigliandosi, della sua divinita viene a partecipare].[3]

In England, as John Guillory has shown, the Protestant epic poet would seek to modify traditional neoclassical sources of authority. The closure of the biblical canon went hand in hand with a strenuous defense of the poet's authority and led to a renewal of the ancient figure of inspiration. By invoking the participation of divinity in the personalized act of poetic production, Spenser and Milton projected the beginnings of the use of the imagination as a source of legitimation.[4] However, legitimizing the author's voice by "something of divinity" put a considerable burden of unity and representativity on the institution of authorship—a burden especially heavy given the shifting conditions of circulation that obtained after the advent of print in the marketplace. The premises of authorization that confronted the writers of pamphlets, prose fictions, and texts for the London theaters were markedly different from both the inspirational authority in the Protestant epic and the widely accepted validity of the "universall consideration" in neoclassical poetics.

How, in the absence of any metaphysically or aesthetically sanctioned writerly authority, did these early modern genres cope with the need for legitimation? In view of the gulf between the uses of secular writings and those of Scripture, it must have been difficult for the new authorship to benefit overtly from any link between the political economy of the products of the printing press and the Reformation mode of self-authorization. In the first place, such a link would appear to presuppose a degree of secularization in Protestant culture that was not available in the Elizabethan or early-Stuart period. And as soon as considerations of universality and divinity ceased to provide any telos to the act of writing and the effects of reading, the business of authorization must have been reduced to a more purely pragmatic level of justification. Here, again, the question was whether the circulation of secular texts, resulting in the communication of worldly knowledge and entertainment, could be considered legitimate outside the context of moral aims and public values.

The answer to this is complex. The new world of early modern ideology with its abstract motivations was interlocked with "politizing" uses of religion, with new validations of "discovery" and progress, and with a variety of causes associated with the rise of sovereign states and imperial nations. True enough, as Thomas More and Erasmus show rather impressively, humanist precepts could still be read as aloof from these. Even so, there emerged at least one area in which humanist concepts of language could be made to embrace politically charged perspectives on public uses of speech, which would vitally affect the issue of authorization in learned as well as popular modes of writing. This was the humanist notion of the authority of speech as informed by social custom and consensus. As against scholastic logicians and grammarians, distinguished humanists such as Lorenzo Valla, Juan Luis Vivés, Erasmus, and More had redefined the knowledge of language as *scientia de sermone*, privileging the spoken language, *usus loquendi*, as a vessel of the foremost authority. As Lisa Jardine, Martin Elsky, and others have shown, the humanists, in rejecting ontological positions in logic, substituted "place-logic," which was particularly suited to the needs of rhetoric and literary studies. At the same time, this modification of the scholastic uses of logic helped bring about conditions of discourse hostile to "base authority from others' books," and favorable to "discovery" and the public impact of new ideas.[5]

This link between humanist antischolasticism and experimental discovery was complicated by a continuing search for a revitalized political telos in the relationship of things and thoughts, outer and inner sources of articulation. As humanists sought to redefine the foundations of order and public responsibility in terms of individual as well as public uses of language, the emphasis on *sermo* as a vital medium of knowledge had practical (as well as ideological) consequences. In the curricula of Elizabethan grammar schools, for example, redesigned according to humanist precepts, future writers developed an esteem for truthful uses of speech that went hand in hand with an acknowledged "reverence for the very idea of the author." As Elsky (following T. W. Baldwin) has further suggested, the emphasis on *vox* was widely viewed as "at the center rather than the periphery of language."[6] Elsky skillfully and on the basis of a vast amount of Renaissance material rejects the Derridean notion "that the distinction between speech and writing is a duplicitous attempt to justify the autonomous subject and the objective world" (3). It is only "by ignoring an intellectual movement as important as humanism" that (à la Foucault) "one can argue that writing and not speech provided the theoretical basis for understanding language in the Renaissance" (4). (This emphasis, incidentally, was part and parcel of the "small Latin" to which Shakespeare was exposed in his grammar school.) At the same time, the humanist positioning of the writer as a creative and responsible agent between interior and exterior modes of expression helped fortify the public plane and moral status of authorship. If on such a plane the discursive constructs of order failed to promote the political health of the state or nation, the nature of this failure was political as well as linguistic.

There is convincing evidence that such English humanists and pedagogues as Richard Mulcaster, Sir Thomas Elyot, and Roger Ascham conceived of language, and primarily of *usus loquendi*, as a thoroughly public article in the culture of the commonwealth. In doing so, they presupposed a "connection between morally disposed political power and the verbal health of a nation."[7] This emphatic link between linguistic and political levels of power could be seen as enhancing the interaction between true verbal competence and the external locations of government; ideally, such an interaction would involve more than submission to the state. Once it was possible for the former (*auctoritas*) to be interiorized in terms of a much-desired convergence between the tongue, the heart, and the book, the latter (the authority derived from *potestas*) could not be reduced to a purely external mechanism of might and obedience. Writing, in this dialectic, would as a matter of course be authorized as, and find its legitimation in, a public institution dedicated to the fine art of verbal *and* political action.

Again, to describe the humanist project as one of closure and cooperation is not to suggest that contemporary fiction or drama tended to identify with idealistic positions such as these. The practice of authorization in narrative and drama certainly did not consistently subscribe to dictates of either interiorization or the recuperation of political order; on the contrary, even among those writers crossing the boundaries between the learning of humanism and the writing of entertainment there was, as Elsky notes in reference to Ben Jonson, an awareness of "the frailty of language in the face of adverse social and political forces."[8] And even when it was possible for a humanistically trained poet such as Marlowe to aggrandize blank verse to the summit of dramatic eloquence, such verbal empowerment—in *Tamburlaine*, for instance, or in *Doctor Faustus*—could be seen as having a deeply unsettling effect on the humanist logic of good speakers producing good societies (and vice versa). Marlowe's uses of rhetoric in *Tamburlaine* were designed to enhance dramatic images of the political and military power of a rebellious shepherd, rather than those of a legitimate representative of sovereignty.

Although, then, the political implications of the authority of such eloquent uses of *sermo* could readily be embraced on the popular stage, this did not quite affirm the humanist concept of interdependence between linguistic order and political stability. As Shakespeare was to show in his extraordinarily varied handling of relations among power and eloquence (in plays from *Richard II*, *Henry V*, and *Hamlet* to *King Lear*, *Coriolanus*, and *Timon of Athens*), there was a good deal of contingency in these dramatized coordinates of eloquence and order: continuity between verbal and political parameters of authority could be viewed ironically as well as strategically. Hence, the humanist search for possible areas of interaction between the verbal and the political must have suggested some stimulating dramatic interrogations and revisions. In the theater's radically different context of circulation and authorization, the search for order through the representational uses of discourse led to an abortive result that, paradoxically, revealed the humanist project at its most vulnerable. The humanist project of reason in its autonomy—"that noble and most sovereign reason" (*Hamlet* 3.1.160)—could tragically be "o'erthrown," "Blasted with ecstasy," as could the supreme balance in humanism's view of man, the great reconciliation of authorities, intellectual and powerful, scholarly and military—"The courtier's, soldier's, scholar's, eye, tongue, sword" (154–63).[9]

Thus, unlike humanist discourse, with its considerable areas of convergence among diverse locations of authority, early modern drama and prose narrative were bound to assume a more volatile and divided space for authorization. In assimilating some heterogeneous and divisive material, the new fiction sought to explore areas of friction and conflict among competing sites of authority. Similarly, as this fiction responded to diverse expectations in its audience and to contingent conditions of circulation, neoclassical concepts of generic order and literary decorum were dispensed with; traditional humanistic poetics proved neither congenial nor adequate to the representation of circumstances in which, for instance, in Thomas Nashe's *Unfortunate Traveller*, a picaresque page "with a Dunstable tale, made up [his] market."[10]

Here, the redefinition of authority in the production and circulation of literary texts was not so far removed from related sites of rupture and contingency in the political economy of cultural circulation. For example, in the new world of exchange relations, traditional warrants tended to be gradually emptied of their fixed legal substance. As the outward authority of ancient writ and conveyance gave way to modes of legitimation that were more abstract and contingent, conservative forms of entitlement surrendered to the law of supply and demand. Similarly, released from the fixed circuit of a predictable type of audience response, literary authority was free to inform a much wider ensemble of representational forms and functions. There was a connection between the rise of these vulnerable and unpredetermined strategies of representation and the awareness of crisis in the dichotomous drift of relations between political *potestas* and intellectual authority. Like the theater, Elizabethan prose furnished "a laboratory of representational possibilities for a society perplexed by the cultural consequences of its own liquidity."[11]

It is in this respect that the negotiation of authority in early modern prose fiction came to establish the most illuminating analogy for the comparable project in the theater. Both genres found themselves in a situation in which the diminishing viability of traditional types of authority allowed for unprecedented apertures in representation, in which circumstances both drama and prose narrative appeared to thrive. But although the theater—except for an occasional prologue or epilogue—usually precluded a self-conscious articulation of the new author-function, contemporary fiction was free to elucidate a new kind of authorization—and it could do so in the emerging point of view of author-narrators. Authors of prose fiction, unlike dramatists, were in a position to spell out the crisis of authority as a problem of

111

representation within their own texts. This was possible on premises (shared, for instance, by Rabelais and Nashe) that did not entirely dissociate the fiction from the very real business of its communication and signification, thereby suspending and yet consummating "the passage from minstrel as actor to minstrel as auctor."[12]

8

Authority in Relations of Orality

In order to pave the way for this approach to authority in early modern prose narrative, it seems useful to begin by establishing a historical perspective on some communal grounds of authorization, a perspective that may serve as a kind of foil. Traditional modes of authorized discourse can be traced in a cultural context in which the assertion of authority was directly and unselfconsciously associated with a social occasion for the recital and reception of narrative. Standards of proficiency were linked to the more immediate social circumstances; these in turn were inseparable from the culture's use of communication as a symbolic means of validating the norms of existence. Long after communitas, in the words of Victor Turner, had ceased to be "symbolically affirmed by periodic rituals" and festivities,[1] the narrator's competence continued to be gauged according to the rules of the cultural occasion. Under these rules, the cultural transaction was marked by a good deal of continuity between author-function and narrative performance. In simple terms, there tended to be more homogeneity than difference among the production, the reproduction, and the reception of narrative.

In these circumstances, authority was neither the function of a personalized medium of rhetoric and inspiration (as in the Renaissance epic) nor a matter of the provision of pleasure in a competitive marketplace of cultural commodities. Instead, whatever legitimation was called for helped associate diverse areas of cultural practice in a context that—throughout medieval culture—marked elements of a transition from a nonliterate to a literate society. In western Europe, this transition was of course a somewhat problematic concept that, as Brian Stock has shown, at once calls for qualification. There was

> no clear point of transition from a nonliterate to a literate society. For, even at the high point of oral usage, let us say, in the medieval context, continental Europe during the tenth century, writing was not by any means absent from everyday transactions; and, when literate norms were firmly re-established in law and government, that is, by the mid-twelfth, the spoken word did not cease to play a large cultural role. The change, as suggested, was not so much from oral to written as from an earlier state, predominantly oral, to various combinations of oral and written.[2]

Moreover, the 'transition' in question was entirely uneven in various cultural areas. Although, for example, by the end of the thirteenth century the authority of unrecorded memory, as witnessed by custom or by uninscribed symbolic tokens (such as Earl Warenne's conquering sword), was generally superseded by written charters, chirography, testimonials, and related memoranda and certificates, in other fields of discursive practice this was not the case.[3] For instance, in the telling and reception of heroic epic matter, knowledge in its inscribed form did not necessarily provide adequate levels of validity, even when—as in the case of *Beowulf*—oral recital was based on a cultural reference system that did presuppose the existence of a written text. Once these complications are fully taken into account, this highly sporadic process of 'transition' may well be said to have been marked by a growing dissociation between author and narrator, as well as between the text's meaning and the audience's belief. It is this dissociation that, ultimately, gave rise to the early modern convention of fictionality and to strategies of representation that profoundly reconditioned the ends and means of authorization.

This, however, drastically condenses a paradigm for narrative authorization that needs to be further differentiated in at least some of its basic aspects. Since to recapture the communal context of a purely

114

oral narrative in western Europe is for all practical purposes impossible, we need to turn to the work of anthropologists in order to reconstruct any consistent preliterary norms of authority in symbolic communications. Here Pierre Clastres's study of the uses of chants and narratives among the Guarini Indians is most revealing: among the Guarini, there is a discursive practice that appears to be authorized by an extraordinarily comprehensive grasp of both the practical and the mythological uses of language.[4] The kind of competence associated with the performance of these "hymnes, chants et prières" is undifferentiated in that the *sage-chamane* disposes of a remarkable *prophétisme sauvage* that—in a tradition going back at least to the sixteenth and seventeenth centuries—seeks to cope with "political significations of crisis in a society without a state."[5]

To a certain extent, this language of mythical narrative reproduces a kind of integration of practical, religious, and political concerns. All these concerns appear to share elements of a semantic space that, in pre-Socratic writings, relates to a matrix of *technē* and myth within which pre-Platonic uses of mimesis may well have to be situated.[6] The immutable strength and the continued viability of this language seem to be closely linked to the structure of its authority. In his most exalted moments, the sage-narrator abandons, as it were, his own utterance to the voice of the gods (and their knowledge): the medium—the sage who is representing—is carried away by what is represented, that is, "la parole prophétique." In his exaltation "to tell what the Guarini possess as their most precious," the narrator, "having lost all constraint . . . forgot . . . that he was a human and spoke as if he had become a god."[7] What ultimately authorizes the utterance is "la magie du verbe que s'empare totalement de l'orateur et le porte à ces sommets où sèjourne ce que nous savons être la parole prophétique" (123). It is the exalted use (and a corresponding concept) of language as the Word that is at the bottom of this authority: "La Parole, comme signe et substance de l'humain . . . la substance à la fois du divin et de l'humain" (25). Hence, the chant is sacred "en ce qu'il est le langage des hommes s'adressant aux dieux" (29).

In his remarkable if somewhat partial reading of this material, Jean-François Lyotard has developed a paradigm of premodern narrative legitimation that, in the present context, is illuminating. According to his reading, "knowledge" in the language of the Guarini is served by a discursive practice whose authority is only minimally differentiated. There is on this level no concept of *savoir* except one that simultaneously embraces all fields of knowledge: *savoir-faire*, *savoir-vivre*, and *savoir-écouter*. Since this type of knowledge goes beyond *connaissance* (in Lyotard's usage, the "determination and application of the criterion of truth"), it can easily embrace "criteria of efficiency (technical qualification), of justice and/or happiness (ethical wisdom), or the beauty of a sound or color (auditory and visual sensibility)."[8]

In a premodern context, then, the narrative uses of this undifferentiated type of knowledge do not necessarily serve the function of representation. Insofar as the narrative does allow for representational functions, authority in this discourse is geared equally to the levels of both its enunciation and its performance. The standards of legitimation appear comprehensive, the process of authorization indivisible. This purely oral discourse brings together, as it were in one voice, the know-how for the composition and for the narration of stories. The *savoir-vivre* has to do with the 'relation' of these stories as a relation of, and in relation to, the practical awareness of the circumstances "through which the community's relationship to itself and its environment is played out" (21). This type of awareness is joined to the *savoir-écouter*, the capacity for listening, responding, and comprehending. In other words, the authority of the early poet-narrator's voice is informed first of all by an ability to listen to, to comprehend, and to preserve tribal memories, horizons of hope and despair expressed in the form of myth. Such a connection between speaking and listening makes it difficult, as Lyotard notes, "to imagine such a culture first isolating the post of narrator from the others in order to give it a privileged status in narrative pragmatics, then inquiring into what right the narrator . . . might have to recount what he recounts, and finally undertaking the analysis or anomnesis of its own legitimacy" (22–23).

Unlike this radically foreshortened perspective on preliterary patterns of narrative legitimation, the uses of authority in medieval narrative are inseparable from an extremely complex and changeful spectrum of interactions between orality and literacy. The interlocking of the two appears especially important when, as is the case with *Beowulf*'s textuality, narrative authority in its written discursive form is not primarily that of books.

For Anglo-Saxon writers such scripted or literary authority was already available. In the case of *Beowulf*, the author must have been familiar with biblical poems of the Caedmonian cycle and at least somewhat cognizant of classical models, not to mention Anglo-Saxon secular poems of the type exemplified by *Finnsburg, Deor,* and *Waldere*. Although *Beowulf* is generally assumed to have been put in its present form only in writing,[9] it may be assumed that the poem was composed as remembered from having been heard and, once written down, intended in turn to be read or sung aloud. As Hans-Jürgen Diller suggests, the strategies of reference identification used in the poem are "consistent with oral delivery"; a number of other features as well "are best explained as left-overs from the habit of oral composition."[10]

Although the clerical author, privileged in his connection with an Anglian court, addressed himself in writing to an aristocratic audience, the recurring gestures of authorization remained in many ways characteristically oral. At this distance we can only speculate about the actual proximity of *auctor* to minstrel, but there is quite conclusive evidence that the writer did not aim at devaluing the discursive activity of the *scop* as presenter. Nor did the author set out to reduce the cultural memory of his contemporary audience. On the contrary, the anonymous writer inscribed the desire of the *scop* to legitimate his recital by displaying a far-ranging type of knowledge that was orally transmitted. In order to demonstrate his competence—his ability to revitalize the cultural code of his audience—the poet-presenter went out of his way to establish what might be called the distinctiveness of his memory. The phrase used repeatedly to assert the special dignity and the unique authority of his epic knowledge qua recital is "ne hyrde ic"—"never have I [the narrator] heard the like of it." This dignity, however, was not primarily that of the person who recollects, but rather that of the event recollected in narration. Consider, for example, the passage in which the narrator says that he had never heard of a ship equipped "more splendidly" [ne hyrde ic cymlicor ceol gegyrwan] (l. 38).

What legitimates the narration is the particular quality and the abundance of evidence of a knowledge that has been orally transmitted, as in the recurrent phrase "as I have heard say" or "as I have learnt by asking."[11] The *scop* is privileged by his capacity for "learning," for "hearing of" things "far and wide." Again and again this capacity is indicated by "ge-frignan," as in the phrase "Da ic wide gefrægn" (l. 74), which denotes an ability shared by both the hero, Beowulf (l. 194), and the collective "we" (l. 2)—the *scop* who had been and the audience that now is listening.[12] Thus, a comprehensive knowledge constitutes the authority by which the author-narrator may, in telling his story, present himself as the knower of names, the one who has spoken to, and heard of, many.

If the "unity of sentiment"[13] of ancient epic is anywhere inscribed in the text of *Beowulf*, it is through this central figure of orality, "ge-frignan," with its connotation of learning or hearing "by inquiry."[14] The force of authorization may be quite different each time the figure appears, but the language authorizing the poet-narrator's knowledge is never far removed from that denoting the sources of awareness in both his audience and his characters. In other words, the *discours* that is representing is semantically related to the verbal configurations, the *histoire*, of what is represented.

Even more important, in the opening lines of the epic, the "we" establishes a community among the teller and those who are told the tale, and it is in this social setting that this prominent figure of orality can best authorize the undifferentiated sources of knowledge.

> Hwæt, we Gar-Dena in geardagum,
> þeodcyninga þrym gefrunon.
> (ll. 1–2)

The "we," much like the "Uns" in the opening line of the *Nibelungenlied*, is designed to link the audience and the narrator in a common act of remembrance. "We . . . gefrunon" is very much a conventional formula (as used, for instance, in *Exodus* and the opening of *Andreas*)

118

by which oral sources of a memory common to all present were appealed to and stimulated.[15] These pronouns are meant to emphasize and draw authority from a sense of community among poet, *scop*, and audience. But although the poet-narrator in the written text is anxious to authorize his poem and its presentation, he submits to that "dissolution of the performing self in the performance style,"[16] which Susan Stewart has traced in the traditional ballad.

The inscription of an oral structure of authority in a strictly literary text appears all the more remarkable when we recall that a different type of authority, one derived from the reading of books, was easily available to the clerical author. To illustrate this we need only glance at Ælfric's homilies, in which he often appeals to a distinctly literary authority in order to fortify the authenticity of what his own text endeavors to say. This is the case, for instance, when he refers to "wyrdwriteras," those who write about kings, or adds "swa swa hit awriten is ge on hæþenum bocum ge on Bibliothecan" [as it is written in heathen books as well as in the Bible].[17] As he notes, the intention behind providing sources for these literary quotations is "þætan us gelyfe" [so that we may be believed].

Abbot Ælfric's clerical basis of legitimation seems deliberately to reject the almost diametrically opposed inclination in *Beowulf* to sustain an oral context as a strongly supplementary ground on which to validate what is represented. His emphasis on what "the books tell us" betrays an author-function pitted against the collective recollection of the more recent history of the Anglo-Saxons.[18] In contrast, the clerical writer of *Beowulf*, far from obliterating these recollections, used them as a central site of compatibility between what was representing and what was represented. What his text relates is achieved by the rehearsing, through the writing itself, of *relations* of orality. It is by recapturing and transmuting these relations (among the teller, the tale, and its listeners) into textuality that this rehearsal implicates a socializing performance of epiphanic knowledge.

9

Minstrelsy and
Author-Function in Romance
Malory

This brief glance at the uses of authority in early narrative may appear to have taken us some distance away from Renaissance representation. But a matter of considerable consequence has been established: where an undifferentiated type of cultural occasion prevails, and the dissociation of author and narrator remains limited, the structure of authority can retain considerable elements of homogeneity. In premodern narrative there is a relatively homological relationship between *histoire* and *discours*. What is represented maintains considerable continuity with what and who is representing. The two types of discursive knowledge combine complementarily; they are received as all the more authoritative in that they serve to recreate what must have been valid significations of heroism, justice, hope, and expediency. In this traditional author-function, the poet's memory of names and places and the presenter's competence in rehearsing them seem to be fused with common acts of evaluation. Authority, then, appears inseparable from these capacities for denotation, connotation, and judgment; together, they provide a structural correlative to the undifferentiated social context itself.

While on this level the process of authorization precedes, and perhaps precludes, the deliberate uses of fiction as artifice, this is no longer true once a differentiation between author and presenter sets in. In terms of the literary history of narrative, the beginnings of such differentiation can be seen in chivalric romance, as when Chrétien de Troyes in *Erec et Enide* goes out of his way to dissociate the written work of the poet from the oral presentation of the minstrel. As he notes in the prologue, "Crestiiens de Troies . . . tret d'un conte d'a-vanture / Une mout bele conjointure."[1] This disjunction between the matter of narrative ("conte") and its refined composition ("bele con-jointure") constitutes a radically new point of departure in represen-tational strategy. In the words of Rainer Warning, this point reflects "the basic pragmatic difference between oral and written form."[2] What is even more significant is that the poet sees beyond a simple assertion of pride in his work; he is not merely content to derive "from a story of adventure a pleasing argument."[3] In *Erec et Enide*, Chrétien, in fact, links the awareness of his own compositional achievement with an attempt to denigrate the authority of those mere presenters "who earn a living by telling stories" [qui de conter vivre vuelent] (l. 22). According to the poet, their purely oral presentations "mutilate and spoil" [depecier et corrompre] (l. 21) the chivalric matter in the presence of noble audiences.

The polemical differentiation between poet and *conteor* must have affected the issue of authority at the very point where an important difference in the strategic uses of representation came into the picture. Here, unlike in the traditional polemics against incompetent com-petitors in the *chansons de geste*, it is the author who seeks to establish his own identity. This is precisely what Chrétien does when, writing of himself in the third person singular, he introduces his name and even, in a later composition, a list of his writings. This is how he be-gins his *Cligés*: "Cil qui fist d'Erec et d'Enide . . ."—"He who wrote of Erec and Enide, and translated into French the commands of Ovid and the Art of Love, and wrote the Shoulder Bite . . . will tell another story now."[4] Listing his credentials as a writer, the poet seeks to cir-cumscribe a literary text (as distinct from its transaction) as the site of authority. On this basis he can guard his composition from the "mutilating" or "corrupting" process of oral transmission. What, in the opening lines of *Erec et Enide*, is authoritative is not the social occasion, with its undifferentiated celebration of "gefræge," but a differentiation of types and uses of knowledge that allows for the discrimination evidenced by the phrases "panser et antandre" and "prover et savoir":

> So Chrétien de Troyes maintains that one ought always to study and strive to speak well and teach the right; and he derives from a story of adventure a pleasing argument whereby it was to be proved and known that he is not wise who does not make liberal use of his knowledge so long as God may give him grace.[5]

> > [Por ce dit Crestiiens de Troies
> > Que reisons est que totes voies
> > Doit chascuns panser et antandre
> > A bien dire et a bien aprandre,
> > Et tret d'un conte d'avanture
> > Une mout bele conjointure,
> > Par qu'an puet prover et savoir
> > Que cil ne fet mie savoir,
> > Qui sa sciance n'abandone
> > Tant con Deus la grace l'an done.]
> > (*Erec et Enide*, ll. 9–18)

This type of "sciance" is inseparable from literacy; the privileged location of it, so conducive to the poet's sense of "conjointure," is, in *Cligés*, referred to in no uncertain terms:

> This story, which I intend to relate to you, we find written in one of the books of the library of my lord Saint Peter at Beauvais. From there the material was drawn of which Chrétien has made this romance. The book is very old in which the story is told, and this adds to its authority. From such books which have been preserved we learn the deeds of men of old and of the times long since gone by. (91)

> > [Ceste estoire trovons escrite,
> > Que conter vos vuel et retreire,
> > An un des livres de l'aumeire
> > Mon seignor saint Pere a Biauveiz.
> > De la fu li contes estreiz,

> Don cest romanz fist Crestiiens.
> Li livres est mout anciiens,
> Qui tesmoingne l'estoire a voire;
> Por ce feit ele miauz a croire.
> Par les livres que nos avons
> Les feiz des anciiens savons
> Et del siecle qui fu jadis.]
> (*Cligés*, ll. 18–29)

The new location of this "panser" and "savoir" is marked by its in-scription: "we find written in one of the books" what now serves as Chrétien's *histoire*. Instead of drawing on the oral repertoire of jon-gleurs and minstrels, Chrétien uses a source that, like his own medium, is a written one. The authority of this "very old" book de-rives from knowledge that is distinctly literary and is appropriately located in a library. For the poet, a library seems more trustworthy than the richest memory, whose power of legitimation appears gravely impaired precisely because it cannot call up the original (that is, the most reliable) "learning" about "the deeds of men of old."

Less than two hundred years after the composition of *Beowulf*, the distance between writer and presenter had become so great that the language and performance of the presenter was no longer reflected in the text of the courtly epic. This is not to deny that Chrétien may well have been his own narrator in the sense that he probably served as a reader of his own manuscripts. Nor does this mean that Chrétien's ac-tual author-function and his conception of the narrator's part in the story are identical. On the contrary, Chrétien, as a poet, uses a per-sona; he speaks *through* the role of a narrator, which he may associate with a patron's instruction or the *auctoritas* of a written source. He does not go nearly so far as does Chaucer in *Troilus and Criseyde*; the latter appears in a fascinating spectrum of roles, from that of mere translator to those of courtier and lover, epic poet, philosopher, and moralist. But even though Chrétien nowhere uses the role of narrator as Chaucer does in *The Canterbury Tales* (where "Chaucer" serves as an element proper to both fiction and biography), Chrétien does use the space between writer and narrator deliberately. He wrests the figure of narration from the jongleur's tradition of orality in order to use the area of nonidentity between *auctor* and narrator as a site of fiction.[6]

As the author took on the role of fictional narrator, the presence in the text of the performer was either displaced or transmuted into artifice. It was in this new space for projecting a fiction (*fingere*) that the author claimed his own authority as the maker of a "well-joined" composition. This authority to treat the story of adventure in terms of "une mout bele conjointure" legitimated the composition—the bringing together—of what customarily was represented piecemeal, by the standards of a mere "conte." At this point, the advent of fictionality consistently helped "join" the various signifiers that were representing and the various signifieds that were represented. Through the elimination of most of the extraliterary traces of the cultural transaction, the fictional world of representation succeeded in constituting its own "bele conjointure," which was so much more than a jongleur's piecing together of exploits one by one.

Thus, the representational uses of fiction stipulated not just the dissociation of poet and presenter, but also the supremacy of the authority that resided in and reflected the specific needs of the written text. Once the authority in the literary (or, *mutatis mutandis*, the dramatic) text was considered paramount, the voice of a minstrel (or an actor) could only mar the act of representation.[7] Literary representation here sought to privilege a conception of the text as independent of the circumstances of orality, including the social traffic between a minstrel's voice and his listeners' ears. The cultural space of this oral and aural transaction might then be appropriated as a site on which the poet, assured of the growing authority of his written text, could himself fashion the fictionalized image of a performer's function.

The division between *auctor* and minstrel-as-actor is of far-reaching importance to pre-Renaissance fiction and drama because it aggravates the process of differentiation between the authority represented and the authority representing. In order to study the textual complexities of this process a little more closely, I propose to glance at Sir Thomas Malory's version of the Arthurian romance, *Le Morte Darthur*. This text, which preceded most Renaissance narratives, appears at the out-

124

set to dispense with undifferentiated modes of social communication. When Caxton in his edition appeals to a "dyvers" audience, the question of reception is complex in that relations of orality, together with their verbal correlatives, appear to linger in a distinctly literary context (such as, for instance, in the homiletic tradition of preaching).[8] In his preface (1485), Caxton cites the lively interest in the story of King Arthur on the part of "many noble and dyvers gentylmen of thys royame of Englond."[9] As he explains in his prologue to *Eneydos*, he is not averse to bringing out "symple and rude translacion[s]" so long as these appear to be "entendyble and understanden to every man." As Caxton further notes there, although "every man" was not to be understood as "every rude and unconnynge man," the sense of the phrase was certainly not restricted to "clerkys and very gentylmen"; in any case, it referred to an audience wider than one composed solely of the literate.[10] Caxton himself hints at a mixed audience when in his preface he refers to "gentylmen or gentylwymmen, that desyre *to rede or here redde* of the noble and joyous hystorye of . . . kyng Arthur."[11]

The following text, portraying "how Arthur was chosen kyng," inscribes (even in its syntax) the *gestus* of a mode of authorization that may be compared revealingly with the matter of representation:

And thenne stood the reame in grete jeopardy long whyle, for every lord that was myghty of men maade hym stronge, and many wende to have ben kyng. Thenne Merlyn wente to the Archebisshop of Caunterbury and counceilled hym for to sende for all the lordes of the reame and alle the gentilmen of armes that they shold to London come by Cristmas upon payne of cursynge, and for this cause, that Jesu, that was borne on that nyghte, that He wold of His grete mercy shewe some myracle, as He was come to be Kyng of mankynde, for to shewe somme myracle who shold be rightwys kynge of this reame. . . . Soo in the grettest chirche of London—whether it were Powlis or not the Frensshe booke maketh no mencyon—alle the estates were longe or day in the chirche for to praye. And whan matyns and the first masse was done there was sene in the chircheyard ayenst the hyhe aulter a grete stone four square lyke unto a marbel stone, and in myddes therof was lyke an anvylde of stele a foot on hyghe, and theryn stack a fayre swerd naked by the poynt, and letters there were wryten in gold aboute the swerd that saiden thus: "Whoso pulleth oute this swerd of this stone and anvyld is rightwys kynge borne of all Englond." Thenne the peple merveilled and told it to the Archebisshop.[12]

Clearly, the issue here is the representation of authority: the episode is about how, despite some resentment of the "berdles boye" (17), Arthur's legitimacy is established. In this great fable of legitimation, an indisputable authority is bestowed on Arthur, now king of England, first among the glorious knights of the Round Table. What makes this text so suggestive is that authority, in the process of being represented in the world of the story, simultaneously betrays its own implications in the very structure of the discourse. Authority represented as a fiction here implicates authority as an actual agency in writing *and* narrating—an agency that, in the very act of representing, legitimates its discursive practice in the world of history. As part of a cultural production and transaction in the real world, this agency is tied to the reality of communicating the text beyond the circumstances of a predominantly oral culture. It is in this sense that the text reveals the two basic discursive dimensions of "authority": one is a represented fiction; the other is the cultural reality of representing that fiction.

A glance at the represented fiction of authority in the world of the story suggests that it is inseparable from the narrated legitimation of young Arthur's royalty. This legitimation is represented in such a way that the process of achieving it is conspicuously free from any modern gesture of self-authorization. The young Arthur, in fact, does not even dream of promoting, let alone fashioning, his own identity and social status. Whatever authorization his claim to the throne has is something that *happens* to him.

The paradox is, however, that this traditional version of legitimation is complemented by the representation of a contingent world of everyday motivation and forgetfulness not found in Malory's source, "the French book." As Malory has it, Arthur wrests the sword out of the anvil through sheer coincidence. Note how, as if deliberately, contingent circumstances are made to feature in this story, such as when Arthur's brother Kay (who "had lost his suerd, for he had left it at his

126

faders lodgyng") sends his presumed younger brother to fetch it.
Arthur, ready to please, "rode fast after the swerd," but when

> he cam home the lady and al were out to see the joustyng. Thenne was
> Arthur wroth and saide to hymself, "I will ryde to the chircheyard and
> take the swerd with me that stycketh in the stone, for my broder sir
> Kay shal not be without a swerd this day." So whan he cam to the
> chircheyard sir Arthur alight and tayed his hors to the style, and so he
> wente to the tent and found no knyghtes there, for they were atte
> justyng. And so he handled the swerd by the handels, and lightly and
> fiersly pulled it out of the stone, and took his hors and rode his way
> untyll he came to his broder sir Kay and delyverd hym the swerd. (13)

Except for the tug on the sword's handles, Arthur obtains the token
of legitimacy effortlessly. Again, the paradox in the representation is
that this moment involves highly contingent and yet quite miraculous circumstances. Young Arthur does not sense that he is being appointed, nor is he at all ambitious. Much like young Parzival in Wolfgang von Eschenbach's courtly epic, Arthur is naive; though both are
strong and vigorous, neither hero is aware of how authority is
achieved. Arthur lacks the self-consciousness to see his extraordinary
feat as a symbol of some title to spiritual greatness in addition to
physical strength and dexterity. In the absence of any sustained meaning in this fable of legitimation, therefore, a written text is needed to
convey the signification: "there was sene in the chircheyard . . . a grete
stone four square . . . and letters there were wryten in gold aboute the
swerd that saiden thus."

One notes not only that this supplementary text reveals who "is
rightwys kynge borne of all Englond," but also that the same text demands no interpretive skill on the part of those who, apparently without effort, decipher its *literal* meaning. Unlike Wolfram's holy grail,
the text is not symbolically encoded; its reading is unproblematic. So
"all the lordes wente to beholde the stone and the swerd. And whan
they sawe the scripture some assayed such as wold have ben kyng"
(13). The "scripture" here clearly is considered authoritative. Its role
in the process of legitimation is as effective as it is unambiguous. This
inscribed agency of authority is very much part of what is represented

in the story, precisely because it serves to sustain the previous absence of symbolic meaning. Since the reluctance to symbolize the authoritative dictum seems obvious, written signifiers are here used as both a representing and a presenting medium of authority. Relinquishing the need for the hero to achieve symbolic qualities, and renouncing the author's privilege to explain and justify, the text on the sword witnesses a dissociation—highly characteristic of late-medieval narrative—between its semantic or thematic dimension and its *sensus moralis*.[13]

The textually prescribed form of authorization remains unquestioned; it is miraculously given before, and continues to be accepted after, the events of the story could conceivably interrogate or qualify it. What is more, the supplemented agency of authorization (the text of the sword) is satisfied by an almost effortless response. This act, the drawing out of the sword, will be repeated seasonally in ritual fashion under a "pavilion" at Candlemass, during "the hyghe feste of Eester" and on "the feste of Pentecoste" (15). It is only when all the others have "assayed" and failed that the miraculous bestowing of legitimacy leads, through general acclamation, to the coronation. But when the coronation proper is finally mentioned, it is dispensed with in two sentences—in marked contrast to the extended treatment in Malory's source.[14]

Thus, Arthur's legitimacy, in terms of his own hereditary rights, is dealt with almost casually. The issue in this fable of legitimation is not the establishment of true lineage or, for that matter, the fulfillment of contractual relations. Rather, the act of legitimation leading to Arthur's royal authority is conceived as a public ritual whose outcome, far from being achieved symbolically, is preordained. The representation of authority in this epiphanous space of *histoire* accords well with what has been called "the heroic temper of Malory's conception of the Arthurian story."[15]

Since authority on the level of the *story* of Arthur's coronation is represented as somehow given before its complicated consequences unfold, it should come as no surprise that this story of authorization calls for no self-reflexive uses of *discours*: the political economy of this discourse is not marked by a need for any self-justifying appropriation of language. It is true that, as distinct from older versions of the Arthurian *matière*, there is a remarkable sense of time, place, and circumstance. As Elizabeth Pachoda suggests, Malory started with the assumption that chivalry was "the practical means for instituting and maintaining the governmental structure" as well as "the corporational thinking of his time."[16] But the contemporary *sens* that the discursive strategy of Malory's adaptation undoubtedly pursued was bound to fail vis-à-vis the overwhelming strength, the unquestioned dignity and self-sufficiency of the Arthurian *matière*. It may well be said, therefore, that the demands which Malory's political thinking made on the story could not be satisfied, especially when the *sens* in Malory's own *conjointure* collides so heavily and on so many levels not only with the traditional *matière* at large but also with such *sens* as was previously grafted on the level of chivalric *conte*.[17]

Despite awkward digressions and repetitions, and an overgrowth of adventure, Malory's text attempts more than condensation. Unlike a vast assemblage of ever-supplementable stories in his sources, Malory's structural emphasis is on new standards of coherence, linearity, and closure. There is an endeavor to impose transparency and consistency on a bewildering accretion of layers and branches—an endeavor culminating in the newfound center of a tragic choice between two loyalties in the tale of the death of King Arthur.[18] But although this groping for a modern structure of authority in writing must on no account be underestimated, it cannot conceal "that throughout Malory's work two conflicting conceptions of structure are pulling violently against each other."[19] For despite the remarkable extent of Malory's rewriting and unraveling, the author-function in the discursive project of translation and adaptation was apparently not sufficiently self-assured for Malory to legitimize a sustained attempt to sort out the tensions between sense and source.

This is why Malory so often accepts the authority of "the Frensshe booke"—and, hence, that of his *matière*—as unquestionably given. In doing so, he succumbs to (even as he qualifies) the validity of the endeavors of his predecessors. His writing accepts as part of its own authority the labor already invested in the invention of a great story with widely known events and characters. The traditional structure of this authority achieves its strength not through the assimilation of an unknown world, as in modern fiction; rather, it achieves it through straightening out, through rearranging and making more self-contained, a given repertoire of narrative strategies, norms, and values. This may involve the scrapping of such symbolism as enhanced *courtoisie* in Chrétien and even in the thirteenth-century prose version. For instance, as Eugène Vinaver has shown in his reading of *The Knight of the Cart*, Chrétien's "charette," just like the "chariot" in the prose version, ceases to support Malory's use of the cart as a symbol of the ignominy to which Lancelot would stoop in the service of his lady. Nor is there room for the mysterious dwarf who drives the cart; for Malory, the magician's vehicle is turned into a woodman's wagon, which the hero forcefully takes over and uses, not because courtly duty to his lady demands self-inflicted humiliation but because "his armour is too heavy and uncomfortable to walk in." Hence, "the cart loses all symbolic value."[20]

Even so, authority in Malory's discourse has a great deal to do with competence in the affirmation, through modification, of an already known code. Both the continuing strength of the old code and the inscribed need for its renewal are evidenced in Malory's text. So even when the adaptation does appear sufficiently self-assured to question the authority of its source, the elements of rewriting can at best assert themselves in a question mark: "Soo in the grettest chirche of London—whether it were Powlis or not the Frensshe booke maketh no mencyon—alle the estates were longe or day in the chirche for to praye." Here, for the first time, Malory's source is introduced, but its limitations are also shown; it fails to provide information as to some more precise location. "The Frensshe booke" refuses to be explicit about "a local habitation and a name." But even when Malory's source proves deficient in that it provides no authority for topographical identification, it is unquestionably accepted as valid. The narrator's intervention is unmistakable; ironically, it affirms as authoritative the very source that does not quite satisfy.

What we have, finally, is an author-function precariously poised between the traditionally given authority of "the Frensshe booke" and that more modern authority derived from verifiable uses of poetic language and fancy, including referentiality, linearity, and contemporaneity in writing. As the two codes and concepts of narrative came to affect one another intertextually, "the Frensshe booke" ultimately did not stand in the way of the formation of a peculiarly composite author-function. On the one hand, the awareness of time and place was sought in order to enhance a new sense of contemporaneity, as against the perpetual present in the traditional representation of Arthurian norms and ideals; on the other hand, these norms and ideals, by being exposed in their vulnerability, were—far from being canceled out—to assume modified functions inseparable from their precariousness.

It is one thing for critics to draw attention to the author-narrator's emerging presence in the text, to his many interventions, to his surprisingly accurate plan of the geography of the story, including his alterations "so as to make Arthur's journey across the continent resemble Henry V's itinerary," and even to his "originality";[21] it is an altogether different matter when these remarkable indices of Malory's modernity are seen as engaged by and transcribed into a larger text whose structure of authority is far from being one-dimensional. If any one formula can do justice to the text at large, it may perhaps be said that a certain amount of authority came to be derived from assimilating visions of the world to the revision of the matter of chivalry. Even so, the text of the latter retained an authority of its own, partially independent of this revisionist rewriting. Insofar as both locations of authority could be complementary, their joint effect was not unconnected to the question of how appropriately the textual corpus itself was (re)appropriated in the world.

By and large, this convergence of authorities was not far removed, historically speaking, from the solution that Chrétien had arranged in the "two endings" to his *Conte de la Charrette*, where, as "perhaps the only way to get at authenticity in expression," he sought "to balance the weight of poetic *matière* with the flight of poetic fancy."[22] But then "fancy," much like *conjointure* (insofar as both can be traced to an authorial agency), already involves "a conflation of roles," which disturbs any linear flow of authority construed along the lines of the chain "writer—text—reader." As David F. Hult suggests in his study of readership and authority in the first *Roman de la Rose*, the place of the scribe (as the extraordinary intervention of Gui de Mori witnesses) and the medieval model of the author, as based on the role of both the scribe and the oral performer, greatly modify the medieval view of the author. (The author himself is, in a more faithful sense of the word, a reader of other texts that go into his own.) Hence, an awareness of the medieval context of circulation not only helps trace authorial activity on the level of "the imaginative refashioning and reinterpretation of inherited materials" but redirects our attention "toward the reader and his active participation."[23]

10

Allegory and the Authorization of Folly

Erasmus

Apart from the romance of chivalry, the type of discourse most deeply affected by the late-medieval crisis of traditional forms of authority and authorization was allegory. Allegory, as Walter Benjamin has noted, confronts us with the "abyss between figurate being and meaning" [Abgrund zwischen bildlichem Sein und Bedeuten].[1] In our context, allegory is a paradigmatic mode of representation through which authoritative decisions about the order of words and things are made and communicated. At its most basic level, this order implies that language is persistently kept at one remove from what it claims to present. Allegory—as Quintilian first said—presents one thing in words and another in meaning; or, as Angus Fletcher put it in the twentieth century, it "says one thing and means another."[2]

Although obliquity is at the basis of the allegorical *modus dicendi*, this indirect manner of signification presupposes a good deal of certainty in the way of presumed knowledge about the correspondence between signs and meanings. In postulating corresponding chains of detail and generality, the sense and the spirit, the visible and the invisible, allegorical writing stipulates a unique authority of comprehension, together with the possibility of a universally connecting knowledge. But once these correspondences between sensuous fiction and metaphysical truth are securely posited as *a part of* a larger whole of realia, allegory will continue to emphasize their divergence, treating each *apart from*, or even as opposed to, the other. In this way, "allegory tends to be at odds with itself, tending to undermine itself by the very process that sustains it."[3]

Authority in allegorical representations, therefore, may be said to be as peremptory as it is vulnerable. In particular, to communicate ideas, attitudes, and moral values by personifying them involves decisions that are nothing if not authoritative; but at the same time to subject each sensuous image to a transcendental notion of good and evil overstates the power of this rhetorical figuration. As Stephen Barney has rather daringly put it, allegory "bears the same relationship of control to the whole world of discourse that a laboratory experiment bears to nature."[4] But the vulnerability of this type of knowledge has less to do with any arrogance behind its show of comprehension than with the simultaneous attempt to conceal, while protecting (and while apparently ignoring), an irreversible disjunction of signifier and signified. Such a disjunction is problematic where the signifying level (the first or literal "meaning") is made to suggest the presence of a universally valid signified, as if such (absent) second-order meaning does not involve a process of hidden codification and signification all its own.

However, allegory constitutes a vast field of cultural semantics in which the sociolinguistic context of discourse needs to be specified if the uses of authority in representation are to be defined adequately. For instance, the cultural semiotics of the "abyss" in allegorical personification is profoundly affected as soon as the uses of allegory begin to respond, as Stephen Greenblatt suggests, to "periods of loss, periods in which a once powerful theological, political, or familial authority is threatened with effacement."[5] Allegorical personification in such periods of crisis undergoes significant changes in function and structure. For one thing, the element of obliquity can find quite specific uses "in critical and polemical atmospheres," when—as Joel Fineman notes—"for political and metaphysical reasons there is something that cannot be said."[6] Under these circumstances, the gap between figuration and meaning could significantly be developed and transformed. For example, it was possible for Spenser to revitalize the "veil of Allegory" and to fortify the traditional even when the universalizing meaning of allegorical form was mutilated under conditions of major disorder. The danger was that the allegorical veil turned easily into some "impenetrable barrier, blocking movement in both directions," and finally compelling "the retreat of allegory (or its movement) into self-critical irony."[7]

Second, and closely associated with such a "profigurative pattern,"[8] there is a good deal of hybrid growth of allegory in Renaissance narrative and drama. At least some of this hybrid growth is linked to coping with increasing incertitude vis-à-vis the cultural uses of semiotic rupture. As the usable dimensions of invisible meaning associated with the medieval realia declined, it was possible to accommodate the personification of universals to the *configuration* of actually operative agencies of social conflict and power. Insofar as this involved an extension of fictional (as opposed to transcendental or universal) meaning, these more strictly representational forms could be used to bolster the authorization of what in juridical and political discourse was codified as an immutable world of order, punishment, and obedience. As an initial illustration (I have elsewhere studied the play at greater length), the allegory of "Authority" in *The Tide Tarrieth No Man* may here be referred to in passing: as a hybrid personification, the figure inscribes nonallegorical uses of "authority" in contemporary judicial discourse, while its allegorical garment continues at least partially to block modern restlessness in the movement among signs, meanings, and their cultural referents.[9]

If such uses of allegory in the context of the morality play did not fully sustain the blockage, the reason was that again and again they could be challenged theatrically, by grotesque, farcical figurations of evil and subversion. Undermining the dualism in the psychomachian order of good and evil from within the largely undetermined potential of their own vicious significations, these figures of vice in Tudor drama came closest to whatever cultural space there was in early modern fiction for a carnivalesque appropriation and transmutation of allegorical form. In this process, both Erasmus and Rabelais adapted discursive practices linked to contemporary institutions of farce and folly, thereby undermining not only the dualism between vice and virtue but also, and perhaps more consequentially, bridging the chasm in allegorical representations between figurate form and meaning.

The Praise of Folly positively thrives on the crisis of authority in allegorical form, using this crisis as a distinct point of departure for the development of new strategies of representation. The importance of this departure can best be assessed when Stultitia, a highly performative vehicle of self-praise, is viewed in the context of contemporary versions of folly. Erasmus had chosen a remarkably shifting, unfixed personification of folly, one that refused to submit to the humanistic certitudes in the traditional demarcations of writing and living. Even more aggressively, Stultitia by herself created a vital confusion among the allegorical distinctions among (and the traditional uses of) the letter, the spirit, and the body. In contrast to this scandalous flux in the relations of figured signs and received meanings, the orthodox medieval tradition of 'folly' had posited a remarkable degree of fixity in its representational strategies. As late as in Sebastian Brant's *Ship of Fools*, folly was identified with sin or insanity, and the polemic against it was part of a larger "opposition of darkness and light, darkness identified with folly and detachment from God and his light, reason."[10]

In that respect, *The Ship of Fools* provides a highly revealing foil for Erasmus's work. Published in German in 1494, *The Ship of Fools* was widely acclaimed, translated into Latin in 1497, adapted in 1507 in an English prose version by Henry Watson, and in the same year freely translated from Latin, French, and Dutch by Alexander Barclay. But Brant's version of folly is a satirical catalogue of the various medieval estates, crafts, and professions, depicting altogether 112 types of folly and fools who journey aboard an imaginary ship down the Rhine. This encyclopedia of vice and foolishness was designed to reassert authoritative norms of behavior in a highly stratified vision of late-medieval society where the dominant repertoire of social values was not in question. As Barbara Swain notes, Brant and Barclay "projected no better picture of life on earth and no fuller vision of heaven than that given by a sincere, pedestrian, static comprehension of feudal and Catholic teaching."[11] In the context of this world-picture, their particular use of the topos of the fool finds its legitimation: a fool is conceived of as someone who does not properly conform to the order of norms and choices associated with the various estates and institutions in society. In this sense, this vast catalogue of human folly is continuous with one of the largest among the late-medieval transcendental signifieds, that of disorder and sin.

In contrast to this remorselessly satirical treatment, Erasmus's *Encomium moriae* projected an altogether different strategy of authorizing and signifying folly. Departing from medieval tradition, Erasmus went back to the classical Lucianic genre of paradoxical encomium (or ironic praise), only to adapt it to a wide-ranging late-medieval spectrum of nonclassical strategies for authorizing the inscription of unsanctioned thought and experience. Among these strategies, those associated with the folk-fool (as in *Marcolf and Solomon*) and the licensed court fool, as well as with ritual occasions (the *sociétés joyeuses* in France, *Fasching* or carnival societies in Germany and the Netherlands), must have loomed large. Erasmus himself pointed to some of these sources when, in a long letter to Martin Dorp, he claimed for *The Praise of Folly* "the same freedom which the uneducated allow in popular comedies," where "the insults hurled at kings and priests and monks and wives and husbands" are "frequent and free."[12] Erasmus grafted onto the mock-heroic form of facetious praise not only the seemingly extemporal, oral tradition of spontaneous speech but the irreverent laughter of the marketplace, the release associated with popular festivities, the whole Dionysian world of sensuality, the pleasures of the table, the passions of the sexes, the gleeful penetration of the veils of civility, the illusions, self-deceptions, and vainglorious aspirations of self-love. In doing all this, Erasmus immeasurably broadened, even as he undermined, the scope of allegorical representation.[13]

At the beginning of the narrative, Folly, like a theatrical figure of farcical wisdom, presents herself through a self-conscious *mise en scène*; the audience is immediately invited to cooperate with her. Half creating and half prodding her audience's initial response—"happy, congenial laughter" (9)—Folly proceeds to set the tone for "an extemporaneous speech" (12), invoking the horizons of expectation associated with the appearance of "pitchmen, low comedians, and jokesters" (10). This opening, among other things, prepares for a thorough reauthorization and reappropriation of the subject of folly; whereas Brant's representation of the ship of fools was designed to meet or fail the authority of church, estate, and degree, Erasmus makes his protagonist suggest a different pattern of legitimation: "what can be sweeter or more precious than life itself?" (18). But the pathos of "life itself" is presently suspended in irony and laughter. For Folly, as Michael Bristol notes, laughter "offers a capacity to revitalize fundamental impulses of love and belief by dissolving the authoritative claims of temporal institutions such as church and state."[14]

The allegorical configuration is already blurred when the meaning of Folly is made to appear as complex as that of life itself. Departing from "the path worn by the common herd of rhetoricians," Folly refuses "to explain [her] subject matter—[herself]—by a definition" or "to divide it into parts" (12) [me ipsam finitione explicem porro ut dividam, multo minus].[15] Rejecting traditional uses of the arts of rhetoric and the scholastic preoccupation with Aristotelian logic, Folly in her own way appeals to "th'attest of eyes and ears" (*Troilus and Cressida* 5.2.122) and asks, "what good would it do to present a shadowy image of myself by means of a definition [umbram atque imaginem finitione repraesentare (408)] when you can see me with your own eyes, standing here before you face to face?" (13). Scorning "what the ordinary run of nobles and wisemen do" (11), she is not content simply with exposing those "wretches," those "foolosophers" or *morosophers* who "are most foolish in fact but try to pass themselves off as wisemen and deep philosophers" (13). Her challenge to the authority of these "wisemen" is a challenge to some of the representational norms and strategies in contemporary uses of rhetoric and allegory.

Folly simultaneously hints at an alternative principle of representation that will enlarge the typical register for, and broaden the scope of, representativity.[16] In view of Folly's domineering claims, this must not be read in terms of some egalitarian politics. For her "to subject the whole world to [her] dominion, lording it over the greatest lords"

(17), does, however, imply some claim on the representativeness of her language, which, it appears, is much larger than the discursive practice of church and schools alike. Appropriating to her retinue representations of self-love, pleasure, madness, and sweet sleep, Folly marshals a new order of what can be or needs to be represented. She broadens the scope of what constitutes the "precious" quality of "life itself." Encompassing the passions of sensuality, the procreation of life, the consummation of old age in death, this new scope allows for a broadened sense of what in the culture's relations of language and existence *is* representative and what is representable in discourse. Here we have a new measure of representation that, perhaps unwittingly, exceeds the bounds of neoclassical decorum and of whatever authority had previously constrained the conventions of representational practice. To characterize the cultural correlative of this new breadth of articulation is to hint at the social function of what Mikhail Bakhtin has characterized as the carnivalization of late-medieval patterns of stratified living. Expanding the range, even—in her reference to madness and procreation—beyond the prescribed limits of the representable, Folly projects a new openness in her standards of what meaning there is in life, a more inclusive register of validity.

It is here that the alternative uses of authority find their raison d'être: in some encompassing perspective on humankind, some foolish wisdom of comprehension and inclusiveness that "enjoys the combined worship of all kinds of creatures" (13). Moving beyond the limits of stratified norms of propriety in the class-ridden society of her day, Folly leaves behind the compartmentalization of the various late-medieval estates and professions. What is more, she blurs not only the dominant systems of social and rhetorical classification but the dividing line, so rigid in dramatic allegory, between vice and virtue. (This must have pointed the way to a discursive practice such as that of farcical evil in the drama, which refused to acknowledge the boundaries between wantonness and vitality, idleness and convenience, greediness and pleasure.) Rejecting "the narrow limits of a definition" (12) (along lines such as those set forth by Sebastian Brant's 112 types of sinful foolishness), Erasmus aims at a new, more nearly irreducible principle of legitimation by which to authorize, together with these new, unsanctioned uses of folly, the unlicensed range and incontinence of his own narrative.

The foremost representative of European humanism thus set out to chart a broadening space for representation; this space could not be appropriated in his writing without upsetting the traditional allegorical order of signs and meanings. As Walter Benjamin has shown, the departure from traditional norms of signification resulted in the increased potency (*Mächtigkeit*) of signs and their signifying performance—which made the question of meaning incommensurate in terms of its more profane referential substratum.[17] (This qualification must always be taken into account, for, as opposed to the profane [or secular] uses of language, there is in Erasmus and his contemporaries one ultimate and irreducible grounding of authority—what Erasmus in his debate with Luther calls "the inviolable authority of Holy Scripture.")[18] But although postmedieval allegory continued to serve as a "vessel of biblical authority" ("Ausdruck der Autorität"),[19] the Erasmian transformation of allegorical form could not leave untouched the metaphysical opposition between vices and virtues, damnation and salvation. In this respect, representational practice in *The Praise of Folly* transgressed the boundaries of medieval allegory without obliterating whatever movement and tension remained in the clash between particularizing and generalizing dimensions of signification.

In its transgressive capacity, the signifying process in *The Praise of Folly* was affected on at least two levels: first, as Folly's language of irony and innuendo amply illustrates, predictable relations between signs and their meanings were constantly called into question. As Sir Thomas Chaloner noted in the preface to his 1549 translation, "Erasmus, the autour therof, delited to mocke men, in callyng it one thyng, and meanyng an other."[20] The allegorical "abyss" between signifier and signified is reopened when the transcendental signifieds themselves cease to follow their own traditional codification. The whole semantic order of words and things begins to totter when the key notions of wisdom and folly are put into doubt. Walter Kaiser has drawn attention to that "vertiginous semantic labyrinth" that the Erasmian uses of folly hold in store:

For the praise of folly, being a *mock* praise, is in fact the censure of folly; but if Folly is thus censuring folly, Wisdom would presumably praise folly. Or, to look at it from another angle, if the praise of folly is, by its mock-encomiastic nature, actually the praise of wisdom, Folly must be praising wisdom. But if Folly praises wisdom, then Wisdom would presumably censure wisdom.[21]

In this ironic use of language, the semantic fields of "folly" and "wisdom" become blurred to the same degree that the relations of signs and meanings are marked by instability and a remarkable potential for distance. If in this mock encomium the mocking itself is mocked, the allegorical figuration, even when avoiding representational closure, disrupts its own conditions of meaning. Compare with this Folly's ironic reference to the fruits and glories of authorship, when authors' names are advertised in front of the booksellers' shops, sounding (in their Greek or Latinized forms) "like the strange words of a magician's spell. Good lord! what are they after all, but names? [Quae . . . quid aliud sunt quam nomina?]" (83; 460). Just as the uses of signs can diverge from the semantic space of their signifieds, so the name of the author can be severed from the person who bears it; what remains, then, is a mere word, a sign whose capacity for establishing meaningful identity is limited.

However, if Folly's own use of language can undo opportunities for certain types of representation and symbolization, and can preclude predictable relations of identity and meaning, it can simultaneously serve to open up vast unused areas for representation. But this emerging representational space is not an extension of the allegorical dualism of idea and figuration; it lies apart from the line of difference between the universals of meaning and the particulars of signs and bodies. Once the binary order of the old metaphysical realism is suspended, signifiers can be both relieved of an old burden and subjugated to a more stringently representational function of language. In line with this second strategy Folly proposes to use signs quite transparently, as the "truest mirror of the mind":

But why even bother to give you my name [Quamquam quid vel hoc opus erat dicere], as if you could not tell at a glance who I am, "prima facie" as it were, or as if anyone who might claim I am Minerva or

> Sophia could not be refuted by one good look at me, even if I did not
> identify myself in speech [etiam si nulla accedat oratio], "that truest
> mirror of the mind." For I never wear disguises, nor do I say one thing
> and think another. I always look exactly like what I am [sumque mei
> undique simillima], so much so that I cannot be concealed even by
> those who most jealously arrogate to themselves the character and title
> of wisemen, strutting around "like an ape in the king's clothes" or "the
> ass in a lion's skin." (13; 408)

To reject "disguises" and to "identify myself in speech" is to propose a perfect continuity between signifier and signified, even when
such representational closure is simultaneously disrupted by irony.
But this self-conscious concern with closing the gap between appearance and reality cannot altogether be shrugged off as yet another
ironic, deceptively naive strategy for misleading the uninitiated
reader. In the first place, Folly's version of "I know not seems" (*Hamlet* 1.2.76) needs to be seen in conjunction with her preference for "extemporaneous speech" (12) and for privileging unstratified thought
and syntax in her language. Note the reference to her father Plutus,
who "now as ever throws things holy and unholy into a mingle-mangle" (a more adequate translation than Clarence Miller's overcolloquial
"he keeps the whole pot boiling" [15]). Plutus, the god of riches, con-
notes the confusing effect of trade and exchange-value; the political
economy of his signification would not allow the allegorical gulf between elaborate images and transcendental abstractions.

Similarly, when Folly rejects "disguises" and says that she never
feigns, never "say[s] one thing and think[s] another," the textual design is to hide (without permanently concealing) the allegorical abyss
between figural appearance and perceived meaning. No doubt the emphasis on continuity is deliberate: for all its obvious irony, an element
of congruity between what Folly is and what she says she is cannot be
denied. No need, then, to read her allegorically, as "Minerva" or
"Sophia" would be deciphered in, say, some mythological context of
allegorical personification. It is a short step from this ironical subversion of a semiotically secure form of identity to an exclusive emphasis on its inward quality, as when Juliet, disparaging Romeo's affiliation with a hostile system of lineage, asks, "What's in a name?" (*Romeo*

and Juliet 2.2.43). For Folly to refuse to "bother to give you my name" is a different matter, since it implies an entirely different antiallegorical skepticism, or at least some reluctance to use so general and traditional a sign to signify adequately the complexity of her meaning.

The paradoxical capacity for simultaneously suspending and achieving representational closure is central to what this postallegorical treatment of the allegory of Folly is about. Folly herself points to the paradox in her uses of language when she cites two proverbial ideas that, as Clarence Miller notes, are contradictory: in the first, a person's true nature may be judged merely from that person's appearance; in the second, only from the person's speech.[22] Let me suggest that the contradiction is not inscribed inadvertently; rather, the idea is to link the uses of visual and verbal signs so as to add to the density of the ground on which the legitimating function of knowledge is to be redefined. For Folly is determined to reject those who

> though they know nothing at all . . . profess to know everything; and
> though they do not know themselves, and sometimes can't see a ditch
> or a stone in their path [cumque se ipsos ignorent, neque fossam
> aliquoties, aut saxum obvium videant (462)] . . . nevertheless they claim
> that they can see ideas, universals, separate forms, prime matter, quid-
> dities, ecceities, formalities, instants—things so fine-spun that no one,
> however "eagle-eyed," would be able, I think, to perceive them. (86)

But if this text refuses to authorize a proposition of "universals" when "a ditch or a stone" cannot be substantially perceived, it is because the Erasmian author-function can no longer be defined in terms of the medieval philosophical opposition, so central to orthodox allegory, between realism and nominalism. According to the new requirements of knowledge, to "see ideas, universals," is not primarily a question of epistemology but rather one of sorting out a novel sense of proportion and priority between the spirit and the letter—without ever disowning the (for Erasmus) fundamental distinction between them. What results is a type of knowledge that, the implication is, can truly legitimize discourse—not one that professes "to know everything" by universals but one that is in a position to know something of the spirit with the help of the letter.

Consider some of the central presuppositions of this type of knowledge in its historical context. There was from the early days of Erasmus's association with the Brethren of the Common Life at Deventer a distinct strain of *devotio moderna* in his thought.[23] This harsh anti-scholastic upbringing went hand in hand with an emphasis on the New Testament and an element of spiritualization that made for considerable analogies not so much with Lutheran as with sectarian practice. As Johan Huizinga, in his biography of Erasmus, and such historians as H. J. Hillerbrand have noted, Erasmus remained indebted to these roots of his. With their help, he was able to encompass a wide discursive space beyond the divisions of outward/inward and visible/invisible.[24] This kind of division in religious thought was widespread in the radical Reformation; for a representative of spiritualism such as Sebastian Franck, "the division between 'inward' and 'outward' was a basic principle" in his writing.[25] But for Erasmus this involved a more complex perspective on both the gaps and the links between appearance and reality.

Under these conditions it was possible for Erasmus to develop a profound sense of diverse courts of appeal without altogether losing sight of outward authority. He disparaged the *ceremonia Judaica* as mere "superstition": "Il lui manquait au sens de l'autorité de l'Ancien Testament."[26] But again, although he had from the outset decided in favor of the spirit and against the letter, in favor of Christian *pietas* and against church discipline and the sacraments, he was in no way prepared to break with the discipline of the old church or even to endorse sectarian enthusiasm. This position must not be regarded as cynical or as one that follows the proverb quoted in *The Praise of Folly*, "which admonishes us that in the absence of the reality, the appearance of it is the best thing." That proverb is referred to by Folly as one of those "great authorities who have spread my fame." And since these great foolish "authorities" will stick to the letter or heed appearances, Folly is only too prepared to follow their mode of authorization: "so I will cite authorities just as they do—that is, 'quite apropos of nothing'" (117).

This has nothing to do with true "scriptural authority" (126), which alone can establish the "true meaning" of "the sword of the spirit" (125). This "sword" must not be read as the symbol of a violent weapon, of "the kind brandished by robbers and murderers." Nor is it a "great image" of the kind of authority—*potestas*—that obtains when "a dog's obey'd in office." Rather, the definition of this discursive type of authority involves the tension (including some mutual interrogation) between the discourse of Folly and the author-function inscribed therein. In more traditional terms, it may be said to thrive at the point of intersection where the language of Folly ("Stultitia loquitur" is the opening phrase of the narrative) is bound to collide with, and to be differentiated from, the voice of the author. But "Erasmus loquitur" is a discursive function whose own authority is incomplete, especially when it is so usurped by that of the medium of discourse that Folly can actually speak of "meus Erasmus."[27] Clearly, the meaning of the text is nowhere given when it is enacted in a process of negotiation between postallegorical form and early modern author-function.

This process, which includes the mediation of the one by the other, is part of a representational project that, a priori, is marked by neither rupture nor closure between signifier/actor and signified/role. What we have instead is a more dynamic and unstable relation between signs and meanings, where irony is very much a part of the nature of the negotiation between them. To make Stultitia both the narrator and the subject of her encomium was, as Walter Kaiser notes, "to conceive of 'Moriae' as being simultaneously both objective and subjective genitive." And since such a title "doubles back upon itself, it tends to cancel itself out in the fashion of a double negative."[28] But irony in the relations of "Stultitia loquitur" and "Erasmus loquitur" provokes an even greater complexity than this: it constitutes a performance game that assimilates for its material the suppressed (in more than one sense) biography of the author, while the author, himself *playing* with the comic persona of Folly, can in his own role condone the instability so marked in the semiotic and cultural moment of his discourse.

This instability, however, is part of the contingent world—Erasmus might say play-world—of history. Since the Erasmian commitment was first and last to *verba*, not to *res gestae*, his preference for an allegorical reading of *fabula* as conducive to *historia* must be assumed.

But even though he did not anticipate any of the neat neo-Aristotelian distinctions (which will be discussed below in relation to Sidney's poetics), this must not obscure Erasmus's conviction that historical people as actors must "perform in the *fabula*, the play."[29] True, Erasmus's own performance—except for his "meus Erasmus" and in his friendship with More—was not visibly inscribed in the text or title of *Encomium moriae*. Even so, as the suppressed biography of the author interrogates (and is interrogated by) the imperious discourse of folly, the process of signification becomes less predictable in its effects. Whatever meaning is projected by the writer and whatever signified is predetermined by the genre involves a complex constellation: one by which either the discontinuity between signs and meanings can provisionally be bridged or the relative continuity between them can be broken. To put it quite schematically: Folly is foolish (and thus the structure of her meaning involves representational closure) *and* Folly is wise (and her meaning involves ironic discontinuity between what represents and what is represented).

This, finally, is at the center of the Renaissance revolution in signification: language deliberately uses, even as it redefines, the "abyss" between what is said and what is meant. In orthodox allegory, the gap between them is largely immutable; in secular dramatic allegory, which continues to enrich the Elizabethan court plays of John Lyly, this gap can already be used topically, satirically, or mythologically so as to obtain "a stimulation of larger senses of meaning from the literal sense of the play."[30] But in the ironic mode of early modern drama and narrative, the depth, the purpose, and the nature of the gap are subject to renegotiation, not only between discursive conditions and authorial designs, but also between the reader or spectator and the undetermined significations in the text. Authority in the wider range of these representations is no longer given prior to the writing and reading. Rather, authority in early modern representation—and here Erasmus points the way to Rabelais, Sidney, Shakespeare, and Cervantes—awaits its precarious consummation in the contingent conditions of possibility to which the new subjectivity in writing and reading is itself subjected.[31]

11

New Authority in Signification

Rabelais

The Erasmian *Praise of Folly*, like More's *Utopia*, stands apart from humanist discourse, which was not (to use Sidney's dictum about the historian) "captivated to the trueth of a foolish world." Humanists took pride in the use and promotion of the printing press, but in doing so they usually sought to disseminate their educational positions, domesticating the *usus loquendi* by assimilating it to the inscription in print of the norms of classical rhetoric. Conceiving of language as oratory, long after *sermo* had surrendered its actual substratum in orality, many humanists conserved more than a little of the Aristotelian notion of speech in its twofold link to categories of convention and reference, halfway between the mind and reality. As Richard Sherry noted in his *Treatise of the Figures of Grammer and Rhetorike* (1555), such an alignment between "usual wordes" ("that be in use of daily talke") and "proper words" ("that belong to the thing, of which we shall speake") would presuppose a state of balance and even harmony between the conventional and the referential dimensions of language. But both would somehow subserve the signifying process: "Neither be properties to be referred only to the name of the thyng, but more to the strength & power of the signification."[1]

This notion of "signification" was conservative, retaining an element of scholasticism in its attempt to come to terms with the issue of authority. No doubt Sherry attempted to strike a balance between a residual element of validity in *usus loquendi* ("daily talk") and the legitimacy of inscription, with its referential bracketing of "the name" and "the thyng." Situating "signification" somewhere between convention and reference, Sherry, like other humanists, neither took the position of a "historian" confronting "a foolish world" nor addressed the political economy of circulating texts through print as a new medium of cultural exchange in the sixteenth century.

The changing relationship between authority and authorship thus remained by and large outside the humanists' ken. As the inevitable dissociation of textual from oral (and mnemonic) locations of authority was minimized, there was no attempt to reassess the shifting premises, in the new medium itself, of authority in signification. Nor was there any attempt—in, for example, Montaigne's *Essays* or Burton's *Anatomy of Melancholy*—to come to terms with the unalterability of the circumscribed book. This was a far cry from the awareness evinced by Bacon of "a blighting authority" in the circulation of printed matter—that is, of the possibility that "the very nature of the book automatically endows it with the authority of closure."[2]

If, then, "the strength & power of the signification" was subject to negotiation in mid-sixteenth-century writing, the issue of authority was bound to come up where the new conditions of authorship were seen as most open, tentative, and experimental. The world of "trafficke and travell" worked to undermine fixture and predictability in circulation; authorship, therefore, came to reconstitute its role in relation to a larger and more differentiated audience of readers and listeners. Once the exchange and property status of discursive practice had begun to change, the question of who was writing for which readers allowed of no easy answer. Having crossed the threshold of the marketplace, authors came to apprehend the mode of production of their work in its difference from an increasing number of alternative modes of production and reception in society.

The writer's response to the traditional repertoire of narrative themes, stories, and kinds of writing now proved to be much less secure, but also more flexible, experimental, and potentially searching. Writing could no longer presume to authorize itself merely in reference to what a given source (such as Malory's "Frensshe booke") had already provided in affiliation with previous recollections and inventions. Rather, authorship appeared best able to establish its authority (and its function) by relating to other discourses as, in Foucault's words, "objects of appropriation."[3]

To do so, however, required more than an awareness of the exchange-value of a given text—its property status. A text now had to be bought or acquired to be made one's own, but beyond this, a reading author's relation to texts as juridical "objects of appropriation" had to be complemented by their reception as subjects of appropriation—as agencies of knowledge, pleasure, energy, and play. Complementing Foucault's preoccupation with the property status of an author's works, the issue of authority in writing for the printing press suggested the *use-value* of an author's *work*. Although the juridical status of a text as property was of immense importance, its fully authorized reception (and "acquisition") was impossible without appropriation of both the text in the world and the world in the text. The link between juridical acquisition and nonacquisitive acts of intellectual assimilation was basic in the new process of (re)constituting authority in the reception and reproduction of form and meaning in early modern prose narrative.[4]

However, appropriation, as Marx has shown, is inseparable from alienation. The early modern market for cultural products involved a particularly virulent connection between the two. As such critics as Jean-Christophe Agnew and Douglas Bruster have described them, "the seemingly wayward impulses of market exchange"[5] amounted to an inventory of the gaps between what a person desired as his or her own (meaning, reading, possession, identity) and what actually was quite alien, part of an elusive and abstract circuit or circulation. As "the personal properties of the self were becoming as ambiguous as the 'real' properties"[6] to which authors might lay claim through their authorship, the assimilation, through reading and new writing, of *matière*, of a story, of a configuration and its meaning became, if not entirely elusive, at least imbued with a good deal of indeterminacy.[7]

The early modern modes of cultural circulation, whether commercially institutionalized in the public theater or in the profit-oriented printing press, had to accommodate "the crisis of representation that a volatile and placeless market had occasioned."[8]

This crisis implicated the uses of signs and meanings at the point where new conditions of authorship and previously established notions of authority collided. By selecting signs and incorporating significations into their texts, sixteenth-century writers of narrative took the question of authority beyond the limits of sources and conventions, of reference and consensus. The traditional repertoire of signs and symbols offered by popular lore or the romance of chivalry (or the mode of allegory, for that matter) could no longer be counted on as fixed, valid, or satisfying. Whatever narrative strategy an author might use was undetermined in the sense that it no longer followed as a matter of course a traditional treatment of a given "book" as a literary source. For an author of romance such as Malory it was possible again and again to refer to his own repertoire in terms of what "the Frensshe booke seyth," but the early modern writer's idea of authorship could not be confined to the rewriting of a matter already authorized. It now became unthinkable for such writers to discontinue their own author-function simply because they found (as Malory said, in concluding book 21) "no more wrytten in bokis that bene auctorysed."

No longer was there an unquestionably given narrative tradition or any one specific "auctorysed" mode of narration. Rabelais, Nashe, and Cervantes (like their characters) needed by their "owne choice, and working" to choose an "unknowne order" of procedure.[9] No less important, they had to cope, within the text as well as outside it, with the order of particularity deemed appropriate for the task of the "historian." The "foolish world" that (and in which) they inscribed was one of contingency. What was thus at issue was a somewhat unprescribed use of signs themselves—the appropriation of these signs on the threshold of both new invention and traditional repertoire, of authorial signification and the readers' unpredictable interpretation of meaning.

In the case of François Rabelais, the spectrum of mediations between these was particularly wide and intriguing, as *La vie très horri-*

fique du grand Gargantua suggests. Superficially resembling a traditional treatment of a widely known popular source, this text uses and,
through parody, abuses a complex, heterogeneous space in which the
author-function is free to appropriate (and ironically to alienate) its
own means and modes of narrative representation. Signifying practice
itself is foregrounded—is, in fact, 'thematized'—through the inser-
tion, in and against a traditional text, of the early modern author's revision of that text's traditional modes of signification. In this respect,
the ninth chapter is perhaps the most revealing:

> Gargantua's colours were white and blue, as you may have read above,
> by which his father meant it to be understood that he felt a heavenly
> joy. For white signified to him gladness, pleasure, delights, and rejoic-
> ing, and blue anything to do with Heaven.
>
> I quite realize that on reading these words you will laugh at the old
> boozer, and consider his interpretation of colours most ungentlemanly
> and infelicitous. You will say that white stands for faith and blue for
> steadfastness. . . .
>
> Who is exciting you now? Who is pricking you? Who is telling you
> that white stands for faith and blue for steadfastness? A mouldy book,
> you say, that is sold by pedlars and ballad-mongers, entitled *The Blason
> of Colours*. Who made it? Whoever he is he has been prudent in one re-
> spect, that he has not put his name to it. For the rest, I do not know
> which surprises me more, his presumption or his stupidity: his pre-
> sumption in daring, without reason, cause, or probability, to prescribe
> by his private authority what things shall be denoted by what colours;
> which is the custom of tyrants who would have their will take the place
> of reason, not of the wise and learned, who satisfy their readers with dis-
> play of evidence. . . .
>
> In a like darkness are involved those vainglorious courtiers and jug-
> glers-with-names who, when they wish in their devices to signify *hope*
> (espoir), portray a *sphere*, put birds' *plumes* (pennes) for *pains*, . . . *a bed
> without a tester* (lit sans ciel) for a *licentiate*: such an absurd, stale, clown-
> ish, and barbarous collection of puns. . . .
>
> The sages of ancient Egypt followed a very different course, when they
> wrote in letters that they called hieroglyphs—which none understood
> who did not understand, and which everyone understood who did under-
> stand, the virtue, property, and nature of the things thereby described.

[Les couleurs de Gargantua feurent blanc et bleu, comme cy dessus avez
peu lire, et par icelles vouloit son pere qu'on entendist que ce luy estoit

une joye celeste; car le blanc luy signifioit joye, plaisir, delices et resjouissance, et le bleu choses celestes.

J'entends bien que, lisans ces motz, vous mocquez du vieil beuveur et reputez l'exposition des couleurs par trop indague et abhorrente, et dictes que blanc signifie foy et bleu fermenté. . . .

Quis vous meut? Quis vous poinct? Quis vous dict que blanc signifie foy et bleu fermenté? Un (dictes vous) livre trepelu, qui se vend par les bisouars et porteballes, au titre: *le Blason des couleurs*. Qui l'a faict?

Quiconques il soit, en ce a esté prudent qu'il n'y a poinct mis son nom. Mais, au reste, je ne sçay quoy premier en luy je doibve admirer, ou son oultrecuidance ou sa besterie; son oultrecuidance, qui, sans raison, sans cause et sans apparence, a ausé prescripre de son autorité privée quelles choses seroient denotées par les couleurs, ce que est l'usance des tyrans qui voulent leur arbitre tenir lieu de raison, non des saiges et sçavans qui par raisons manifestes contentent les lecteurs. . . .

En pareilles tenebres sont comprins ces glorieux de court et trans-porteurs de noms, lesquelz, voulens en leurs divises signifier *espoir*, font protraire une *sphere*, des *pennes* d'oiseaulx pour *poines*, . . . un *lict sans ciel* pour un *licentié*, que sont homonymies tant ineptes, tant fades, tant rus-ticques et barbares. . . .

Bien aultrement faisoient en temps jadis les saiges de Egypte, quand ilz escripvoient par lettres qu'ilz appelloient hieroglyphiques, lesquelles nul n'entendoit qui n'entendist et un chascun entendoit qui entendist la vertu, proprieté et nature des choses par icelles figurées.][10]

Here the traditional alliance between signs and resemblances crumbles, and the question of signification in narrative is reopened. If allegory is characterized by an "abyss between figurality and meaning," so that "the particular involves the loss or negation of generality,"[11] then the thrust of the passage is decidedly antiallegorical. What Rabelais here explores is an altogether different type of relationship among signs, matter, and meaning: it is not one in which authorship is simply a function of a given mode of signification but, rather, one in which signification is made to serve, even partially to constitute, the author-function itself.

This, of course, radically oversimplifies the matter; signs and appearances, as Rabelais's prologue to *Gargantua* warns us, are deceptive when a "sustantifique mouelle" ("substantial marrow" [58]) contradicts the surface of a cornucopian vessel. But the rhetoric of *copia* is (and is not) actually suspended in meaningful substance. Such a "self-eliminating theory of allegory," to use Terence Cave's term, is one that both recommends the allegorical reading and rejects it as a falsification. In its Janus-faced structure, the prologue—like Panurge's quest in the *Tiers livre*—constitutes an ambivalent 'neither-nor' in the space between signs and meanings, one that "performs a pantomime of its own autonomy and productivity." It is here, Cave continues, that

> Rabelais displaces the whole of the allegorical question as formulated in the early 1530s by making it a topic of the comic fiction, an ineradicable fold in its surface. In consequence, the impasse of allegorical theory, as pure theory, is overcome. By undercutting the reader's right to systematize its meaning, the text gives full licence to its prodigal surface. Deviation, evasion, the blocking of the reader's desire for coherence, are the means by which a fallen text asserts its "authenticity" and the proliferation of its "significance."[12]

The question of signification in regard to "les couleurs de Gargantua" is part of a strategy that is at the heart of the issue of authority in representation. The reader's wish for meaningful identification is titillated, but his or her satisfaction is deferred; the desire for interpretation is roused, but the grounds for exegesis are made to appear unsafe. And yet such semiotic instability in the text does not lead readers into a void when what is at issue is the exciting, teasing "power of the signification" itself. Its major source and sustenance are inseparable from what "productivity" the text, as appropriated in the world, invests in its own assimilation of forms and meanings.

In contrast to both the allegorical and the neoclassical modes, these pages challenge the unthinking use of fixity in the links between symbolic signs and their signifieds (such as white for "faith" and blue for "steadfastness"). Although this basic challenge recalls Erasmian (and anticipates Shakespearean) "productivity" in writing, it says little about what authority actually does sustain the author's function, except that the author's position is incompatible with two traditional modes of signification. One is the mode of those who, by no authority but their private interpretation, seek to establish which "choses" allegorically or emblematically shall be signified by which colors. The other mode, equally unacceptable, is that of "ces glorieux de court et transporteurs de noms," who arbitrarily indulge in formal patterns of similitude where resemblance is achieved on the level of "homonymies tant ineptes, tant fades, tant rustiques et barbares."

Rather than following any emblematic method of similitude, the new narrative proceeded to explore a different strategy of achieving and perceiving significance in fiction, "which none understood who did not understand, and which everyone understood who did understand, the virtue, property, and nature of the things" figured thereby. The emphasis, it appears, was on the signifying process, on the processing of the meaning derived from "the strength & power of the signification" itself. This "strength" does not reside in any "autorité privée," in any 'tyrannical' gesture of closure between signifier and signified, in anything that is "sans raison, sans cause et sans apparence"; nor does its "power" issue from convention as a given set of measures of semiotic and semantic order. Hence, neither *le Blason des couleurs* nor, for that matter, the alternative interpretation of "white" and "blue" (as offered by Gargantua's father) can be said to have much authority or "strength" in its mode of signification. While the latter ironically claims to be superior ("blue" after all is the color of open skies), the former's authority is literally expropriated when Rabelais denies the text the name of its *auctor*—which it actually possessed. As A. J. Minnis notes in his *Medieval Theory of Authorship*, anonymity was "regarded as 'apocryphal' and believed to possess an *auctoritas* far inferior to that of works which circulated under the name of *auctores*."[13]

What "the power of signification" was all about, then, was neither convention nor reference but the act of figuring relations through the appropriation not simply of signs, but of the symbolizing correlations among signs, things, and meaning. This signifying process, unthinkable outside the trivium tradition of dialectic and rhetoric, questions the existence of given stable relations between signifier and signified. As Rabelais's treatment of Panurge's quest suggests, the use and reception of signs in narrative involve the negotiation of a meaning that is not given prior to the author's use, the hero's experience, and the reader's understanding of the symbolizing ("hieroglyphic") power of language in regard to the things "par icelles figurées."

The emphasis is on the playful exploration of indeterminacy, where the rhetoric of prescribed proof, the quotation of authorities, itself can lead the reader astray. It is the absence of fixity in the semiotics of cultural relations that points to the premises on which a new power in signification becomes available. This goes hand in hand with an enhancement of the author's capacity for signifying, which is conducive to a proliferation of meanings, a proliferation conspicuously absent in Malory and the tradition of romance. It is only in early modern discourse that—to use Foucault's term—we have a "foisonnement de signification": "weaving relationships so numerous, so intertwined, so rich. . . . Things themselves become so burdened with attributes, signs, allusions that they finally lose their own form. Meaning is no longer read in an immediate perception, the figure no longer speaks for itself; between the knowledge that animates it, and the form into which it is transposed, a gap widens."[14] But if, from that point on, meaning "is no longer read in an immediate perception" and "the figure no longer speaks for itself," it is because signification constitutes itself through and within the very processing of instability between signs and things, whose acknowledgment can best promote an understanding of how the "nature of things" relates to the uses of texts.

Rabelais's concern here is with no less than the premises on which representations in early modern fictional discourse engage a semiotic order that is not preordained. The element of instability in the new mode of signification arises because neither any "private" nor, for that matter, any traditional *autorité* can henceforth authorize an adequate use of signs. As against these, a more viable agent of narrative authority is hinted at in the phrase "la restitution des bonnes lettres": the reference is to those wise and learned men (for Rabelais, surely, Erasmus is here included), "saiges et sçavans qui par raisons manifestes contentent les lecteurs." But although they, unlike the others, do not proceed to write or read "sans raison, sans cause et sans apparence," yet their "raisons manifestes," if conducive to standards more universally applicable, ironically seem to create new difficulties in the achievement and perception of meaning.

It is at this point that the appearance of a vaguely ironic preference for a strictly modern, referential relation between the word and the world finally ceases to be associated with the text. Hinting at unprecedented complications in the order of signs and things, the writing refers itself not to a modern but to a preclassical order, that of "les saiges de Egypte" and their "lettres qu'ilz appelloient hiero-glyphiques." It is the most revealing of metaphors: *their* meaning is symbolic and accessible only by laborious decipherment. The new language of fiction, much like those "hieroglyphiques," follows the pattern of a "bifold authority" according to which fictional images and their symbolic meanings, being divergent, require collation. The direct reference of the sign to the "nature of things" is deceptive, for the emphasis on things does not reduce the indirection in the use of figures. What finally counts is the negotiation and projection of a more complex, collateral form of interplay, an "unknowne order" between the things of the world and the figures of the word.

It is tempting, given the structure of the language used ("lesquelles nul n'entendoit qui n'entendist et un chascun entendoit qui entendist"), to suspect a Renaissance renewal of dialectic. Dialectic, which formed part of the traditional trivium, could be viewed not simply as the building of linguistic units into balanced edifices of reasoned speech, but "as analysing natural relations as embodied in discourse, and manipulating language to gain insight into the natural world."[15] Although this practice was worlds apart from Bacon's project of modernization, the object of both endeavors was to subordinate grammar, and even rhetoric (as overlaid on discourse), to a reformed concept of a dialectic that could be made available for pragmatic or, in Lisa Jardine's phrase, "opportunistic use." Far from constituting an unambiguous element of modernity in Rabelais's discourse, the issue of signification was revisited at the point where a reforming humanism set out "to discover truths unknown at the outset (and not contained in the premises of the argument)."[16]

At the same time, the language of Rabelais, ironically or otherwise, drew on a wide spectrum of impulses, on a "plurality" that, as Terence Cave notes, "is always in excess of any gloss, any analytic discourse which may be added to it."[17] On the one hand, this language harks back to the order of similitude that, thriving on the rhetorical figure of *copia*, dominates several planes of catalogues and correspondences. On the other hand, the allusion to "les saiges de Egypte" must be seen in a Neoplatonic context, as when Plotinus described how "the wise of Egypt . . . indicated the truth" through indirection and imagery rather than through imitation and linear reference: "they drew pictures instead, engraving in the temple-inscriptions a separate image for every separate item."[18]

Here, there are multiple uses of *copia* on the levels not only of dialectic or rhetoric but also of (anti)allegorical signification; the prologue to *Gargantua* anticipates both the discussion of the meaning of colors and the introduction of the issue of significance in the *Tiers livre*. In the prologue, Rabelais expressly rejects both an exclusively universal and a consistently referential discourse; he repudiates the involved allegorical interpretation as well as the unambiguous reference to "ce que concerne nostre religion, que aussie l'estat politique et vie oeconomique."[19] But if neither the allegory of universals nor the transcription of history appears satisfying, the exuberance of timeless release, the carnival world of "mocqueries, folasteries et menteries joyeuses"[20] must, as an alternative, appear equally unacceptable. The oral culture may have retained its immense vitality in transcribed form, especially in direct address, exclamation, and the sonic quality of rhetoric associated with town criers, carnival societies, and the premodern element in an older, public type of author-function. But in the historiographic *fabula* of the Renaissance the authority of oral utterances was no longer good enough. In the last resort (and in contrast to Bakhtin's view),[21] the utopian impetus from the carnival world of discourse must have surrendered to the ascendancy of an alphabetized culture. In that culture, the problem of significance was a "hieroglyphic" one in the sense that it emerged after scrutiny, thus allowing for all the splendor and deceit associated with the state of illusion and the gesture of verification.

The historiographic order of early modern narrative resides, if anywhere, in a "silenus"—that deceptive little box (to which, in the prologue, Socrates is compared) that shares its name with the satyr, "maistre du bon Bacchus."[22] An ambiguity is inherent in the two versions of the medium, because in the *Cinquièsme livre* (chaps. 38–40), in the story of the temple mosaics, Silenus emerges as an altogether unreliable source of interpretation, one that induces a fatal misreading of the strength of the enemy. His visualized presence in "history minus words" serves as a metaphor of the proximity of illusion and historiography. This fiction of historical unreliability suggests "a clearly historiographic problem having to do with critical distance, the proximity, at least in historical narrative, of the eyewitness vis-à-vis the event."[23]

The difficulties contained within the new mode of signification were truly Socratic in that they began on the level of the proper definition of the elusive order of meaning within the fiction. Hieroglyphs can be downright baffling; the historiographic message associated with Silenus, precious vessel of truth and confusion, was equally tantalizing: things in history are not what they appear to be. Insides and outsides contradict each other: the box cannot be opened to reveal the truth; the actual "sustantifique mouelle" cannot be sucked out like the marrow from a bone. Rabelais's position in the prologue is richly ambiguous,[24] but the ambiguity points to some confusion in discursive practices among the functions of poetical and historical discourses. This is why his reference to the enigmatic characters reveals insights through perplexity: a hieroglyph, according to the *Oxford English Dictionary*, is "a picture standing for a word or notion, esp. one symbolizing something which it does not directly figure . . . hence, a figure, dance, or sign having some hidden meaning."

The new author-function brought forth, in the world of history, a hidden meaning of *fabula*. So it *was* possible for the figuration of Panurge to be "captivated to the trueth of a foolish world," to be caught in representations of the everyday world in a search for some "hidden meaning." This is what happened when Rabelais, beginning in the ninth chapter of the *Tiers livre*, provided news about "how Panurge consulted Pantagruel as to whether he should marry." Turning to the everyday world of *historia*, he does so *fabula*-wise, so to speak, in the universalizing manner of a comic parable. Panurge's quest for an answer to the most vital of his problems is inordinately protracted because, among other things, it serves as a parable of the exasperating burden of signification on the discourse of this fiction itself. The question is on what grounds to authorize meaning in the contingency of a *sermo humile* that is not concerned with "the divine consideration of what may be and what should be" but, simply, with what is. The quest (which is also a quest for an answer to this question) has many layers of falsification, but perhaps the most striking representational strategy involves an image of a character's new mode of producing and understanding meaning in the "foolish world" of his own life, which is a fiction.

The basic pattern of Panurge's quest is that of unavailing consultation with ambivalent authority: for a solution to his problem he is made to consult, among others, Pantagruel, Virgil, his own dreams, a dumb man, a dying poet, a theologian, a doctor, a philosopher, a fool, and the Sybil of Panzou. But the answers he receives are such that no advice is helpful, no prophecy is reliable, and no authority is unambiguous. Since he receives riddles rather than clarifications, Panurge is thrown back on himself. He develops an astonishing capacity for willfully interpreting the texts and responses he is given. His mistake—as eventually the Dive Bouteille makes clear—is to believe that any ready-made answer to his question can be found outside his own efforts to pose and solve the problem himself. In other words, whatever particularized meaning is available must be appropriated through his own search and action.

This is the hidden imperative in the last of the enigmatic texts placed on the bottle itself: the German word *Trinch*!—denoting drink. This is the most directly physical way of making its contents one's own. *Trinch* is the order of discourse for which hieroglyphs are noted. In this respect it might be said of Bacbuc, who provides the interpretation, that the answer for once is unambiguous: "Soyez vous mesme interpretes de vostre entreprinse" [You must be your own interpreters in this matter].[25] This is the last word; it comes at the end of Panurge's quest, but it also provides a parable of the humble, contingent mode of postclassical signification. Still, this is the privileged function, the self-fashioned authority of the author's labor: to make the means and meanings of the fictional enterprise his own. Anterior to this function, and beyond the indeterminate course of its fulfillment, there is no valid production of significance in modern fiction.

12

Historia in *Fabula*
Nashe

As the stories of chivalry and the figures of allegory became vessels emptied of an authority that for centuries had legitimized (as well as prescribed) a given, specific use for them, these traditional forms became both subjects of ridicule and objects of experimentation. At the same time, the crisis in the legitimation of these forms and genres, coinciding with the rise of an innovative type of writing, was only in part compensated for by the rise to literary preeminence of neoclassical models and the inauguration of humanistic poetics. Below the prestigious culture of the humanists and the official teachings of the church there was plenty of space for 'incontinent' language, which, on the common stages and in the pages of Elizabethan fiction, tended to break down barriers among the various types of literary discourse. At about the time of Polonius's description of the new theatrical experiments of "scene individable" or "poem unlimited" ("tragedy, comedy, history, pastoral, pastoral-comical, historical-pastoral, tragical-historical, tragical-comical-historical-pastoral" [*Hamlet* 2.2.397–400]), there was a comparable crisis in narrative in the demarcation of discourses, a similar hodgepodge of poetry, divinity, historiography, and jesting.

Thomas Nashe, more than any other Elizabethan author-narrator, provides a self-conscious instance of this highly experimental writing that, breaking down barriers between traditional types of discourse, moved from criticism, theology, and history to the jest-book and the pamphlet, and thence toward a largely unknown mode of early modern fictionality. Nashe sought to align the rhetoric of academic learning and the colloquial speech of the tavern; his best-known piece of fiction, *The Unfortunate Traveller*, thrives on the depleted authorities of all these modes: the *matière* of chivalry, the mode of allegory, the manner of the jest-book, even the project of humanist poetics.

The humanist arts of rhetoric and dialectic could here be used "unredeemed"; they could without much fuss be dissociated from the neoclassical project. True, the latter continued to provide what was clearly the greatest publicly acknowledged authority in sixteenth-century poetics. Identified as it was in Renaissance England with the person, the poetry, the aesthetic theory, and the thought of Sir Philip Sidney, this project stood for a triumphant vindication of the vatic nature of poetry. Although he confronted (and rejected) the rival claims of both philosophy and history, Sidney tended to align poetry more closely with the "universall consideration" of philosophy. The main and truly revealing differentiation he made was between the discourse of history and that of poetry. The particularizing historian is "captivated to the trueth of a foolish world" and, hence, "bound to tell things as things were"; the poet, according to high-Renaissance doctrine, is more philosophically concerned not with what is but with "the divine consideration of what may be and should be."[1] So for "the fained language of Poetrie" to associate itself with more universally valid ideas of beauty, virtue, coherence, and propriety, it was necessary to claim superiority over "the Historian" for at least two reasons: the latter "scarcely gives leisure to the Moralist" (12); at the same time, the historian appears "captivated" not simply to a contingent world but also, and more insidiously, to a much more barren (and questionable) mode of "authorizing." The historian, Sidney noted,

> loaden with old Mouse-eaten Records, authorising himselfe for the most part upon other Histories, whose greatest authorities are built uppon the notable foundation *Heresay*, having much ado to accord differing

writers, & to pick truth out of partiality: better acquainted with a 1000. yeres ago, then with the present age, and yet better knowing how this world goes, then how his owne wit runnes. (12)

In view of these charges, the marriage of fiction and historiography in Elizabethan narrative and drama must have appeared quite unwarranted, if not proscribed by neoclassical doctrine. It was all very well for Sidney, on a general level, to postulate in poetry a union of the universal and the particular; once the "universall consideration" was identified with "precept" (à la philosophy), the "example" would either be an "Application" (21) or be suspected of "partiality." The irony was that what appeared most objectionable from the point of view of humanist poetics was precisely what the writer of the most innovative mode of Elizabethan fiction and drama stood for.

Nashe had at least one thing in common with Sidney's "Poet": he "never affirmeth, the Poet never maketh any Circles about your imagination, to conjure you to believe for true what he writeth: he citeth not authorities of other histories" (29). Both, then, rejected "base authority from others' books" (*Love's Labour's Lost* 1.1.87), albeit for different reasons: Sidney's poet, "even for his entrie, calleth the sweet *Muses* to inspire unto him a good invention" (29). Nashe, however— even when he did seek recourse to "a Muse of fire" (*Henry V* prol. 1)— usually saw no reason to dispense with what Sidney, with unconcealed irony, called "the notable foundation *Heresay*." On the contrary, the innovative writer remained closer to the historian in that he did have "much ado to accord differing writers"—as well as differing genres and levels of style. It was for just such "dainty" matching of "horne Pipes and Funeralls"—for, in a word, "mongrell Tragicomedie" (39–40)—that Sidney took the popular writers to task. (The context in which the neoclassical objection was rooted is easily overlooked: in Sidney's own words, that context had to do with the ignorance of those who "do . . . not know that a Tragedie is tied to the lawes of *Poesie* and not of *Historie*" [39].) Because "in themselves, they have as it were a kinde of contrariety" (40), these writers quite congenially tended "to accord differing writers" and to encompass the minglemangle of types of discourse in their impure (and unsanctioned) strategies for discovering meaning in contingency precisely by picking "truth out of partiality."

This departure from the authority of neoclassical poetics was characteristic of Elizabethan popular drama and fiction. In both genres, the new authority in representation (marked by some "scene individable, or poem unlimited") could only with great difficulty (if at all) be reconciled to humanist doctrine. The potent interaction of diverse cultural forms and discourses was important because it made it easier for dramatist and author-narrator alike to undermine the gap between idea and reference, "precept" and "example." Sidney's taunt that, as against the poet, the historian presumes to know better "how this world goes," appears strangely contradicted when, in a great scene in *The Tragedy of King Lear* (4.5.145–46), these same words become resonant with a grim, profoundly poetic vision of "the trueth of a foolish world" caught between the language of poetry and the awareness of the ordinary history of contemporary vagrancy.

Nor was a late-Elizabethan writer of fiction such as Thomas Nashe less radical in discarding the authority of humanist doctrine. For him, not to heed the prestige of neoclassical precepts was one way to celebrate, in the words of Walter R. Davis, "the temporary liberation of fiction from ideas."[2] In Nashe's case, this "liberation" was more an emptying out of universality than the inscription of an intensely particularized experience. Exemplifying the antiallegorical and antichivalric direction of Nashe's representations, this writing had certain parallels with the new narrative of such author-narrators as Gascoigne, Greene, Lodge, Dekker, and Deloney, as well as with late-Elizabethan pamphlets. In all these, the authority of neoclassical decorum was at least partially ignored, and sometimes disrupted: the distinction between *fabula* and *historia* ceased to provide grounds for legitimation. On the contrary, the respective modes of poetic and historiographic discourse tended to intertwine until, against Sidney's own "precept," "the fained Image of Poetrie" and "the particular truth of things" (14) ceased to appear diametrically opposed. The classical demarcation between fictional "pictures, what should be" and true "stories what have bin" (29) was no longer operative. In a rapidly changing social, cultural, and communicative situation, the function of discourse tended to reconstitute itself so that altogether new levels of correlation between the universal and the particular became a discursive strategy of the new representation.

Because it seems difficult, on such a general level, to characterize this constellation adequately (with all the far-reaching implications for the Elizabethan chronicle play), I propose to look more closely at Thomas Nashe's *Unfortunate Traveller*. The (ir)resolutions in this text between *fabula* and *historia* are conspicuous—one might say precariously central. This is especially so when the author in his dedication smoothly attempts to link the "phantasticall" and the historical by promising to give "in this phantasticall Treatise . . . some reasonable conueyance of historie."[3] The use of "historie" without an article is suggestive in that the narrative (or, to use Hayden White's term, "narrativity")[4] carries a certain right or authority to treat within the feigned images of the fiction a number of actual events and persons.

Indeed, within the framework of his narrative, Nashe provides an account of Henry VIII's siege of Terrouanne (or "Turwin"); gives a description, partly based on Holinshed, of the outbreak of the sweating sickness; proceeds to his own version of the battle of Marignano (in 1515); dwells at some length on the defeat of the Anabaptists at Münster; and has a considerable number of historical personages assembled in this "phantasticall Treatise" (among them, Luther, Erasmus, More, the duke of Saxony, Cornelius Agrippa, Pietro Aretino, and Henry Howard, the earl of Surrey). It may seem a large claim that Nashe, as G. R. Hibbard puts it in his critical biography, "had stumbled on the historical novel long before anyone else."[5] But by tentatively subsuming such historical material under the "fained Image" of fiction, Nashe could not help making the fiction historical and the history fictional—could not help, that is, interrelating, on highly uneven levels of discourse, the "phantasticall" and the historiographic, *fabula* and *historia*.

This is not the place to detail the actual situation in Elizabethan society in which the social uses of historiography were stimulated at a time when authorship could more freely relate to multiple social functions and conflicting cultural expectations, drawing as it did on both the declining institution of patronage and the still-immature market for products of the printing press. Suffice it to say that Nashe's narrative, insofar as it transcribed these circumstances, was simultaneously traditional and scandalous, rhetorically stylized and very much down-to-earth. In this rapidly changing, transitional situation there was plenty of room for what Jonathan Crewe in his book on Nashe insists was a powerfully disruptive function of "unredeemed rhetoric," whose "violent negativity" could contaminate logic and subjugate truth.[6]

I shall return to the important question of Nashe's rhetoric, but suggest here that the "unredeemed," disruptive force of rhetoric in *The Unfortunate Traveller* cannot be simply opposed to historiography and representation. If we are to grasp its self-authorized recklessness, we must note the concurrence as well as the incongruity of rhetorical performance and the representational uses of *sermo humile*. As the neoclassical distinctions broke down, as the "universall consideration" ceased to fulfill the lofty demands of the humanist project, and the loss of decorum, balance, and proportion became irretrievable, the hybrid mode of fantastical historiography helped transcribe the welter of cultural possibilities and social realignments in this period. The unsanctioned use of rhetoric (for example, when it transgressed neoclassical decorum) must be seen as participating in a historical moment of cultural change and experimentation, one that the convergence of poetic and historiographic modes of discourse helped bring about. Such a conflation, even in its experimental form, was no small achievement; it helped open up a new and promising space for representation and performance, far beyond the didactic order of the Tudor chronicle in prose and the universalizing humanist definition of poetry. The new narrative could provide "the instruments by which the conflicting claims of the imaginary and the real are mediated, arbitrated, or resolved in a discourse."[7]

In Nashe's case, the site of convergence remained structurally undeveloped; the nature of his historiographic activity was nevertheless fundamentally and (as G. R. Hibbard has shown) deliberately different from both the chronicler's mode and the greater scope of an epic subject matter "under the authority" of the poet's "pen."[8] As opposed to these, Nashe's fiction is authorized by a strategy of contrariety: in his response to the chronicles Nashe invoked the standards of poetry, while in his objections to the "worn-out impressions" of the chivalric romance, he invoked the standards of historiography, such as recording "the particular truth of things."

Although the chronicle form was close to his own point of departure in narrative, Nashe deplored its deficiency in the art of poetry. As he wrote in *Pierce Penilesse his Supplication to the Divell*: "your lay Chronigraphers, that write of nothing but of Mayors and Sheriefs, and the deare yeere, and the great Frost . . . want the wings of choise words to fly to heaven, which we have: they cannot sweeten a discourse, or wrest admiration from men reading, as we can, reporting the meanest accident" (1:194). The "we" in this text implies the superior gift of poets as reporters of "the meanest accident." Surprisingly, they are assumed to take a position of both affinity with and distance from the chronicle mode of discourse. The distance is that between the wings of Nashe's own heavenly muse and the flatness of poetical figuration in the chronicles, but this does not preclude a congenial, if condescending, kind of affinity between the chronicler and the poet. It is startling to find how easily Nashe, at the outset of his writing career, was prepared to sacrifice Renaissance decorum for his fascination with representing "a foolish world."

This passage from *Pierce Penilesse* is an early theoretical statement, but in his later discursive practice Nashe revealed similar positions regarding both the proximity of and the disparity between the historiographic and the poetic modes of discourse. As he notes in the concluding sentence of *The Unfortunate Traveller*, unless his fantastical conveyance of "historie" pleases, "I will sweare upon an English Chronicle never to bee out-landish Chronicler more while I live" (2:328). In his proudly good-humored self-mockery, Nashe confesses to be a chronicler, but one with a difference. The outlandishness of his chronicling mode refers to more than the continental localities his traveling persona visits; there is the self-assertive awareness of innovation in what he himself calls "a cleane different vaine from other my former courses of writing" (201). But the originality of the "out-landish Chronicler," although justifiably claimed, could at this date in Nashe's career be exaggerated, since similar interactions between poetic and historiographic modes of discourse can be traced much earlier in *Pierce Penilesse,* and even in Nashe's satirical sketch of Gabriel Harvey in *Have with You to Saffron-Walden,* which despite its brevity has been called "the liveliest life written in England in the sixteenth century," a notable biography in which fantastical figuration turns a historical person into almost "a mock-epic hero."[9]

Nashe, then, was perfectly capable of *poetically* "reporting the meanest accident"; his own version of "the trueth of a foolish world" refused to acknowledge a good many traditional barriers between poesy and contingency. As an illustration, note how Nashe renders his memorable encounter with Harvey in a Cambridge inn, and how, in representing an actual person and presumably a real event, he uses both historical allusions and rhetorical figures to convey his archenemy's stature and complexion:

> It is of an adust swarth chollericke dye, like restie bacon, or a dride scate-fish; so leane and so meagre, that you wold thinke (like the Turks) he observ'd 4. Lents in a yere, or take him for the Gentlemans man in the *Courtier,* who was so thin cheekd and gaunt and starv'd, that, as he was blowing the fire with his mouth, the smoke tooke him up, like a light strawe, and carried him to the top or funnell of the chimney, wher he had flowne out God knowes where, if there had not bin crosse barres overwhart that stayde him; his skin riddled and crumpled like a peice of burnt parchment; & more channels & creases he hath in his face than there be Fairie circles on *Salsburie Plaine.* (3:93)

This, indeed, is a fantastical conveyance of a historically existing person, whose accidental appearance is universalized into sheer comedy. Far from emancipating itself from the "duty of representation," this unredeemed rhetoric of hyperbolic figuration helps establish a highly effective kind of mediation among verbal signs, historical objects, and, to use Charles Sanders Peirce's term, their "interpretants."[10] This mediation not only has affective force; it also is effective as representation in that the process of figuration involves a much wider and more nearly universal spectrum of activities—imaginative, emotional, and empirical—than a purely factual inscription of biographical data would allow.

Although in this instance the art of rhetoric helps create the poetic

image of a historical person, in *The Unfortunate Traveller* the images of
Surrey, John Leiden, Luther, Aretino, and others exist side by side
with purely fictional figures and events. But whereas actually existing
people can—like Harvey—be metamorphosed into creatures of historical fable, the purely fictional characters are treated to the same representational logic by which empirically verifiable vehicles serve to
convey fantastical impressions of history. Compare the "crosse barres"
inside the Tudor chimney (realistically barring Harvey's fantastical as-
cent) with the extraordinary amount of social history that goes into
the building up of a presumably purely fictional figure of *fabula*, the
cider merchant in Jack Wilton's opening story:

> There was a Lord in the campe, let him be a Lord of misrule if you will,
> for he kept a plaine alehouse without welt or gard of anie ivybush, and
> sold syder and cheese by pint and by pound to all that came. . . . This
> great Lord, this worthie Lord, this noble Lord, thought no scorne
> (Lord, have mercie upon us) to have his great velvet breeches larded
> with the droppinges of this daintie liquor, & yet he was an old servitor,
> a cavelier of an ancient house, as might appeare by the armes of his an-
> cestors, drawen verie amiably in chalke on the in side of his tent dore.
> (2:210–11)

The chalk used for representing the arms of noble ancestors is, presumably, the same with which "this peer of quart pottes" was "count-
ing his barrels and setting the price in chalke on the head of them"
on the day Jack Wilton visited him. At this entirely fictional encounter the narrating poet again stoops to "reporting the meanest accident," such as what took place in "a backe room" into which Jack
was led by his host, "where after he had spitte on his finger, and pickt
of two or three moats of his olde moth eaten velvet cap, and spunged
and wrong all the rumatike drivell from his ill favored goats beard,
he bad me declare my minde" (211).

The representational logic of this (unhistorical) portrait draws on
a sense of social history that is inseparable from the violence with
which the rhetoric in this narrative overthrows the postulates of decorum. For a brief moment, the meanest of these accidents, such as the
picking of two or three motes off the cider merchant's velvet cap,
achieves both the exuberant status of a carnival performance of rhetor-

ical misrule and the representational status by which this accidental gesture mimetically attests to the embarrassing moment of apprehension before Jack Wilton's "secret" is out. As this strutting "Lord of misrule" is transformed into the trembling host of the camp, the memories of timeless jests and the arts of unbounded rhetoric are used to authorize a different type of discourse, one that can appropriate figures and images of the historical world in which "*Henrie* the eight (the only true subject of Chronicles), advanced his standard against the two hundred and fifty towers of *Turney* and *Turwin*" (209).

Nashe, who had scorned to consider as poetry "the feyned no where acts, of Arthur of the rounde table" (1:11), was obviously concerned to establish a local habitation and a historical name for the meanest of narratives, including those commonly associated with the jest-book tradition. If, in this endeavor, he failed to cope with the persistent gulf between chronicled events in history (such as the advance of King Henry's standard) and the historicizing mode in fiction, the reason is obvious. The mimesis of sponging and wringing a beard in tense expectation can without difficulty be integrated into the representational logic of a socially and psychologically defined image of a fictive person, and this person can even be associated with the historiographic setting of an army in a state of siege, but these specifics are considerably easier to handle than the conceiving of language, plot, character, and setting in terms of a comprehensive narrative strategy. In other words, it must have been possible for Nashe to cope with the differentiation of discourses, in particular with the *historia-fabula* gap, but it must have seemed impossible for him to integrate historiography globally into the plot sustaining his innovative text. However, even to suspend the order of difference between the fantastical conveyance of *historia* and the historically concrete conveyance of *fabula* was no mean achievement, especially when it both contained and superseded a jest-book type of anecdotal narrative.

There is in Nashe's representations an awareness of the social correlatives of appropriated language that, in the late-Elizabethan context, is unrivaled outside Shakespeare's dramatic compositions. Note how in *The Anatomie of Absurditie* a firmly established past tense combines with a distinct social underside in Nashe's metaphors so as to inspire his rhetorical raid on the language of chivalric romance. The authors of these romances—"these bable bookemungers"—seek

> to repair the ruinous wals of *Venus* Court, to restore to the worlde that forgotten Legendary licence of lying, to imitate a fresh the fantasticall dreames of those exiled Abbie-lubbers, from whose idle pens proceeded those worne out impressions of the feyned no where acts, of Arthur of the rounde table, Arthur of litle Brittaine, sir Tristram . . . with infinite others. (1:11)

Here the language of romance is taken to task for having been associated with a cultural past that is firmly situated in a pre-Reformation context, where the uses of allegory and chivalry were characterized by inactivity, imprecision, and depletion. For Nashe, it must have appeared helpful to remind his readers that the "forgotten Legendary licence of lying" is categorically distinct from his own liberty in the more complex use of the contradictions between fictional and nonfictional discourses.

Nashe himself, though, seems to have been singularly free from the Renaissance storyteller's sense of a dilemma regarding fact and fiction. His own insensitivity to the charge of lying and his disregard for any "authoritative and circumstantial proof of . . . historicity"[11] reveal the self-assuredness with which his innovative muse took the conventions of fictionality for granted. The purely fantastical figures of romance were unsatisfactory not because they were fictional as such but because their naive conventions did not allow for the fine interplay between fantasy and experience, for playfulness *in* meaning. As opposed to their discredited authority, Nashe's own writing, by intertwining the discourse of *fabula* and that of "historie," could actually thrive on the contradiction between fictional and existential levels of significance. Nor was Nashe, even when he anticipated in certain aspects the early-eighteenth-century "public and popular news/novels discourse," in any way concerned about the "benefit of lying about the truthfulness of a work."[12] The "idle pens" and "dreames of those exiled Abbie-lubbers" were "phantasticall," but so was, according to his self-styled definitions, his own "Treatise" called *The Unfortunate Traveller*. Obviously, then, the "licence of lying" and the liberty of inventing a "phantasticall Treatise" were not the same; it was not fictionality that presented a problem but the way its contradictions were either ignored by "idle pens" or used by more active spirits.

It was the new parameters of his author-function that really mattered. On their strength Nashe proceeded to challenge the more learned and purely literary type of authority derived from classical studies and neoclassical poetics. This was the innovative, aggressive position from which Nashe set out to ridicule not only the pedantic language of the learned Harvey, but the failure, in its pragmatic dimension, of the Petrarchan mode of figuration, as in the language of Jack Wilton's "Heroical Master," the earl of Surrey. In prison, the two characters meet the beautiful, tempting Diamante, but although his master "wold praise her beyond the moone and starres," Jack "caught the bird: simplicitie and plainenesse shall carrie it away" (2:262–63). Here the feigned image of poetry fails to communicate the particularities of earthly seduction. Surrey's unpragmatic signification precludes not only an efficacious use of language in the world but, equally, an appropriation of worldly lust through discourse. Surrey, we are told, "out of the incomprehensible drossie matter of cloudes and aire," thrust with his tongue "the starres out of heauen, and eclipsed the Sun and Moone with comparisions" (270). Observing "the true measures of honour" and "glory" (278), Surrey then indulges in the emblematic language of knighthood during the absurd tournament at Florence, culminating in the unintentionally self-revealing allegory of the fifth knight: "*Nos quoque florimus*, as who should say, we haue bin in fashion" (274).

The veil of allegory looks threadbare when—in a long catalogue of ridiculous emblems—its main function is ironically to reveal its inadequacy as a locus of both privileged ceremony and ordinary sexuality. In his servant's eyes, Surrey "was more in love with his own curious forming fancie" than with its purported referent. But what makes the ironic uses of the Petrarchan conceit as well as those of emblematic allegory so suggestive is that the gap between words and their meanings is suspended as well as exposed. It is suspended when the gap in signification is actually used *mimetically*, as a mirror of inadequacy in purposive action: in Surrey's case, "with his own curious forming fancie," the gap in question serves to *represent* and characterize a socially significant readiness to sacrifice vital matters in favor of considerations of high style and status. In the case of the fifth knight, the allegorical rupture between emblem and existence is, as in Erasmus and Rabelais, ironically acknowledged but simultaneously closed. The gap is mimetically suspended in what now serves as a representation of the outdated historicity of the allegorical form of chivalric emblems.

In both cases, these signs of cultural authority appear to have lost their previous validating functions. They now emerge as part of a spurious language of social privilege that, paradoxically, is not nearly so qualified to represent an artificial person in the fictional world of his or her purported aims and interests as are the indecorous signs of *sermo humilis*.[13] The authority by which Nashe mockingly challenges the indiscriminate uses of Petrarchism as well as those of allegorical emblems appears to be based on a more stringent view of how, in a fiction, representation and existence can cogently be made to connect in their vulnerability and contingency. What is validated is the "unredeemed rhetoric" invested in the "attempt to reflect and engage actuality, in contradiction to those idealizing and self-referential forms of art" that seem entirely to displace the merciless moment of instability in the use and reception of early modern fiction.[14]

At this point, two conclusions suggest themselves. First, Nashe's perspective on the (dis)junction between speaking and living was inseparable from the historiographic moment in his narrative. This perspective could admittedly not cope with the remaining gaps between historiography and rhetoric, but, even in the face of the contradiction, the attempt to link the universal consideration of *fabula* and "the trueth of a foolish world" was one way of coping with the absence of fixture and determinacy in the (dis)junction in question. Second, it must have been impossible for Nashe to develop the hybrid mode of his representation without some awareness of the position of his own authorship and author-function. This can be traced in (even when obscured by) combined conventions of complaint and apology, layers of pride, delusion, and self-mockery—such as when, through the thinly disguised persona of Pierce Penilesse, he speaks of his poetry as "my vulgar Muse" (1:157).

The position of authorship and the function of fictional writing being so precarious, however, Nashe was inordinately attentive to the criticism and commentary his writings received from others. Among his contemporaries, it was Harvey who referred scornfully to Nashe's language as that newfangled "naturall stile," with its "piperly phrases and tinkerly compositions," as derived from "Tarletons surmounting Rhetorique, with a little Euphuisme, and Greenesse inough,"[15] by which that "gosling of the Printing-house" made up "the whole ruffianisme of [his] brothel Muse."[16] Nashe was self-consciously aware of the weight of such charges; he defended himself by the argument, remarkable for its perhaps unintended implications, that "there is no newfanglenes in mee but povertie" (3:31). As Nashe accepts "newfanglenes" as a correct rating of his discursive practice, he applies the criterion of historical function to the writings actually produced by his own pen: he thus relates the "newfangled" nature of his pen (30) to a concrete situation of social independence and poverty "which alone maketh mee so unconstant to my determined studies" (31).

The contemporary realities of this author-function, the peculiar market conditions under which literary texts would be sold or dedicated, appropriated or expropriated, obviously mattered to Nashe, and he used them both as a constant source of complaint and as a platform for the freedom by which his authorship came to constitute, and rely on, an insecure authority distinctly his own. In this respect, Nashe (for all his conservatism) was indeed a modernist, and Harvey's judgment appears discriminating: "The witt of this and that odd Modernist is theyr owne."[17] To possess one's own wit, to have (as Nashe postulates) "invention or matter. . . of [one's] owne" (2:251), is to appropriate the means of one's own poetic labor and thereby to fulfill the conditions under which the neoclassical poetic becomes obsolete. In the traditional dedication, prefixed to *The Unfortunate Traveller*, just before proceeding to address a wider audience in the marketplace, he triumphantly declares the joys and promises of innovation that this narrative (so different from his previous writings) seems either to anticipate or to have at least partially fulfilled: "a new brain, a new wit, a new stile, a new soule will I get mee" (202)—a bold promise in which representation and existence come together in the pathos of renewal, derived from and thriving on past periods of supposed instability.[18]

Out of the constraints of a socially precarious position, Nashe with his "Mercuriall fingers" proudly snatched a modicum of freedom and experiment; nevertheless, the full weight of the contradiction between *fabula* and *historia* could not, for all the originality of its conception, finally be held in suspension in *The Unfortunate Traveller*. There are moments of triumph through innovation, as for instance when he begins to break down barriers between traditional types of discourse, moving toward that undefined and, for him, largely unknown mode of modern fictionality that sought to align the imaginary and the real through the integration, in one "tale," of the most heterogeneous modes of discursive practice. This, as far as it goes, is the achievement of *The Unfortunate Traveller*. It is a work that, in narrative form, equaled the remarkable hodgepodge of Elizabethan drama, defined by Lyly in terms of a similar mingle-mangle of signs, genres, and representations.

Lyly's younger colleague Thomas Nashe might have traced a similar gallimaufry in narrative, a mingle-mangle of poetry, divinity, and history; he too might have wondered how deeply Time affects consciousness, and consciousness the matter and the language of narrative. The exuberance and resignation, strangely mixed in the rhetoric of gallimaufry, by which language in the theater represented its own confidence in finding acceptance and audience participation, was not, however, shared by Nashe; although he too confronted the challenge of social and cultural change, the odds were much more strongly against him. In the language of narrative, the sheer burden of integration was far heavier, especially when the author toward the end of his tale appeared still vexed by an unexpectedly deep gulf between the literary genres and the representations of social classes that he had hoped to bring together in his writing. Thus the playful admission of failure and despair when Nashe in propria persona usurps the first-person-singular viewpoint of his medium and says: "This tale must at one time or other give up the ghost, and as good now as stay longer; I would gladly rid my handes of it cleanly, if I could tell how, for what with talking of coblers, tinkers, roape-makers, botchers, and durtdaubers, the mark is clean out of my Muses mouth, & I am as it were more than duncified twixt divinity and poetrie" (2:241).

The classical tradition behind Nashe's not-so-vulgar "Muse" never ceased to revolt against the historical representation of "coblers, tinkers, roape-makers" and the meanest accidents of their political history. Was, then, the reopened gulf between poetry and history one that, for Nashe, in the end remained unbridgeable? It would be possible to argue that the combined reference to "divinity and poetrie" helps link the writing of religious pamphlets and that of fiction, especially when we follow Ronald B. McKerrow in glossing "the mark is clean out of my Muse's mouth" to mean, simply, "my muse has become old and worn out" (4:270). But this reading is somehow at odds with the immediately preceding context, where the "talking of cobblers, tinkers, roape-makers" and so forth does not suggest weariness so much as a need to finish on a note of closure and decorum that would not be "clean out of my Muses mouth."

In order to appreciate the daunting gulf, for Nashe, between the awareness of decorum and the desire to exploit contingency and sensational action, it seems best to return to the representation of the Anabaptists' rule at Münster. Here, in view of a particularly violent (and sensational) crisis of authority in the rise of radical Protestantism, difficulties in integrating divinity, history, and story are especially marked. Here, as Mihoko Suzuki suggests, "the problem of authority in the political and spiritual realms is brought together with the problem of authority in the linguistic realm."[19] The apparent incongruity between the historical-theological pamphlet ("divinity") and the fictional "tale" seems bewildering, as the self-consciously described dichotomy between the two levels of discourse betrays. For Nashe to say that he is "duncified twixt divinity and poetrie" is, on the surface, to dramatize the central difficulty arising out of the combination of increasingly distinct strategies of discourse. Although labeled by Harvey the "gosling of the Printing-house," Nashe could not associate himself with the post-Reformation alliance among preachers, printers, and players. As the author of a printed tale, he was, in the end, unable to close the gap between the fiction of the traveling page—a purely imaginary invention—and the nonfiction of the anti-

Puritan pamphlet, which contains the historical account and the theological critique of the German Anabaptist rising at Münster.

At this point, the difficulties in both the "universall consideration" of poetry and the representation of "vulgarity" are suspended in Nashe's use of rhetoric to communicate, through the author's voice, a stylized version of his difficulties in controlling the combined effects of these discursive strategies. Undoubtedly there is, on the surface of this verbal action, an element of nonfictional confusion and perplexity, witnessed by the use in this context of the verb *duncified*. But although Nashe "would gladly rid [his] handes" of this tale, his putative despair ("if I could tell how") itself appears somewhat fictive. In fact, the rhetorical figure through which the dilemma between poetry and pamphlet is communicated undermines the validity of the classical distinction between *fabula* and "historie." To use the verb *duncified* in this connection is to suggest a countercurrent of continuing experiment, innovation, and integration. According to the *Oxford English Dictionary*, the verb *dunce* is used in the sense of "to puzzle, pose, prove to be a dunce; to make a dunce of." But in conjunction with the suffix *-ify*, the implied sense of "bringing into a certain state" can be given a jocular or trivial overtone.

This would correspond with the odd mixture of complaint and self-mockery that Nashe, from the introduction to *Pierce Penilesse* to his *Lenten Stuff*, used throughout his writing. And yet the element of self-mockery is not, I think, to be read exclusively as another self-conscious touch of the popular performer. Beyond the self-styled irony, the use of *duncified* involves a historical referent in the person of John Duns Scotus. The allusion is to the scholastic theologian, the Subtle Doctor of medieval Oxford, whose works on theology, philosophy, and logic must have been familiar to any Elizabethan university graduate, either as outdated textbooks or as traditionally sanctioned authorities. In the sixteenth century, the scholastic system of the learned doctor was repeatedly attacked and ridiculed by humanists and reformers, and the Scotists or Dunsmen (as they were called) rallied against the aggressive polemic of the new learning. The point is not simply that Nashe, being a humanist-trained author, was anti-Scotist from his early days at Cambridge—at least as early as 1589, when in his pref-

ace to Robert Green's *Menaphon* he attacked the pragmatic orientation
in "the doting practice of our Divinitie Dunces" (3:318). (In his writings, including *The Unfortunate Traveller*, he talks of "the dunsticall
incorporationers of *Wittenberg*" (2:247) and again of the "dunstically
set forth . . . devout Asses" of Leyden and the Anabaptists [233].) The
point is, rather, that Nashe's longstanding opposition to scholastic
learning must have suffused the metaphoric language of his self-
dramatization, in the sense that the noun *dunce*, as the *Oxford English
Dictionary* notes, had become synonymous with "hairsplitter" and
"caviling sophist," as in reference to the "farrago of needless entities,
and useless distinctions" with which the Scotist system had become
associated.

When, therefore, with a curious mixture of circumspection and
emphasis, Nashe says, "I am as it were more than duncified twixt divinity and poetrie," he in his self-mocking fashion transforms the jocular language of antischolasticism into a provocation of humanist doctrine and authority. The rhetoric in his self-representation adopts a
strategy by which the humanist position in poetics is severely interrogated: the rhetorical repertoire of scholastic meaning is so freely
reencoded that the underlying ironic distance is turned into a historical distance from its humanist critics. The cultural memory of scholasticism (in the referent of "needless entities, and useless distinctions")
is made to associate with what is troublesome in the dichotomy, endorsed by humanist poetics, between universalizing fiction and particularizing historiography.

The dilemma is that of the new authorship, with its vague, opportunistic standards of legitimation. In view of the continuing friction
between pamphlet and tale, history and story, the author-narrator's
strategy turns out to be a desperate one. The sheer diversity (concealing an unprecedented jumble of social and cultural functions) is supposed to be contained by the rhetorical figure used to convey the difficulty of effectively bridging their incongruities. But what makes
these difficulties so crucial is that they are linked to the attempt to
map out a major road of representation in the vernacular culture of
the Renaissance. Here we have, in one highly experimental text, more
than just the transcription of actual events and figures into the nascent

language of fiction. We have, in this process, a number of shrill voices that sound forlorn, caught as they are between the authorization and the performance of a new type of narrative.

The complex text of *The Unfortunate Traveller* suggests that the crisis of neoclassical authority in writing involved an extraordinary opening for another, larger space for representation. Emerging from the crumbling Renaissance humanist principles of composition, rhetoric, and poetics, new norms and choices in writing (and in reading) suggested themselves. Superseding the allegorical as well as the neoclassical versions of universality, the paradox of closure in a divided space offers itself: an unfixed mode of representation, according to which what represents may cease to be (dis)continuous with what is represented. So the gaps come to exist side by side with a new type of link, one that brings together, even as it divides, the assimilation of words through a new awareness of the order of things and the appropriation of a new relation of things through words—embracing the words as part of a larger system of signs in contractual, monetary, property, and exchange-value relations. The breakdown of authority in neoclassical poetics—following the one in the universals of allegory and the even earlier one in the matter and ethos of chivalry—may have been as unsettling as it was inviting to unprecedented uses of representation.

The author-function was thus subjected to changing patterns of legitimation associated with a new type of validity that resided in the pleasure, the knowledge, and the exchange-value of the signs themselves. These patterns were hardly imaginable without a sense of the profit and prestige that the narrative and its hero would gain in the marketplace. At any rate, Nashe in the "Induction" went out of his way to drape the new exchange mechanism in mocking hyperbole: "Everie Stationers stall they [his readers] passe by, whether by daie or by night, they shall put off theyr hats too, and make a lowe legge, in regard their grand printed Capitano is there entombd" (2:208). There is a connection between the author's "Mercuriall fingers" and his capacity for snatching "a new wit, a new stile, a new soule" for his writing. Even more crucially, if "the witt of this . . . odd Modernist is [his] owne," he expects his readers to show a similar "newfangleness." As they enter the market for the products of the press, they need to accept the low life of Jack Wilton as, potentially, a sparkling 'chip off the block' of his own biographer. The tossed-about hero is one of their own, to be greeted in effigy and honored for his wit: he is implicated in their own lives and yet he stands on display as "their grand printed Capitano"—inviting particular consideration of what, positively or negatively, "may be and should be" in their own lives.

In this respect, the self-inscribed wit of the early modern intellectual was representative in a new sense: piercing the boundaries of old, this penniless, unaccommodated wit opened a textual monument, albeit a marketable one, to both scrutiny and empathy. The circulation of wit between author and hero (and reader) was "entombd" so that there might be wit in others. The narrative, rather than merely being subjected to given types of authority, through the act of its reception constituted a little brief authority of its own. Part of the power of its mimesis came from the power of the knowledge, the mobility, and the pleasure of its readers. From this point on, the appropriation of the world in the text could more potently be linked with the appropriation of the text in the world. This heightened interaction between writing and reading was part and parcel of a larger constellation of cultural exchange where, as Jean-Christophe Agnew notes, "the market was made meaningful at the very moment that meaning itself was becoming marketable."[20]

13

Textual Ownership and the New Reading

Cervantes

A s the author-function in the writings of Thomas Nashe— "gosling of the Printing-house"—suggests, the sense of ownership through appropriation affected both the language of authority and the conditions of its reception. The ties between product and producer had by this stage become so close and so personal that the process of appropriation was often sanctioned by metaphors of procreation. The author-function is not to reinvent and redefine (as Malory did) what "the . . . book says"; now the book, far from reconstituting any previously established authority, aimed at a self-fashioned validity, in the sense that the story, the characters, and the multiplication of significance largely resulted from the author's and the reader's own invention and labor. But the political economy of the product (the text in the marketplace, the book as a unit of exchange-value) could be almost obliterated in the biological metaphor of procreation, which suggested the process of 'bringing forth one's own.' The author's function, even outside its traffic in the marketplace, was naturalized into that of a parent: for Sidney, the sheets of the *Arcadia* were "this child, which I am loath to father";[1] for Cervantes, the narrative was defined as "hijo del entendimiento" [the son of my understanding],[2] and none would understand who did not understand the nature of *this* understanding.

What, ironically, the images (and illusions) of procreation actually obscured was that the presumed autonomy of the new author-function presupposed a greater amount of socialization through exchange. The narrative served a greater variety of cultural functions in relation to society at large. On the economic level, the individual acquisition of the narrative could not help being geared to its exchange-value: individual ownership plus the use of the printing press made circulation imperative. On the social and intellectual level, the relationship of the narrative to its readers was both broadened and further differentiated; the author-function, moving in the direction of the autonomy of procreation, ceased to be tied to the needs and conventions of any one of the late-medieval estates and institutions.

In the course of the sixteenth century, authors of narrative found themselves able to relate to a considerably wider spectrum of choices in the selection of their own fictional repertoire. Because the available narrative traditions and conventions had more nearly become objects of individual appropriation, the given "schemata" of narration (to use E. H. Gombrich's term)[3] lost the force of their restraint and stringency to the extent that the modifying thrust of the author's "correction" assumed an altogether new dimension. If, as Wolfgang Iser suggests, such "correction" can "only take place through the restructuring of points of significance in the schemata," then—by reconstituting the norms of expectation—it "creates its own condition of reception."[4] The actual restructuring powers of the author's correction, the heightened degree of its potency and effectiveness, must not be viewed as timeless characteristics of rewriting and reception. Rather, these elements are correlated to distinctly historic patterns of discursive practice and author-function that presuppose and promote intellectual (as well as material) appropriations, according to which "the chief objective condition of labor" is not "already there" but would itself "appear as a *product* of labour."[5]

In this respect the most consistently experimental texts, such as *Lazarillo*, *Gargantua*, *The Unfortunate Traveller*, and *Don Quixote*, provide extreme examples of a discourse that creates its own conditions of reception by breaking up long-established schemata, such as those associated with the *Volksbuch* and jest-book traditions and, especially, the patterns of chivalric romance. (Parody, in this connection, can play an important part; in prose narrative as well as in verse—as Pulci and Ariosto confirm—it can serve as a particularly effective way of disrupting traditional modes of discourse from within their own repertoires.) What results is a multiplicity of particularized significations that helps sustain the range and direction of the new "entendimiento" involved in the correction itself. As soon as the author-narrator succeeds in making the "correction" so integral to the work that some "coherent deformation" of the schemata ensues,[6] the new mass of detail and particularity can thematically be used to authorize any divergence from the given forms and genres.

Early modern writers who claimed self-fashioned authority for their texts had to be ready for conflict and displacement. The actual effects of appropriation, the springs of its power and energy, were closely connected to the conflictual quality of the authorial "corrections" and to how their potential coherence throve on the simultaneous availability of both more particularity and a greater design of generality. It was on this level that the contradiction between previous schemata and their "corrective" treatment could be coped with, as when inherited versions of idealized conduct were revealed to be in conflict with "the foolish world" of experience and contingency.

As new authors assumed the function of intellectual and juridical appropriation in regard to the process and the products of their making, their readers were confronted with a communicative situation in which, more literally than ever before, they had to make the text their own in order fully to comprehend and use it. The reader of early modern narrative, after having bought or borrowed a printed copy of the text, was required to adapt his or her own code to a repertoire of social norms and aesthetic choices that was less invariable or predictable than, for example, the traditional schemata in the *Grandes chroniques* of Gargantua or in the *Amadis* and *Palmerin* romances had ever been. (A similar demand was made in the Erasmian *Praise of Folly*, as compared with traditional uses of allegory such as Sebastian Brant's, and in Shakespeare's treatment of postallegorical figures of farcical evil—

Richard III, Iago, Edmund, and so forth—as compared to the uses of psychomachia in the Tudor morality play.)

For this very reason, the intended as well as the actual reader (or spectator) was made to invest more cooperation, imagination, and labor into exploring and assimilating motives, connections, perspectives, and causes. Although the conditions of actualizing the text had become removed from any given social occasion of festive pastime (such as used to prevail even in late-oral cultures), and although the time and place of reception had increasingly become a matter of individual choice and leisure, the narrative texts of Rabelais, Sidney, and Cervantes now offered an "idle reader" a whole network of response-inviting structures that were more complex and exacting than anything found in the traditional genres of prose fiction. Because the early modern texts tended to correspond much less closely to the repertoires already familiar to their readers, they had to produce for themselves a system of equivalences with which to counter the unprecedented deformation of traditional social norms and literary choices. But by doing so, by projecting the imaginative energies and intellectual faculties of their own private understanding into the act of reading, readers could more nearly appropriate the text as a distinct mode of production of their own selves, their culture, their insight, and their sensibilities.

Thus, while the meaning of narrative tends to become a function of the readers' cooperation—of their competence in appropriating the text—that activity itself is closely related to what the understanding of the peculiar mode of textual signification demands. There is a considerable correlation between the action in the text and the act of its reading, but this interaction is based on, indeed presupposes, an increased awareness of the area of nonidentity between the literary profession and public function of the author and the social pursuits and private responses of the author's readers. At the center of this interaction, there is perhaps the most seminal contradiction in early modern prose narrative: the contradiction between fictive matter and "true" meaning, between the autonomous code of the narrative and the search, through the medium of fictionality, for some heteronomous use of narrative in the world of early modern history. For an adequate understanding, the reader must face and somehow suspend the distinction between the matter of fictionality and its meaning in reality. It was at this juncture that, not fortuitously, the drama of the reader who fails to perceive this necessary distinction could be turned into the greatest of early modern narratives.

The prologue to *Don Quixote* is indeed a most revealing instance of the changing function of the reader's activity, at least insofar as the discussion of the new reading is linked with an almost self-conscious awareness of the author-function:

> Idle reader, you can believe without any oath of mine that I would wish this book, as the child of my brain, to be the most beautiful, the liveliest and the cleverest imaginable. But I have been unable to transgress the order of nature, by which like gives birth to like. And so, what could my sterile and ill-cultivated genius beget but the story of a lean, shrivelled, whimsical child, full of varied fancies that no one else has ever imagined—much like one engendered in prison, where every discomfort has its seat and every dismal sound its habitation? Calm, a quiet place, the pleasantness of the fields, the serenity of the skies, the murmuring of streams and the tranquility of the spirit, play a great part in making the most barren muses bear fruit and offer to the world a progeny to fill it with wonder and delight. It may happen that a father has an ugly and ill-favoured child, and that his love for it so blinds his eyes that he cannot see its faults, but takes them rather for talents and beauties, and describes them to his friends as wit and elegance. But I, though in appearance Don Quixote's father, am really his step-father, and so will not drift with the current of custom, nor implore you, almost with tears in my eyes, as others do, dearest reader, to pardon or ignore the faults you see in this child of mine. For you are no relation or friend of his. Your soul is in your body, and you have free will with the best of them, and are as much a lord in your own house as the King is over his taxes. For you know the old saying: under my cloak a fig for the king—all of which exempts you from every respect and obligation; and so you can say anything you think fit about this story, without fear of being abused for a bad opinion, or rewarded for a good one.

> [Desucupado lector, sin juramento me podrás creer que quisiera que este libro, come hijo del entendimiento, fuera el más hermoso, el más gallardo y más discreto que pudiera imaginarse. Pero no he podido yo contrvenir á la orden de naturalexa; que en ella cada cosa engendra su semejante. Y asi, ¿qué podía engendrar el estéril y mal cultivado ingenio

mio, sino la historia de un hijo seco, avellanado, antojadizo, y lleno de pensamientos varios y nunca imaginados de otro alguno, bien como quiense engendró en una cárcel, donde toda incomodidad tiene su asiento y donde todo triste ruido hace su habitación? El sosiego, el lugar apacible, la amenidad de los campos, la serenidad de los cielos, el murmurar de las fuentes, la quietude del espíritu, son grande parte para que las musas más estériles se muestren fecundas y ofrezcan partos al mundo que le colmen de maravilla y de contento. Acontece tener un padre un hijo feo y sin gracia alguna, y el amor que le tiene le pone una venda en los ojos para que no vea sus faltas, antes las juzga por discreciones y lindezas, y las cuenta á sus amigos por agudezas y donaires. Pero yo, que, aunque parezco padre, soy padrastro de D. Quijote, no quiero irme con la corriente del uso, ni suplicarte casi con las lágrimas en los ojos, como otros hacen, lector carísimo, que perdones ó disimules las faltas que en este mi hijo vieres, pues ni eres su pariente ni su amigo, y tienes tu alma en tu cuerpo y tu albedrío como el más pintado, y estás en tu casa, donde eres señor della, como el rey sus alcabalas, y sabes lo que comunmente se dice, que debajo de mi manto, al rey mato. Todo lo cual te exenta y hace libre de todo respeto y obligación, y así puedes decir de la historia todo aquello que te pareciere, sin temor que te calumnien por el mal, ni te premien por el bien que dijeres della.][7]

The emphasis is on possessions, material and intellectual, and the language thrives on the tensions between autonomy and filiation—filiation as a metaphor of ownership through organic descent. From the point of view of the security of the author's property, the theoretical concern curiously anticipates the menacing practice of expropriation and the subsequent need for reappropriation. In this sense the theme of literary ownership is reformulated in the opening of the second part, especially in the complaint made against Alonso Fernandez de Avellaneda, who had threatened to deprive the rightful author of his income—"que me ha de quitar la ganancia con su libro."[8]

At the beginning of each part of *Don Quixote*, the spheres of literary and juridical ownership have already begun to overlap; the reader's response is structured through the awareness that narrative has become an object of both intellectual and material appropriation. What is remarkable is that the occasion for asserting the latter provides a congenial opportunity for more deeply probing the former. The comparison, then, between the reader's property and that accruing from the king's revenues seems as appropriate as the implied links between economic substance and the reader's own "soul . . . and . . . free will." The language of property and the possessive form (as in the recurring "tu") is used not simply to acknowledge (and indeed stimulate) the claim for personal independence and individual judgment, but to project the new mode of appropriating a literary text into the world of early modern history, with its characteristic division between social and private dimensions. The reader's own "soul" and "house" are the basic instances of the intellectual and material possession of the text, the most essential requirements of its economic as well as literary appropriation. But such independence is at the same time part and parcel of a pattern, well known in modern history, of changing connections between the public and private domains of cultural activity. Thus the image of the royal tax money (*alcabalas*) seems suggestive in that it helps reintegrate the private act of appropriation into the larger context of social obligation and public circulation. There is a sense of the reader's activities as already independent of many of their traditional predeterminations, yet still part of a public ensemble of the cultural exchange of goods and values.

Behind the author's studied politeness a new aesthetic of reception is proposed. The readers are summoned to appropriate the text individually and yet to project their own faculties communally, beyond the particularity of class and station. The dialectic is one of appropriation and objectification, and it allows, together with a new rhetoric, an astonishing flexibility in the relations between author and readers. Pointing beyond the older type of collective response, the new relationship involves identification as well as distance: Cervantes' readers are, socially, isolated, private persons who cannot take for granted the reproduction of fixed, given relations to their society. They cannot, therefore, fully relate to the means, the modes, or the authorial language of signification as their own, as a part of *their* own sense of the world—except through a cathartic act of the imagination. Admittedly, each reader can be addressed, individually, as "lector carísimo," but his or her world (and activity) seems clearly differentiated from that of both the author and the author's work—with which the reader

shares little that is his or her own—by way of either family or friendship ("pues ni eres su pariente ni su amigo").

Thus the author approaches the reader respectfully, as an autonomous individual who is under no obligation to accept authorial
legislation in matters of poetic taste and opinion. And yet he acknowledges this independence only in order to invite readers themselves to use it in the service of a new strategy of reading, so as to be
able to dissociate themselves from the all-too-familiar schemata of the
romances of chivalry. The reader is invited imaginatively to identify
not with an image of the order of knighthood, but rather with the
most thoroughly historical and the most historically consistent of all
literary deformations. The timeless acts of chivalry are subsumed under the ordinary experiences of temporality; idealization is suspended
in "the trueth of a foolish world." To follow the destruction of the
schema and yet to perceive balance in the act of its suspension, the
reader's independent intellect is indeed sorely needed. There is a necessary affinity between the readers' need to use their own souls and
free wills and the author's freedom in the deformation (in the form of
parody) of the time-honored theme of chivalry.

But in order to use the images of "a foolish world" as an informing
source of their own authority and cultural energy, the readers of this
type of *historia* must provide and validate the "consideration" that, according to Sidney, not *historia* but "Poesie dealeth with." To characterize the demands made by the new amalgamation of history and
story, it is not enough to say that the reader must appropriate the two
modes of discourse at the same time. What the reception of this new
type of historiographic fable presupposes is the assimilation of the
"fained Image" of *fabula* in terms of the function of that different kind
of discourse which, as *historia*, is "captivated" by the ordinary and particular. And vice versa: the "trueth" of the world has to be assimilated
in a historical sense, but at the same time through the images of in-
vented stories. In other words, the truth about the world must be read
metaphorically, whereas the metaphoric function of the new fictionality is to be viewed as related to the world as conceived of in the text.

In bringing all this together, the new fiction not only combined the historian's and the poet's demands on the reader's code formation but summoned him or her to participate in the comprehension and resolution of the contradiction between the fictive dimension and the discursive practice actually performed in the narrative. For readers to move between what was represented (in a fiction) and what was doing the representing (in actuality), they had to acknowledge the distance between their own world and that of the story, but at the same time they had to be involved in bridging the gulf between the two worlds. When Cervantes acknowledges the reader's property—her or his independent head and "free will"—he does so not in order to limit the scope of the interplay between the world of the reader and the world of his own *hijo* but, on the contrary, to bring out the full extent of the distance between what was (in the story) alien and what (in the reading) nevertheless might be made one's own.

To connect the discourses of *historia* and *fabula* must have been a difficult undertaking. Cervantes seems wary of putting too great a burden on his readers when he has his protagonist say that the understanding of his own story, since it was written in the random style of history, would require a special interpretation ("Y así de ser de mi historia, que tendrá necesidad de comento para entenderla").[9] But the "necesidad de comento"—the need to guide or prefigure the reader's responses—turned out to be unnecessary when the distance between the *historia* in the story and the history in the reader's life could be imaginatively bridged; the meaning of the text emerged as a function of the reader's own experience in reading. Thus, the act of reading had, in its turn, become so much a function (and theme) of the narrative that there was no need for the author to follow convention and appeal to his readers outside the fabric of his story ("ni suplicarte casi con las lágrimas en los ojos, como otros hacen"). Nor was there, as Cervantes says in the prologue, any need for the author to embellish his story with *sententiae* or erudition of any other kind. The activity of the reader had become an independent one, and the world of the book had its own validity; it was only from within the story that the interaction between feigning and meaning could be realized.

From the point of view of the cultural uses of appropriation, then, the relationship between the assimilation of the world to the book and the assimilation of the book to the world had become complex, and the two had, as never before in fiction, become interconnected. To assimilate the narrative in the world of early modern history involved readers in a dual communicative situation: they were supposed to "believe," that is, to accept the feigning as an effective force in their own imaginations. But at the same time they were supposed to "know"— that is, they had to make out the told events as false, as fictive happenings, if ever the readers were in their own lives to use these events with an understanding of their true meaning. If the readers failed to do that, if they had belief but no knowledge (if they related only to the *fabula* in the *historia* and not the *historia* within the *fabula*), these readers would fail both in the reading of the literature and in their worldly actions, as did the most notorious of all bewildered readers, the ingenious *hidalgo* himself. The drama of mistaken fictionality, in which Don Quixote is a supreme protagonist, began to make sense in a world in which, as never before in early modern history, the discerning appropriation of fictional matter had become one way of coming to terms with that world itself.

Epilogue

Ambivalent Representations
Integrating Difference

In his path-breaking archaeology of representation, Michel Foucault views its "decline"[1] almost as a moment of liberation, a moment when language, recapturing its freedom and movement, is about to triumph once more. At long last, the immense power of representation to order and to command language appears to be nearing exhaustion; the time has seemingly come when the incompatibility of language and humankind will explode and, "since language is here once more, man will return to that serene non-existence in which he was formerly maintained by the imperious unity of discourse" (386). This is not the place to criticize the inverted teleology behind this grandiose panorama of the rise and fall of representation. But if Foucault's project cannot convince us of the *end,* it is certainly persuasive on the *ends* and the *limits* of representation. Nowhere else do we find so fierce a sense of its vulnerability and, especially, of its limitations vis-à-vis the shadowy realms of birth and death, violence and desire, work and sexuality. Failing to encompass this underside of our unspeakable existence, representation cannot but conceal its own inefficacy in the face of the hardness of things, the irreducible and the inexpressible—in short, the nonrepresentable dimension of existence.

Foucault's project may well be the most highly influential, perhaps the one truly classical, study of the subject; it can, in conclusion, provide us with a significant point of vantage from which to view six-teenth-century representational practices in perspective. If, in Fou-cault's project, this perspective seems rather sweeping and conjectural, part of the reason is that it posits an abrupt, unhelpfully rigid hiatus between representations in the Renaissance and their ubiquity and imperiousness in the "classical" and modern periods. According to this view, representation and interpretation in the sixteenth century were guided by "the four similitudes," a rich semantic web of resem-blances whose principal figures were *convenientia, aemulatio,* analogy, and the play of sympathies (17–25). With these figural patterns be-tween him and "the empirical domain," "sixteenth-century man" per-ceived the latter "as a complex of kinships, resemblances, and affini-ties" (54). Representation, in terms of this "sixteenth-century episteme," was posited as "a form of repetition" (17) sanctioned by its "macrocosmic justification." These figures continued to be dominant, at least until, "at the beginning of the seventeenth century, during the period that has been termed, rightly or wrongly, the Baroque, thought ceases to move in the element of resemblance. Similitude is no longer the form of knowledge but rather the occasion of error" (51)—as Fou-cault proceeds to show in his reading of Descartes.

The trouble with this approach to sixteenth-century representations is that too many of their hybrid forms and contradictory functions tend to be obliterated; their instability and their resilience, their pro-found and sometimes scandalous involvement with nondiscursive practices, with market relations and new technologies of distribution, are either ignored or minimized. Foucault has little patience with Gutenberg; he looks neither at Geneva (let alone Wittenberg) nor, strictly speaking, at Port-Royal. Insofar as the latter is referred to, the early apostolic Augustinianism of Bajus and Jansenius with its semi-Calvinist underside is lost sight of in favor of what the sign in "the Classical age" stands for.[2]

I do not dispute the unquestioned penetration and originality of Foucault's readings. But what is problematic is an archaeology of the sign that, more often than not, turns out to be forgetful of the "in-strumentality" of early modern representations, their engagement with the "modalities" of living and communicating, their contributions to "accommodating their writers, performers, readers, and audiences to multiple subject positions within the world that they themselves both constitute and inhabit."[3]

To invoke a prestigious text such as *Les mots et les choses* on the changing paradigms of representation is to invite reflection on what, in the present (far more modest) study, is in the nature of a counter-proposal, especially on the early modern order of things. At the same time, the idea (far from a self-congratulatory one) is to draw attention to those open and disturbing questions that throughout these pages have been touched on rather than cogently spelled out. Foremost among these questions is the issue of authority in those diverging coordinates of material and intellectual power within which representational practices operate in the first place. As most of us have learned from Foucault, talk about representation becomes fairly meaningless unless the concept of 'power' is redefined beyond the haze of those generalities where power is always already repressive. There is a need to reject the identification of power (or authority) with the notion of "repression" as, in Foucault's terms, "a wholly negative, narrow, skeletal conception of power," one that is "quite inadequate for capturing what is precisely the productive aspect of power."[4]

In the emerging modern nation-state, the political apparatus of absolutism with its sovereign control over both church and state could be divorced from neither a repressive nor a "productive aspect of power." The same was true of the nascent machinery of jurisdiction, which, although brutally repressive, emerged as an alternative to fifteenth-century turmoil and the strife-ridden, even more arbitrary rule of local magnates. Here as elsewhere, however, an awareness of this centralization process must not presuppose any monolithic source of power in the period; it must not minimize the ongoing 'unofficial' diversification and differentiation in contemporary uses of authority. Rather, on a rudimentary political, economic, and sociocultural level, the contradiction between centralization and diversification was fundamental to and endemic in the early modern order of things. Without it, neither the reaffirmations nor the crisis of authority can be understood adequately, nor would it be possible to account for those early modern locations of struggle and gallimaufry in which the material and the intellectual sources of authority began to contradict and engage, but also to complement, each other.

It was precisely in view of, and by assimilating, these contradictions that sixteenth-century representations increasingly assumed varied, often opposing directions. Seeking to capture and stand for particular visions, causes, and images in and of the world, representations became manifold and vulnerable, liable to unforeseen uses and abuses. There were links and gaps between the particulars of living, feeling, and thinking and the larger means and overriding coordinates of exchange, "trafficke," education, and a nascent central government. Early modern representations were imbued with and transmuted this problematic linkage: they responded to these circumstances by viewing this particularized world as if it were a whole picture, as something that—in Heidegger's sense of *Weltbild*—had to be imaginatively projected in order to be grasped at all.[5] In light of the resulting diversification in points of viewing, writing, and reading, the notion of one "sixteenth-century episteme" (let alone one dominated by resemblances) is not helpful; it should be discarded in favor of a wider register of representation marked by conflict, debate, and division but also, I suggest, by new levels of alliance, integration, and socialization.

Paradoxically, in early modern culture these two aspects, although they seem to be mutually exclusive, in fact go together. The paradox in question is not unrelated to a recurring ambivalence in the sociohistorical conditions of absolute sovereignty, where the concomitant centralization of government and the emergence of nascent forms of nationwide administration went hand in hand with the gradual formation, and even polarization, of distinct classes, interests, lifestyles, and ideologies. Thus, social historians of the period have noticed "a whole series of developing polarities of speech, dress, manners, living conditions, leisure pursuits and literary interests," most of them resulting from "a process of withdrawal by the gentry and middling groups from a common heritage of assumptions about social integration."[6]

While these changes gradually, on a day-to-day basis, affected elementary conventions of living together in society (involving, for instance, the dislodgment of servants from their time-honored eating place in the hall, and the installation, for their use, of back stairs to guard the gentry's privacy), other developments assumed a more spectacular and dramatic character. As county historiography has shown in recent years, there were regional divisions on a political level that had far-reaching implications on a national scale. For example, according to Peter Clark's study of politics and conflict in Kent, there was, by the end of Elizabeth's reign, "a major expansion" of local government culminating in "the growth of an all-powerful county government centered on quarter sessions." Along with this horizontal expansion of county government there was "a vertical growth in power: the Elizabethan regime sought to intervene increasingly in the running of local communities, wherever possible absorbing functions previously performed on an informal, seigneurial, or neighbourly level."[7] Such sharply opposed views of governmental authority and practice led in many cases to a polarization of the gentry into two coherent and reasonably stable groups, one willing to implement and profit from economic and administrative policies formulated by the central government, the other concerned with upholding the cause of county government, landowning interests, and local privileges. In Norfolk, for instance, as A. Hassell Smith writes, "this conflict between 'court' gentry and 'county' gentry intensified during the 1590s,"[8] especially after the threat of a Spanish invasion had ceased to induce unity. But even earlier, this state of affairs involved "an intensely political situation" that "led to frequent debates about who did what and on whose authority."[9]

Alongside these socially and politically divisive trends, there were different overriding and homogenizing tendencies at work. Closely connected with such factors as an expanding market for exchange-value and the new social mobility, these tendencies were promoted by the new monarchy. But they were also encouraged by a new technology of communication in alliance with the spread of literacy. As Anthony Fletcher and John Stevenson note, "the tremendous expansion of educational opportunity . . . contributed to the growth of a homogeneous national culture"[10]—even while, one should add, it greatly accelerated diversification.

Here as elsewhere, the boundaries between division and integration were fluid. But in the sphere of culture, too, a dichotomy between the divisive and the integrative uses of representation was clearly at work. For an illustration, one only has to look at Elizabethan drama, where this bifurcation is quite explicit in both the theme and the function of representation. Once, as Ulysses says in Shakespeare's *Troilus and Cressida,* "The specialty of rule hath been neglected" (1.3.77), "Each thing meets / In mere oppugnancy" (110), and "everything includes itself in power, / Power into will, will into appetite" (119–20). Dramatic representations could be used to deny that there "be rule in unity itself" (5.2.144): their own dynamic mode of composition and reception could demonstrate "that a thing inseparate / Divides more wider than the sky and earth" (151–52).

However, even in projecting and interpreting "the spacious breadth of this division" (153), Elizabethan representations, out of their own uncertainty, revealed a countervailing direction: the attempt to cope with vanishing courts of appeal could adumbrate new patterns of order *through* difference and differentiation. For instance, John Lyly, in his bewilderment over the loss of authority in the generic rules of dramatic composition, invoked the confusing energies of trade and mobility. Since "Trafficke and travell hath woven the nature of all nations into ours," the trespassing of generic boundaries (at least) "is to be excused." So when "Time hath confounded our mindes, our mindes the matter," the dramatist's perception sought refuge in a new picture of the "whole": for Lyly, "the whole worlde is become an Hodgepodge."[11] Once the traditional order of decorum and propriety no longer applied, dramatic representations themselves were in search of a more inclusive order, one that allowed for a colorful weaving ("like Arras") of the strange and the unknown into what was received as one's own.

Here, early modern representation reveals its own vulnerable groping for form out of both the formless and the placeless market of the time. But the same set of circumstances that made for new division also contained (often in both senses of the word) integrative trends vis-à-vis dislodged boundaries of old. At the turn of the century and shortly thereafter, representations attained a reach and a functioning marked by differentiation itself; the working principle became that of a "scene individable, or poem unlimited" (*Hamlet* 2.2.400). In Shakespeare's plays, Lyly's gallimaufry of generic kinds actually seemed to thrive on the breakdown of generic boundaries ("pastoral-comical, historical-pastoral," and so forth). For the "scene" to declare itself "individable" revealed a somewhat desperate note of defiance, commingled with a new trust in a centripetal dynamic of representation. In engaging the full spectrum of both divisive and "individable" strategies of representation, the language of the theater came near to harboring an element of mutuality, even interdependence, in their respective conditions of possibility. To say that trade and mobility had "woven" the experience of others "into ours," or that "the age is grown so picked" (yet another world-picture, from *Hamlet* 5.1.136), established an imaginative frame of reference for both association and dissociation within this frame: the global and the homely, idea and particularity, could be made to jostle in mutual attraction and repulsion. What was implicated was a more complex sense of both exchange and polarization than any nonmetaphorical reading of "weaving" and "picked" would seem to allow for.

To account for this pictured element of motion in figural form is no easy matter; insofar as it connects with the dichotomy in representation, this connection would seem, first of all, to presuppose an imaginary opening in the uses of language. Here was an opening, entirely absent from early Tudor usage, that reached out to involve an "unknowne order" of inclusion and exclusion in the virtually "unlimited" quality of presentation and duplication of other objects and relations by what was not identical with them. But if, to recall W.J.T. Mitchell's happy phrase, there is no representation without taxation—without, that is, loss in the shape and presence of the represented—then the early modern reaching-out in scope and depth would go hand in hand with an "awareness of difference and the recognition of otherness," because these, especially in times of revolutionary change, coincide "with a heightened perception of a crisis in representation."[12]

This crisis, however, as it is reflected in Lyly's rhetoric of the confusion of mind and matter, came from overtaxing representation, from exacting from it too much presence in the presentation of too many imaginary articles, actions, and relations in a new, movable order of contingency.

This imaginary dimension is an important pointer to a cultural potential of inventive energies that suffused cultural representational practice in the early modern period. In this period there first emerged an increasingly interactive alliance between representation and the imagination, especially where the latter was released from, or had never subscribed to, the order of similitude. The imaginary, and in particular the uses of imagery and related forms of picture making, achieved an unprecedented role in certain areas of discursive practice. No doubt there was a strong link, as Christopher Braider has suggested, between the almost unlimited use of verbal imagery and the early modern promotion of painting "from the lowly status of a mere 'mechanical' art" to Leon Battista Alberti's extolling it as "the flower of every art." To account for this dazzling rise of the pictorial and to understand this "deep and pervasive commitment to forms of picturing"[13] (an impossible task here), one would have to reconsider the humanist interest in the Horatian *ut pictura poesis* in conjunction with a vast amount of material circumstances, from the late-medieval need for pictorial instruction in biblical matters to the nascent middle-class culture of the home, in reference to all of which "pictorial form affirmed its peculiar authority and scope."[14]

At present we do not have anything like a satisfactory account of the imaginary in early modern culture, though John Guillory's study of the changing invocations of authority through the internalization of the muse remains an invaluable contribution to the subject.[15] No doubt it is difficult in this connection to overestimate the Reformation matrix of the transformation, in the course of which the decline of divine inspiration came to constitute, in the teeth of radical Protestant scruples, a unique catalyst to the literary uses of the imagination. Nevertheless, the growing role and (as Bacon says) "authority" of the latter was widely linked to non-Reformation factors, among which the figure of invention and the practice of appropriation loomed large, particularly so since they effected a profound change in author-functions and informed unprecedented semantic as well as semiotic energies in the proliferation of discursive practices.

It was thus possible for Nashe, in *The Unfortunate Traveller*, to congratulate himself (un)ashamedly on "this phantasticall Treatise,"[16] thereby alluding to a self-conscious rôle of fantasy in the invention of fictional narrative. Scorning the obliging deference, à la Malory, to "bokis that bene auctorysed," the new author-function could dismiss "the notable foundation *Heresay,*" only to invoke "the sweet Muses to inspire unto him a good invention" (Sidney). Liberating fiction from the "worn-out impressions" of traditionally prescribed *matière,* the Muses offered lofty "wings" with which "to fly to heaven" (Nashe). These soaring wings, the same author insisted, were "the wings" of his pen, authorizing the middle-class graduate and his aspiring fellow writers to do what the poet behind the chorus in *Henry V* aimed at: to ascend a "heaven of invention" (prol. 2) so as from there to unleash "imaginary puissance" (25).

The early modern impulse behind such "imaginative practices" (to use Paul Ricoeur's phrase)[17] presupposed the decline of "base authority from others' books" (*Love's Labour's Lost* 1.1.87). No doubt these practices themselves were associated with the desire, inseparable from representation, to rely on "ones owne choice, and working" (Sidney) in coming to invent pictures showing the world in the mirror of its worldliness and diversity. *Invention* here is a key term of some conceptual consequence. Despite enormous differences in Renaissance reassessments of the imagination between thinkers as diverse as Marsilio Ficino and Francis Bacon, it seems significant that both locate the imaginary in a discursive space marked by what today might be called a transdisciplinary concept of invention. In book 13 of Ficino's *Platonic Theology,* the human *ingenium*—the creative affinity with nature itself—is inseparable from material constructions and practical inventions, such as the "buildings of the Greeks and Romans, their workshops for metal and glass."[18] The imagination is a unique *potentia media* through which "the inventors of innumerable arts," capable of godlike creation, bring forth an "admirable culture" of the soil and "stupendous constructions of buildings and towns."[19]

Similarly, in Bacon's *Advancement of Learning,* the role of the imagination is discussed in the context of an even broader awareness of the role of invention, both in the "Arts and Sciences" (including their links with a "discovery" such as that of "the West-Indies") and in "Speech and Argument." But "Imagination" in these provinces cannot be reduced to the role of "an agent or *nuncius*":

> Neither is the Imagination simply and only a messenger; but is invested with or at leastwise usurpeth no small authority in itself, besides the duty of the message. For it was well said by Aristotle, *That the mind hath over the body that commandment, which the lord hath over a bondman; but that reason hath over the imagination that commandment which a magistrate hath over a free citizen*; who may come also to rule in his turn.[20]

As remote from a doctrinaire Protestantism as he is from Ficino's apprehension of the "One" who is everything and transcends everything, Bacon makes an important qualification in regard to "matters of Faith and Religion." It is not only that in matters of "Faith" (a capitalized concept preceding "Religion") "we raise our Imagination above our reason"; even more specifically, it is in "divination" that the imagination excels itself. "Astronomer," "physician," and "politique" have their predictions, but when "divination . . . springeth from the internal nature of the soul," the mind—"withdrawn and collected into itself "—is ripe for the most intense form of imaginative activity: "The retiring of the mind within itself is the state which is most susceptible of divine influxions," such as those that derive from "the foreknowledge of God" (380).

Here, there is a tension between Bacon's almost grudging (and largely Aristotelian) reinstitution of the imagination on a functional and intermediate plane and his readiness to grant it "no small authority in itself." If the rather emphatic language of introspection does not in itself convey a proto-Protestant temper in his authorization of the imaginary, the unexpected link between the authority of the imagination and the potential *potestas* of a "free citizen" may well serve an end that substantially goes beyond an Aristotelian conception of the imagination. Unless this reading is wide of the mark, there is a significant investment of authority in those "wings" of choice— an investment that must have been greatly strengthened by a lively in-

teraction between the growth of imaginative and the proliferation of
representational practices. Here the theater again pointed the way;
Theseus's characterization of "strong imagination" as one of the "shaping fantasies" that "bodies forth / The forms of things unknown"
(*Midsummer Night's Dream* 5.1.5, 14–15) dramatically underlines this
interaction. Early modern imagination, far from serving as the inner-
most source and image of subjectivity, here provides a "strong" vessel
for shaping and transfiguring perceptions.

  With this in mind, the dichotomy between division and integration in the uses of representation can perhaps be seen in better perspective. In the absence of a subject-centered location of those "shaping fantasies," the unifying potential of the imagination, so marked
in its Neoplatonic and Romantic versions, cannot, in a good deal of
early modern practice, be said to be predominant. In early modern
England, for one thing, it was not impossible to associate the imaginary with the ambivalence representation itself possessed. In Bacon's
view, the imagination was authorized (or even "licensed") to do both:
to "join" the divided and to "sever" the unified. "Poesy," he writes, is
"a part of learning in measure of words for the most part restrained,
but in all other points extremely licensed, and doth truly refer to the
Imagination; which, being not tied to the laws of matter, may at pleasure join that which nature hath severed, and sever that which nature
hath joined, and so make unlawful matches and divorces of things:
Pictoribus atque poetis, &c." (343). If the true license of "Poesy" in reference to the imagination consisted of making both "unlawful
matches" and unsanctioned "divorces of things," the question of its
cultural function would need to be answered beyond the issue of unity
versus division, as well as beyond any other binary scheme of functions. The need for "rethinking imagination" (as a recent volume on
the subject puts it) in the early modern period seems now to be particularly urgent, all the more so since a preoccupation with Romantic definitions has for so long effectively barred a more balanced view
of it. At a time when universally accepted locations of authority and
cohesion fell into disarray, "imaginative practices" would especially
seek to respond to what Ricoeur has called "the need every group has
to give itself an *image* of itself, to 'represent' itself."[21] The need for self-

identification must have been quite urgent at a time of fast-moving transformations—a time when "the distance between actual practices and the interpretation" of those practices was, inevitably, painfully wide. There was a need to cope with the distance in question; imaginative practices would respond to this need and serve, in Ricoeur's words, an "integrative function" contemporaneous with "the symbolic constitution of social ties themselves."[22]

The point here is that these imaginative practices helped establish in early modern representations a remarkable space for "something of great constancy" (*Midsummer Night's Dream*, 5.1.25). This strange conjuncture, almost unthinkable in terms of our present critical preoccupations, is best brought out by Cornelius Castoriadis, who subsumes under it the cultural capacity for both institutionalization and an "inexhaustible supply of otherness."[23] Such "otherness," comprising but going beyond "the forms of things unknown," would constitute, in Castoriadis's terms, "an irreducible challenge to every established signification." The imaginary, in this sense, is not to be thought of as "an image *of* something"; rather, it is "the 'mirror' itself and its possibility," a puissance of its own, "the unceasing and essentially *undetermined* (socio-historical and psychical) creation of figures/forms/images" (3).

With this perspective on the imaginary in mind, the paradox in the early modern alliance between the conflicted and the "indivisible" in dramatic representations may no longer appear unaccountable. On the one hand, the imaginary—occupying, as an ambidextrous force in representation, the nonrepresentable space "before separation and differentiation" (296–97)—would constitute an "ensemblist-ensemblizing dimension" in the historical constellations of discourse. Castoriadis, even while distinguishing between "représenter/dire social" and "faire social,"[24] underlines a socializing capacity of the radical imaginary for closing the gap between them. "The ensemblist-ensemblizing dimension," being their joint function, constitutes, through socialization, a fundamental link between representation and the ensemble of its users. This socializing and instituting potential, therefore, is "simultaneously a creation and a condition of society, a condition created by what itself is conditioning."[25]

Here, then, is an intriguing dialectic: combining the force of institutionalization and the power to transform this force, the "ensemblist-ensemblizing" functions of the imaginary help constitute society as a unity that is identified by its differential ("unité identique à soi des différents"). Modern society, then, "does not abolish the difference of the elements that belong to it but coexists with it even where it superimposes itself on this difference." Again, "separation and reintegration mutually implicate and presuppose one another" (307).

In this process, the role of representation is more complex than can be defined within the limitations of the subversion/containment alternative. The interlocking of these conflicting functions must not be thought to play down the more overt political positions pro and contra; in the long view, however, the mode of representation—its function, purpose, and strategy—provides us with a site for a political unconscious that can only partially be subsumed under the semantic order of any act of either subversion or recuperation, no matter how important this act in itself can be.

In view of the vast literary output of the period, it is dangerous to generalize here, especially where the narrower focus of this study—Reformation discourse and Renaissance fiction—must be viewed against such extremely heterogeneous kinds of writings as the literature of *civilité,* Protestant conduct books, the new Catholic *artes moriendi,* the highly checkered *Bibliothèque bleue,* to name a few. As Roger Chartier suggests about the *Bibliothèque bleue,* "the variations in the apportionment of sociocultural differences" were significant in that these differences were "fragmenting the market into clienteles presumed to be discrete and establishing new cultural frontiers."[26]

It is difficult, therefore, to define the mode of early modern representation as a site of history and politics except by saying that preordained locations of authority continued to be strongest where "Trafficke," circulation, and gallimaufry within the representational process remained limited and where agencies of conscience, conviction, appropriation, and imagination were weakest in terms of their achieved puissance. Positively speaking, the sites of conscience, choice, invention, exchange, and the imaginary, especially strong where linked, marked the broadest space for innovative practices in and through

representation. Wherever these prevailed, generic boundaries and traditional decorum were threatened, and motion itself assumed an en-
coding force in the semiotics of signification.

Such a sweeping formula, however, must suggest the absolute limits of the potential of "innovative" early modern practices of representation. Sixteenth-century fiction could reject the "autorité privée"
of "presumption" and "stupidity" (à la Rabelais) in redefining
(dis)continuity in the relations of signifier and signified; it was equally
possible to scorn, at least in *historia,* "the notable foundation *Heresay*"
(Sidney) and to dismiss "that forgotten Legendary licence of lying,"
together with all the "worn out impressions of the feyned no where
acts" (Nashe) of chivalrous romance. But even when the new authors'
activity was designated as that of an "odd Modernist" (as Harvey said
about Nashe), Nashe, not unlike Rabelais and Sidney, could only partially claim to have "invention or matter . . . of [their] owne." Clearly
there was no such break with tradition as, only decades later,
Descartes postulated in the image of the tabula rasa. But the writings
of Descartes, not to mention those of Bacon, situated themselves beyond the politics of an alternative between *séparation* and *institution.*[27]
Although the *séparation* from tradition was significant enough in that
it denied Descartes, as Braider notes, "the authority of literary prece-
dent," this very "lack of authority" opened the way for a new type of
authority rooted in "the radically unprecedented and therefore radically unconditioned present of critical, self-consistent thought." It is
precisely because the philosopher was "authorized to begin entirely
afresh"[28] that the loss of source and the gaining of control could go
together in the project of yet another *instauratio magna* that came closest to the formulation of a new *episteme.*

For obvious reasons, the new authority in the representational practice of both Renaissance fiction and Protestant discourse did not attain an instituting stature of comparable magnitude and consistency.
In the writing of fiction in particular, if we except Cervantes, the exuberance of "a new brain, a new wit, a new stile, a new soule" (Nashe)
could only be celebrated in a desperate strategy coping with endless
irresolutions and meanderings in the circulation of authorities old and
new. Although in Reformation discourse authority was much more

consequentially redefined, in the Elizabethan state church polity (at least as represented by Bancroft, Cosin, and Ormerod) the analysis of crisis and the sense of division invariably preceded and predominated whatever instituting gesture was actually inscribed. Here, Richard Hooker's writings alone were of a different caliber, even when the blending of an early version of natural right with Thomas of Aquinas's universalism could not secure much of a future for this grand and profound project.

If, as I posit in the introduction, the alignment of "printers, players, and preachers" (Gardiner) constituted a potent nexus of discursive strategies in the early modern world, it is in the Elizabethan theater more than anywhere else that the forces of integration and separation came to a head. Here, the cultural occasion of the pulpit converged with the new conditions of authority in narrative to create a remarkably powerful and malleable space. Representation in the theater was forced, by the unavoidable presence of diversity in the very occasion of performance, to come to terms with the irreducibility of "Trafficke" and division. Here, it was imperative to establish new grounds of authority even as its traditional sources were enlisted and energized. In this respect, representation in the Elizabethan theater was centrally implicated in the irresolutions of early modern discourse. The recollection of game and sport, the memories of similitude, and the language of "mirror," "image," "form," and "pressure" (*Hamlet* 3.2.22–24) could be subjected to premodern as well as modern uses of theatrical space. The theater provided a platform on which representations themselves were represented through the medium of professional players who were multivocal and not unconditionally bound to any one particular mode and purpose of representation. The theater, though, was exceptional in that it instituted, through bodies and voices, cultural occasions and conventions that by themselves were inherently visual: on the platform stage, *ut pictura* was translated literally into a "speaking picture."

But the transaction of this "picture" was—as in Marlowe's "tragicke glasse"—relayed and no doubt contaminated by the performing agents of the "fond and frivolous Jestures"[29] of which Richard Jones, the printer of *Tamburlaine,* complained. The trouble with these agents was that, thereby, they themselves came into the picture. As long as their style of performance contained something of a "self-resembled show,"[30] these performers, representing something and someone else, also represented themselves. Whether or not their own craft and craftiness were already inscribed in the imaginary act of representation, their histrionic practice must have retained traces of existence and transmission, where the contemporary world with its motion and mingle-mangle could be encoded in the uses of representation.

The kinetic energy in the language and action of Elizabethan drama, and especially in Shakespeare's, must not be viewed as simply reflecting the presence of the player. This theater instituted a partially uncontrolled, highly flexible space between textualized representation in the language of the script and the (histrionic) representation of that (scriptural) representation through the impersonation of common players. When the task was "On this unworthy scaffold to bring forth So great an object" (*Henry V* prol. 1, 10–11), this space was suited for both the use *and* "Th' abuse of distance" (prol. 2, 32). Between the "scaffold" and "the worthiness of the matter itself" (to echo Marlowe's printer) there was a site for both the divisive and the "individable" purposes of playing. It was a site of difference integral to the representational process. The kinetic energy of motion and "travell" could here be invested in the "distance" (or lack thereof) between what was represented and what was representing or, to shift the emphasis somewhat, between the forms of fiction and the force of performance.

In accordance with this historicizing project of sounding the gaps and links in the representational process, the distinction between *histoire* and *discours* has been adapted to the present study of narrative forms between the Reformation and the Renaissance. This distinction, however, can be taken further wherever the gap between the forms of fiction and the force of performance can be viewed as if it were materialized in a spatially potent social relationship. The Elizabethan stage (and, partially at least, the stage in early modern Spain) may well be said to have assimilated this space for both division and continuity between who and what was represented and who and what was, through performative practice, doing the representing. Here, the division *in* representation could be overcome—the gap between actor and role could be closed—when the actor's use of signs functioned as part of the signified system of the role. In contrast to such closure, which occurred at moments of dramatic illusion and verisimilitude, the recourse to rupture—for example, when links between role and actor were suspended—was equally significant. Whichever the gesture, historical practices can be discerned in the differing purposes of playing.

The distinction, schematic though it may be, is not simply theoretical. The constellation of representational practices in the Elizabethan theater marks a profound and complex division of social interests and cultural attitudes. This division derives historically from the existence of an institution whose cultural "choice, and working" was primarily established by the social experience and the political economy of those who ran the playhouse and worked in it, those whose minds and bodies provided the means of signification. But although such performing agents of representation, together with most of the agents of reception, were (as Jean Howard noted in a seminar discussion) drawn from "unsanctioned groups" in society, the performed figures of representation almost invariably were not. In the tragedies and histories the serious dramatis personae almost always come from the nobility and gentry, and even the leading figures in the comedies are portrayed as patricians rather than as plebeians. So, unlike in much of the modern theater, the representing agents and the represented objects of drama were not of the same social order. There were tensions and gaps in experience between roles and actors, between dramatic signifieds and signifying minds and bodies. While in the great scenes of dramatic illusion representation could close gaps and naturalize norms and choices, in other places it also had to cope with "the spacious breadth of this division."

In these circumstances, the stage—unlike written narrative in printed form—could take advantage of the disparity between the agents and the objects of representation. In other words, the theater was in a unique position to process and, sometimes, to foreground the element of (dis)continuity between the representation of authority and the authority of its own performance work, work that culminated in the "imaginary puissance" of actors and spectators alike. Like no other

place in early modern culture, the ground between authority represented and authority (and competence) representing was an open, not
entirely predetermined one that could be used for several purposes,
including both rupture and continuity, divisive and comprehensive
strategies of representation.

To elaborate the theater's own scenario for authority and representation requires a study of its own, for which performance the present
book cannot even serve as a dress rehearsal.[31] This is not to say that
the perspectives on early modern discourse, as here developed, cannot
be of great significance in such an undertaking. In each case it seems
important to approach the issue of authority through the changeful
history of the authorization, distribution, and appropriation of discursive activities in the sixteenth century. To move from authority in
representation to the conditions of authorship and performance is to
explore the social and topographical space in which not only writing,
reading, and interpreting but playing and play-watching were unfolding. The crisis in authority went hand in hand with both a proliferation of discourses and an ambivalent mode of representation in
which the integration of difference could alternate with the differentiation of what had passed for integrity, identity, and institution.
Blurring the lines between the forces and functions of division and
those of closure and institution, the early modern forms of discourse
thrived on, and were profoundly affected by, a groundswell of social,
cultural, and technological change, whose consequences, for better or
worse, are with us late moderns still.

Notes

Introduction: Representation and Division in Early Modern Culture

1. Here and in what follows, my text is William Shakespeare, *The Complete Works of William Shakespeare*, ed. Stanley Wells and Gary Taylor (Oxford: Clarendon Press, 1986). As my use, in the same sentence, of "Renaissance" and "early modern" suggests, the distinction is deliberate in that the latter concept is used for a broader range of cultural practices such as those embracing social, economic, and religious activities, and also oral culture and nonhumanist types of writing. This distinction in part recalls the more profound differentiation that Leah S. Marcus develops in "Renaissance/Early Modern," in *Redrawing the Boundaries: The Transformation of English and American Studies*, ed. Stephen Greenblatt and Giles Gunn (New York: Modern Language Association, 1992), 41–46. Throughout this study both terms are used as heuristic concepts rather than definitive categories, somewhat along the lines of recent contributions by Heather Dubrow and Frances E. Dolan to the Forum discussion in *PMLA* 109 (October 1994): 1025–27.

2. Martin Heidegger, "The Age of the World Picture," in *The Question concerning Technology and Other Essays*, trans. William Lovitt (New York: Harper and Row, 1977), 134, 135.

3. Ibid., 133.

4. Christopher Hill, *The English Bible and the Seventeenth-Century Revolution* (London: Allen Lane, 1993), 5, 4, 6, 29. See Deborah K. Shuger, *The Renaissance Bible: Scholarship, Sacrifice, and Subjectivity* (Berkeley and Los Angeles: University of California Press, 1994), for further ramifications of biblical authority far beyond purely religious and political discourses.

5. See John Guillory, *Poetic Authority: Spenser, Milton, and Literary History* (New York: Columbia University Press, 1983).

6. Vassilis Lambropoulos, *The Rise of Eurocentrism: Anatomy of Interpretation* (Princeton: Princeton University Press, 1993), xi–xii.

7. Ibid., 28.

8. This book was first envisioned in the context of a situation in central Europe in which relations between power and discourse had entered a state of undisguised crisis, as transcribed in the conjunctural subtext of my (East) German essays: "Shakespeare und Luther: Von neuzeitlicher Autorität und Autor-Funktion," *Shakespeare-Jahrbuch* 120 (1984): 7–24; "Mimesis und die Bürde der Repräsentation: Der Poststrukturalismus und das Produktionsproblem in fiktiven Texten," *Weimarer Beiträge* 31 (1985): 1061–99; "Autorität der Zeichen versus Zeichen der Autorität: Statussymbol und Repräsentationsproblematik in *König Lear*," *Orbis literarum* 42 (1987): 221–35; and "Mimesis zwischen Zeichen und Macht," *Zeitschrift für Germanistik* 9 (1988): 133–55.

9. Timothy J. Reiss, *The Discourse of Modernism* (Ithaca, N.Y.: Cornell University Press, 1982), 31.

10. Here and throughout this study, I use 'practice' in the basic sense, specified by Michel Foucault and others, of material or mental "action repeatedly or habitually performed" (*Universal Dictionary of the English Language*, s.v. "practice"). At the same time, I tend to foreground, wherever appropriate, links with praxis, as explored by Pierre Bourdieu, *Esquisse d'une théorie de la pratique* (Geneva: Droz, 1972), for at least two reasons. First, in the light of such praxis, as defined by Marx in his *Thesen über Feuerbach*, the gaps (as well as the links) between representation and existence need to be defined from a point beyond "the sovereign position from which objectivism seeks to order the world" as something out there. Hence, both institutions and language uses can be conceived as "tätige Seite" (Karl Marx and Friedrich Engels, *Werke* [Berlin: Dietz, 1959], 3:533)—that is, in relation to a highly interactive view of activities and circumstances.

Second, and even more directly relevant to my emphasis on what is performing and what is representing, such a concept of praxis resists a binary order or opposition between product (*opus operatum*) and process (*modus operandi*), the latter defined as a practical mode of processing and "mastery." (See Pierre Bourdieu, *Entwurf einer Theorie der Praxis*, rev. German ed. [Frankfurt am Main: Suhrkamp, 1979], 250.) This emphasis contradicts structuralism's panlogism and corresponds, as Bourdieu notes, to Wilhelm von Humboldt's earlier trajectory from *ergon* (objects, acts) to *energeia* (the "principles of production") (263).

11. For my use of 'appropriation,' again emphasizing the (dis)continuity,

especially visible in early modern culture, between material or economic and mental or intellectual modes of assimilation, acquisition, and possession, see my essay "'Appropriation' and Modern History in Renaissance Prose Narrative," *New Literary History* 14 (Spring 1983): 459–95.

12. James Clifford, "On Ethnographic Authority," *Representations* 1 (Spring 1983): 119, 118, 120, 139, 142.

13. Stephen Greenblatt, *Shakespearean Negotiations: The Circulation of Social Energy in Renaissance England* (Oxford: Clarendon Press, 1988), 38.

14. Jacques Derrida, *Of Grammatology*, trans. Gayatri C. Spivak (Baltimore: Johns Hopkins University Press, 1974), 3.

15. Robert Young, *White Mythologies: Writing History and the West* (London: Routledge, 1990), 19.

16. Ibid., 19, 172. Not surprisingly, in this revisionist ethnography, questions of authority and representation loom large. See, e.g., Marie Louise Pratt, *Imperial Eyes: Travel Writing and Transculturation* (London: Routledge, 1972), 6–7, 10–11.

17. Louis Montrose, "New Historicisms," in Greenblatt and Gunn, *Redrawing the Boundaries*, 392–418; 396.

18. John Foxe, *The Acts and Monuments of John Foxe*, ed. Stephen Reed Cattley (London: Seeley and Burnside, 1838), 6:41. See my discussion in chap. 4 below of Gardiner's position on authority.

19. Thomas Hobbes, *Leviathan*, ed. C. B. Macpherson (Harmondsworth, England: Penguin, 1968), 217–18.

20. Ibid.

21. Ibid., 112.

22. Jennifer Loach, *Parliament under the Tudors* (Oxford: Clarendon Press, 1991), 147; the reference here, in her highly cautious reopening of this question, is to the work of Derek Hirst, *The Representative of the People? Voters and Voting in England under the Early Stuarts* (Cambridge: Cambridge University Press, 1975).

23. D. M. Dean and N. L. Jones, eds., *The Parliaments of Elizabethan England* (Oxford: Basil Blackwell, 1990); see the editors' introduction, "Representation, Ideology, and Action in the Elizabethan Parliaments," 1.

24. Ibid., 13.

25. R. Baine Harris, ed., *Authority: A Philosophical Analysis* (University: University of Alabama Press, 1976), 1.

26. Philip Sidney, *The Prose Works of Sir Philip Sidney*, ed. Albert Feuillerat (Cambridge: Cambridge University Press, 1912), 1:3.

27. Miguel de Cervantes Saavedra, *El Ingenioso Hidalgo Don Quijote de la*

Mancha, ed. Francisco Rodríguez Marín (Madrid: Revista de Archivos, Bibliotecas y Museos, 1927), 1:19.

28. Cf. E. H. Gombrich, *Art and Illusion: A Study of the Psychology of Pictorial Representation* (Princeton: Princeton University Press, 1969), 313.

29. Sidney, *Prose Works of Sir Philip Sidney*, 1:206.

30. Michael McKeon, *The Origins of the English Novel, 1600–1740* (Baltimore: Johns Hopkins University Press, 1988), 25.

31. Cf. the definition of poetic "authority" in Jacqueline T. Miller, *Poetic License: Authority and Authorship in Medieval and Renaissance Contexts* (New York: Oxford University Press, 1986), 5.

32. This is one reason (the other is limitation of space) why I must disregard Elizabethan prose romance, with its blending of pastoral, euphuism, and Hellenistic models, as in the works of Robert Greene, William Warner, and Thomas Lodge. The same holds for the somewhat anachronistic but patriotic and highly popular processing of chivalric romance, as in the works of Richard Johnson, Henry Robarts, and Emanuel Forde, together with the adaptations, à la Anthony Munday, of the *Amadis* and *Palmerin* series. For a useful survey of these, see Paul Salzman, *English Prose and Fiction, 1558–1700: A Critical History* (Oxford: Clarendon Press, 1986), 59–82, 98–101.

33. John Bender, *Imagining the Penitentiary: Fiction and the Architecture of Mind in Eighteenth-Century England* (Chicago: University of Chicago Press, 1987), 72.

34. This refers to the debate, in Sidney and Nashe, on the conjunction of *fabula* and *historia*; cf. chap. 12 below.

35. Foxe, *Acts and Monuments*, 6:41.

36. Ibid.

37. See Jonathan V. Crewe, *Unredeemed Rhetoric: Thomas Nashe and the Scandal of Authorship* (Baltimore: Johns Hopkins University Press, 1982), 69–71. My emphasis, although different, is complementary to Crewe's brilliantly developed perception, according to which the punning bifurcation of Jack Wilton's identity "registers . . . the 'migration' of rhetoric from its elevated situation in the court, the academy, and the pulpit to its new (low) situation in the city and on the printed page" (70).

38. The reference is to my forthcoming *Shakespeare and the Power of Performance: Authority and Representation in the Elizabethan Theater*, which will follow up the present study and take its argument further. Meanwhile I have developed the concept of 'performance-game' and related issues in several articles, among them "Textual Authority and Performative Agency: The Uses

of Disguise in Shakespeare's Theater," *New Literary History* 25 (Fall 1994): 789–808.

Part I: Reformation Discord in Authority

1. Thomas Docherty, *On Modern Authority: The Theory and Conditioning of Writing, 1500 to the Present Day* (New York: St. Martin's Press, 1987), 49.

2. Joel Hurstfield, ed., *The Reformation Crisis* (New York: Harper and Row, 1966), 1.

3. For this phrase, from Henry VIII's address to his last parliament, see chap. 3 below.

4. The links between conflicting uses of authority and increasingly "loose" and expanding grounds of representation have remained outside the ken of even the most penetrating (and pioneering) studies in the "poetics of Protestantism." See, for example, Barbara K. Lewalski, *Protestant Poetics and the Seventeenth-Century Religious Lyric* (Princeton: Princeton University Press, 1979), and Andrew D. Weiner, *Sir Philip Sidney and the Poetics of Protestantism: A Study of Contexts* (Minneapolis: University of Minnesota Press, 1978). In "The Poetics of Protestantism and the English Literary Renaissance," *Sixteenth-Century Journal* 11 (1980): 99–102, Carl J. Rasmussen comments: "The English Reformation initiated a profound revolution in the midst of which, beginning in the late 1570s, came the flowering of the English literary renaissance. . . . Was there more than an accidental relationship between these two historical movements?" (99). To answer this question, we need to close the gap between the social history of communication, as in Elizabeth L. Eisenstein's thesis of the printing press as *preparatio evangelica* (*The Printing Press as an Agent of Change: Communications and Cultural Transformations in Early-Modern Europe* [Cambridge: Cambridge University Press, 1979], 1: 370–75), and the work on Protestant poetics and Reformation literary history. See especially John N. King's study of radical Reformation literature within its mid-Tudor context (*English Reformation Literature: The Tudor Origins of the Protestant Tradition* [Princeton: Princeton University Press, 1982]), in which he suggests the far-reaching consequences of the lifting of "restrictions on reading, speech, and publication" (77) during the Protectorate. Among these consequences was unheard-of space for "lay interpretation" of biblical and Reformation texts (131). See, in this connection, James K. McConica, *English Humanists and Reformation Politics under Henry VIII and Edward VI* (Oxford: Clarendon Press, 1965), 104–5, 270, and Arthur B. Ferguson, *The Articulate Citizen and the English Renaissance* (Durham, N.C.: Duke University Press, 1965), 133–34. More recently, Mark U. Edwards, Jr., has

studied the Reformation as a "print event," with Martin Luther as "the central figure in the West's first media campaign" (*Printing, Propaganda, and Martin Luther* [Berkeley and Los Angeles: University of California Press, 1994], jacket copy).

5. Joan Lockwood O'Donovan, *Theology of Law and Authority in the English Reformation* (Atlanta, Ga.: Scholars Press, 1991), 81; this paraphrases and confirms Jasper Ridley's reading in *Thomas Cranmer* (Oxford: Oxford University Press, 1962), 11. Here, as elsewhere, "the issue of authority" could be perceived as a "stumbling block," a moral and intellectual complication "never to be resolved unambiguously" (O'Donovan, *Theology of Law and Authority*, 82).

6. Paul W. White, "Patronage, Protestantism, and Stage Propaganda in Early Elizabethan England," *Yearbook of English Studies* 21 (1991): 39–52; 40, 43.

7. David Bevington, *Tudor Drama and Politics: A Critical Approach to Topical Meaning* (Cambridge, Mass.: Harvard University Press, 1968), 3.

8. Julia Gasper, *The Dragon and the Dove: The Plays of Thomas Dekker* (Oxford: Clarendon Press, 1990), 10.

9. See Margot Heinemann, *Puritanism and Theater: Thomas Middleton and Opposition Drama under the Early Stuarts* (Cambridge: Cambridge University Press, 1984); Martin Butler, *Theater and Crisis, 1632–1642* (Cambridge: Cambridge University Press, 1984); and Donna B. Hamilton, *Shakespeare and the Politics of Protestant England* (New York: Harvester Wheatsheaf, 1992).

10. Paul W. White, *Theatre and Reformation: Protestantism, Patronage, and Playing in Tudor England* (Cambridge: Cambridge University Press, 1993), 163–64, 5–7. Although no doubt the "Reformation involvement with the theatre . . . became considerably more complex in the age of Shakespeare" (174), we should not, except perhaps as a strategic corrective, minimize the enormous contradictions, present throughout the period, in this "alliance."

11. This approach reflects and yet may be said to go beyond its conjunctural moment, as outlined in the introduction.

12. Hamilton, *Shakespeare*, x; this is not taken as indicative of "*the* position that Shakespeare took on church-state issues" (xi).

13. A. G. Dickens, "The Ambivalent English Reformation," in *Background to the English Renaissance*, ed. Joseph B. Trapp (London: Gray-Mills, 1974), 56; cf. A. G. Dickens, *Reformation and Society in Sixteenth-Century Europe* (London: Thames and Hudson, 1971), 101–4. As against Dickens and somewhat against Elton, see the more recent revisionism of such Reformation historians as Christopher Haigh, according to which "England had an ersatz Reformation," a "piecemeal Reformation, to be explained by the chances of day-

to-day politics": "The establishment of Protestantism as a mass religion was thus a consequence, not a cause, of the political reformation. The Reformation brought Protestantism, not Protestantism the Reformation" (introduction to *The English Reformation Revised*, ed. Christopher Haigh [Cambridge: Cambridge University Press, 1987], 7–8). The revisionist view cannot be shrugged off; it carries considerable conviction, such as when the continued viability of religious guilds, confraternities, and related institutions is revealed (see, e.g., J. J. Scarisbrick, *The Reformation and the English People* [Oxford: Basil Blackwell, 1984], 19–39). There is such a thing as "the continuity of Catholicism in the English Reformation" (which is the title of one of Haigh's essays in *English Reformation Revised*), and there is more than a kernel of truth in the suggestion that "the Reformation did not produce a Protestant England: it produced a divided England" (209). But even when it is granted—a main revisionist point—that Protestantism, with its stress on Bible reading, predestination, and justification by faith, "was not, and could not be, an attractive religion at the grass-roots level" (6), the perspective on the Lollard element and the tradition of popular Protestantism, as advanced by A. G. Dickens, is not invalidated. In fact, some of the most vocal elements (and those most in touch with Continental developments) were instrumental in helping sound the depth of the division inside and outside the reformed (that is, the state) church—at least down to the days of Martin Marprelate.

Chapter 1: A Protestant Author-Function

1. This figure was given to me by the historian Adolf Laube, to whom I owe these facts as well as some highly perceptive and helpful criticism.

2. References to Luther's works in the original are from *D. Martin Luthers Werke: Kritische Gesamtausgabe*, Weimar ed., vol. 6 (Weimar, Germany: Hermann Boehlau, 1888). The translation used is *Luther's Works*, ed. Jaroslav Pelikan and Helmut T. Lehmann (St. Louis: Concordia, 1958–86). Further page citations appear in the text. I have bracketed and sometimes retranslated certain passages from the German edition in the text.

3. For the concept of 'representativity,' compare Susan Wells's "typical register of representation" in *The Dialectic of Representation* (Baltimore: Johns Hopkins University Press, 1985), 19–34.

4. Stephen Greenblatt, *Renaissance Self-Fashioning: From More to Shakespeare* (Chicago: University of Chicago Press, 1980), 85.

5. Natalie Z. Davis, *Society and Culture in Early Modern France: Eight Essays* (Stanford, Calif.: Stanford University Press, 1965), 164–69.

6. The links between the Reformation and the German tradition of philosophical idealism are more complex than can be explored here; see, for instance, Erich Franz, *Deutsche Klassik und Reformation: Die Weiterbildung protestantischer Motive in der Philosophie und Weltanschauung des deutschen Idealismus* (Halle, Germany: Niemeyer, 1937).

7. See W. D. J. Cargill Thompson, *The Political Thought of Martin Luther*, ed. Philip Broadhead (Brighton, England: Harvester Press, 1984), 36–78. According to Thompson, this dual notion "provides the core of Luther's political and social theory" (36).

8. See Guillory, *Poetic Authority*: "the original reformers restricted the *Wort Gottes* to the Bible, a finished revelation that is only extended into the present by the act of reading" (14).

Chapter 2: The Spirit betwixt Polity and Scripture

1. See Jean Calvin, *Institutes of the Christian Religion*, ed. John T. McNeil, trans. F. L. Battles (Philadelphia: Westminster Press, 1964), esp. book 4, chap. 20, 1485–1521. Further page citations appear in the text.

2. For a recent translation and annotated edition of book 4, chap. 20, "On Civil Government," see Harro M. Höpfl, *Luther and Calvin on Secular Authority* (Cambridge: Cambridge University Press, 1991), 47–86.

3. Harro M. Höpfl, *The Christian Polity of John Calvin* (Cambridge: Cambridge University Press, 1982), 171, 152.

4. The chapter heading in its original Latin is "De politica administratione." See Joannis Calvini, *Institutio Christianae Religionis*, vols. 3–5 of *Opera Selecta*, ed. Petrus Barth and Guilelmus Niesel (n.p.: Chr. Kaiser, 1957–62), 5:471. Further page citations appear in the text.

5. See the glossary in Höpfl, *Luther and Calvin on Secular Authority*, xxxii–xlv.

6. See ibid., xlii.

7. Höpfl, *Christian Polity of John Calvin*, 46.

8. See ibid., 106–7.

9. Alister E. McGrath, *A Life of John Calvin: A Study in the Shaping of Western Culture* (Oxford: Basil Blackwell, 1990), 97–98. The two chapters on Geneva provide an extremely well balanced critical perspective on Calvin and Geneva as having "one of the great symbiotic relationships of history" (79).

10. See Rupert E. Davis, *The Problem of Authority in the Continental Reformers* (London: Epworth Press, 1946), 131.

11. This is the editor's or translator's summary and subtitle; it is not in Calvin's Latin original. See Calvin, *Institutes of the Christian Religion*, 3:66.

12. Although in book 4 the main thrust of his argument was against the institutionalized location of authority in the papacy and Roman councils, it is not fortuitous that, in book 1, the most ferociously pursued target is that "devilish madness" (93) against which the author of *Contre la secte phantastique et furieuse des Libertins* (1545) was elsewhere to intervene.

Chapter 3: Discord and Identity

1. Patrick Collinson, *The Birthpangs of Protestant England: Religious and Cultural Change in the Sixteenth and Seventeenth Centuries* (London: Macmillan, 1988), 7. This pattern was reversed as the Civil War approached: it was then that "the idea of the elect nation, God's Israel, once a means of consolidating the Protestant Nation, now threatened to distract and divide it" (25). On the concept of "the Protestant nation," cf. Christopher Hill, *The Collected Essays of Christopher Hill* (Amherst: University of Massachusetts Press, 1985–86), 2:28–29.

2. See Stanford E. Lehmberg's study of the origins of the Tudor idea of sovereignty in *The Reformation Parliament, 1529–1536* (Cambridge: Cambridge University Press, 1970), 164–65.

3. G. R. Elton, *The Tudor Revolution in Government: Administrative Changes in the Reign of Henry VIII* (Cambridge: Cambridge University Press, 1953), 427. In *Reform and Reformation: England, 1509–1558* (Cambridge, Mass.: Harvard University Press, 1977), Elton shifts the phase of revolution away from the year 1485, reducing the stature of Henry VIII and the role of the monarchy in general. In this shift, the contribution of Thomas Cromwell is still acknowledged to be paramount. Elton comes closest to exploring the grass-roots level of these forces in *Policy and Police: The Enforcement of the Reformation in the Age of Thomas Cromwell* (Cambridge: Cambridge University Press, 1972). The theory of a Tudor revolution from above, which Elton retains throughout his work, has not gone unchallenged; it was flatly rejected by Penry Williams and G. L. Harriss in "A Revolution in Tudor History?" *Past and Present* 31 (1965): 87–96.

4. For example, in *The Peddler's Prophecy* (ca. 1561) the plebeian unlearned figure of the peddler is authorized, as David Bevington puts it, "to castigate clergy and judiciary unsparingly," insisting throughout the play on his right not only to teach his betters but to "rail upon authoritie" (cited in Bevington, *Tudor Drama and Politics*, 137).

5. Kevin Brownlee and Walter Stephens, eds., *Discourses of Authority in Medieval and Renaissance Literature* (Hanover, N.H.: University Press of New England, 1989), 1–19, esp. 1–4.

6. See Christopher Hill, *Puritanism and Revolution: Studies in Interpretation of the English Revolution of the Seventeenth Century* (London: Secker and Warburg, 1958), 32–49, 56, 323–36.

7. King, *English Reformation Literature*, 32.

8. Wallace MacCaffrey, *The Shaping of the Elizabethan Regime* (Princeton: Princeton University Press, 1968), 4, 9, 11.

9. Frank Wigham, *Ambition and Privilege: The Social Tropes of Elizabethan Courtesy Theory* (Berkeley and Los Angeles: University of California Press, 1984), 3.

10. Cf. chap. 24 of *Das Kapital* in Marx and Engels, *Werke*, 23:741–91. I have discussed the importance of these changes for the history of the theater at some length in my dissertation, *Drama und Wirklichkeit in der Shakespearezeit* (Halle, Germany: Niemeyer, 1958), 13–60.

11. Julian Cornwall, *Revolt of the Peasantry, 1549* (London: Routledge and Kegan Paul, 1977), 4.

12. Ibid., 3. Cf. Ferguson, *Articulate Citizen*, esp. 133–61, where "the rapid growth of public discussion" is richly and convincingly documented and its "revolutionary significance" recognized (133–34).

13. The twenty-nine demands appear in S. T. Bindoff, *Kett's Rebellion, 1549* (London: Historical Association, 1949), 63–66. See also Dickens, *Reformation and Society*, 101–4.

14. See Rosemary O'Day, *The Debate on the English Reformation* (London: Methuen, 1986), 155–59. There is good reason why this debate is largely inconclusive; for instance, one of its most significant elements—the interpretation, on both sides, of preambles and dedicatory clauses to sixteenth-century wills—cannot be made to yield an unambiguous answer to the questions raised.

15. Robert Whiting, *The Blind Devotion of the People: Popular Religion and the English Reformation* (Cambridge: Cambridge University Press, 1989), 267.

16. Ibid., 268. The generalization here is from the situation in the southeast, which is given the most minute attention in this study.

17. Ralph Houlbrooke, *Church Courts and the People during the English Reformation, 1520–1570* (Oxford: Oxford University Press, 1979), 269, 266; see also Richard L. Greaves, *Society and Religion in Elizabethan England* (Minneapolis: University of Minnesota Press, 1981), 676–79.

18. Christopher Haigh, *Reformation and Resistance in Tudor Lancashire* (London: Cambridge University Press, 1975), 157.

19. Joel Hurstfield, "The Elizabethan People in the Age of Shakespeare,"

in *Shakespeare's World*, ed. James Sutherland and Joel Hurstfield (New York: St. Martin's Press, 1964), 39.

20. In *Elizabethan Life: Morals and the Church Courts, Mainly from Essex Archidiaconal Records* (Chelmsford, England: Essex Record Office, 1973), F. G. Emmison mentions "strong anti-clerical feelings": the Elizabethan clergy "received from the laity an abundant offering of slander and hostility" (113, 215). Emmison is certainly right to stress in *Elizabethan Life: Disorder, Mainly from Essex Sessions and Assize Records* (Chelmsford, England: Essex Record Office, 1973) that we must beware of gathering from these instances "an exaggerated impression of discontent or disorder" (65), but his claim that Essex was unique for "outbursts of treasonable sayings" appears unwarranted as long as there is reason to regard the analysis of the records by their Victorian editors as inexhaustive. Compare for instance Emmison's reference to the mere "six Middlesex charges in the whole reign" (*Elizabethan Life: Disorder*, viii) with John Cordy Jeaffreson's statement in his edition of the *Middlesex County Records* (London, 1886): "Having given the abundant evidence, I have forborne to render it superabundant by needless examples" (1:xlix).

21. Thomas Stapleton, *A Fortresse of the Faith* (Antwerp, 1565), fol. 118r, cited in Greaves, *Society and Religion in Elizabethan England*, 98.

22. Thomas Cooper, *An Admonition to the People of England* (1589; reprint, London, 1847), 198; see also the section headed "The Swelling Tide of Anticlericalism" in Greaves, *Society and Religion in Elizabethan England*, 98–104.

23. Dickens, "Ambivalent English Reformation," 50; A. G. Dickens, *The English Reformation* (New York: Schocken Books, 1964), 31–34.

24. S. T. Bindoff, *Tudor England* (Harmondsworth, England: Penguin, 1950), 162.

25. T. M. Parker, *The English Reformation to 1558* (London: Oxford University Press, 1966), 125.

26. Edward Hall, *Chronicle; Containing the History of England, during the Reign of Henry the Fourth, and the Succeeding Monarchs, to the End of the Reign of Henry the Eighth* (London, 1809), 865. Further page citations appear in the text.

27. The *Oxford English Dictionary* traces *mumpsimus* back to R. Pace, *De fructu* (1517); the next occurrence is (characteristically) in Tyndale (1530).

28. Christopher Sutton, *Disce vivere* (London, 1604), sig. A6v, cited in Greaves, *Society and Religion in Elizabethan England*, 3.

29. Henry Medwall, *Fulgens and Lucrece*, in *The Plays of Henry Medwall*, ed. Alan H. Nelson (Cambridge: D. S. Brewer, 1980), ll. 53–56.

30. Thomas Adams, "The White Devil; or, The Hypocrite Uncased" (1612), in *The English Sermon: An Anthology*, ed. Martin Seymour-Smith (Cheshire, England: Carcanet Press, 1976), 1:281.

31. Jean-Christophe Agnew, *Worlds Apart: The Market and the Theater in Anglo-American Thought, 1550–1750* (Cambridge: Cambridge University Press, 1986), 62.

32. Foxe, *Acts and Monuments*, 6:31.

33. Cited in Dickens, *English Reformation*, 70.

Chapter 4: Breach in Authorization

1. Cited in King, *English Reformation Literature*, 132.

2. See Greenblatt, *Renaissance Self-Fashioning*, chap. 2, esp. 93–105.

3. Foxe, *Acts and Monuments*, 6:39.

4. Gardiner here seems to go back on certain positions of the Henrician Reformation, when royal policy was behind the "dismantling of the gilded shrines of Canterbury, Walsingham and elsewhere." See Margaret Aston, *Lollards and Reformers: Images and Literacy in Late Medieval Religion* (London: Hambledon Press, 1984), 192: "Image-breaking became official and entered a new era."

5. James R. Siemon, *Shakespearean Iconoclasm* (Berkeley and Los Angeles: University of California Press, 1985), 143, 178. In his suggestive treatment of the problem, Siemon (143) cites Victor Turner and Edith Turner, *Image and Pilgrimage in Christian Culture: Anthropological Perspectives* (New York: Columbia University Press, 1978), 144 (emphasis in the original).

6. Lear's phrase is in both the quarto (scene 11, l. 99) and the folio (3.4.102) editions; *Henry V* 4.1.235–81; *Romeo and Juliet* 2.1.85; *Hamlet* 1.2.76.

7. John Bale, *A Comedy Concerning Three Laws of Nature, Moses, and Christ*, in *The Dramatic Writings of John Bale*, ed. John S. Farmer (New York: Barnes and Noble, 1966), 17. On Bale's "universe of stark antinomies," see Ritchie D. Kendall, *The Drama of Dissent: The Radical Poetics of Nonconformity, 1380–1590* (Chapel Hill: University of North Carolina Press, 1986), 131; on Bale's dramatic figure of "Idolatry," see 104.

8. See Jonathan Crewe, *Trials of Authorship: Anterior Form and Poetic Reconstruction from Wyatt to Shakespeare* (Berkeley and Los Angeles: University of California Press, 1990), 48–49.

9. See, for example, John A. F. Thomson, "John Foxe and Some Sources for Lollard History: Notes for a Critical Appraisal," *Studies in Church History* 2 (1963): 251–54.

10. King, *English Reformation Literature*, 84; see also John N. King, "Free-

dom of the Press, Protestant Propaganda, and Protector Somerset," *Huntington Library Quarterly* 40 (1976): 1–9.

11. Christopher Hill, "The Problem of Authority," in *Collected Essays of Christopher Hill*, 2:47. For a definition of external authority in relation to "the poetic text," see Miller, *Poetic License*, 5.

12. See Hobbes, *Leviathan*, part 1, chap. 14, and part 2, chap. 18.

13. See chap. 7, "The Anabaptists and the Reformation," in R. A. Knox, *Enthusiasm: A Chapter in the History of Religion* (New York: Oxford University Press, 1950), 117–38, for a modern historical perspective with a special emphasis on links to medieval heresy; see also Irvin B. Horst, *The Radical Brethren: Anabaptism and the English Reformation to 1558* (Nieuwkoop, the Netherlands: De Graaf, 1972), for a revision of Foxe's approach to the radical Reformation (57–58).

14. Oliver Ormerod, *The Picture of a Puritane* (London, 1605), 8; Richard Cosin, *Conspiracie for Pretended Reformation: viz. Presbyteriall Discipline* (London, 1592), 1. Further page citations appear in the text.

15. Cosin, *Conspiracie for Pretended Reformation*, 83.

16. Richard Bancroft, *A Sermon Preached at Paul's Cross* (London, 1588), 33–36. The sermon was preached on February 9, 1588. Further page citations appear in the text.

17. Ibid., 45. The Protestant urge to "search and read" has to do with what Alan Sinfield calls the "Reformation belief of contradictories," insisting "on the need for grace whilst denying any means to obtain it." See his *Literature in Protestant England, 1560–1660* (London: Croom Helm, 1983), 11. Compare in this connection Robert Burton, *The Anatomy of Melancholy* (3:419): "the more they search and read Scriptures, or divine treatises, the more they puzzle themselves, as a bird in a net" (cited in Sinfield, *Literature in Protestant England*, 18).

18. See Hall, *Chronicle*, 865–66.

19. Richard Hooker, *Two Sermons upon Part of S. Judes Epistle* (1614; reprint, Amsterdam: Da Capo Press, 1969), 40; the reference is to Lam. 2.13. For the metaphor in the *Laws*, see Richard Hooker, *The Works of Richard Hooker*, ed. W. Speed Hill, Folger Library ed. (Cambridge, Mass.: Harvard University Press, 1977), 3:146.

20. Bancroft, *Sermon Preached at Paul's Cross*, 52.

Chapter 5: "Bifold Authority"

1. Millar Maclure, *The Paul's Cross Sermons: 1534–1642* (Toronto: University of Toronto Press, 1958), 3–4, 7–8.

2. Annabel Patterson, *Censorship and Interpretation: The Condition of Writing and Reading in Early Modern England* (Madison: University of Wisconsin Press, 1984).

3. Jacques Derrida, "Force of Law: The 'Mystical Foundation of Authority' (Deconstruction and the Possibility of Justice)," *Cardozo Law Review* 11 (July–August 1990): 920–1045.

4. Francis Bacon, *The New Organon*, ed. Fulton H. Anderson (New York: Liberal Arts Press, 1960), 64.

5. Francis Bacon, *The Works of Francis Bacon*, ed. James Spedding (London: Longman, 1864), 3:343.

6. Bacon, *New Organon*, 81.

7. Diarmaid MacCulloch, *The Later Reformation in England, 1547–1603* (London: Macmillan, 1990), 56.

8. Patrick Collinson, "The Jacobean Religious Settlement: The Hampton Court Conference," in *Before the English Civil War: Essays on Early Stuart Politics and Government*, ed. Howard Tomlinson (London: Macmillan, 1983), 44.

9. See Herbert Grabes, *Das englische Pamphlet*, part 1, *Politische and religiöse Polemik am Beginn der Neuzeit (1521–1640)* (Tübingen, Germany: Niemeyer, 1990), 65–67.

10. Dean and Jones, *Parliaments of Elizabethan England*, 11.

11. William Perkins, *The Works of William Perkins*, ed. Ian Breward (Appleford, England: Courtenay Press, 1970), 1:529–30.

12. William Perkins, *The Whole Treatise of the Cases of Conscience* (1606; reprint, New York: Da Capo Press, 1972), 44–45. Further page citations appear in the text.

Chapter 6: Reformation "For Ever After"

1. John Dover Wilson, "The Marprelate Controversy," in *The Cambridge History of English Literature*, ed. A. W. Ward and A. R. Waller (New York: Macmillan, 1939), 3:436; Kendall, *Drama of Dissent*, 176.

2. Martin Marprelate, *The Marprelate Tracts (1588–1589)*, facsimile ed. (Leeds, England: Scholars Press, 1967), 5.

3. E. K. Chambers, *The Elizabethan Stage* (Oxford: Clarendon Press, 1923), 4:263.

4. See Patrick Collinson, *The Elizabethan Puritan Movement* (Oxford: Clarendon Press, 1990), 12, 118–21.

5. Hooker, *Works of Richard Hooker*, 3:146.

6. Cosin, *Conspiracie for Pretended Reformation*, 1.

7. Thomas Nashe, *The Works of Thomas Nashe*, ed. Ronald B. McKerrow

(London: Sidgwick and Jackson, 1910), 2:239. Further page citations appear in the text.

8. Cf. Patrick Collinson, *Archbishop Grindal, 1519–1583: The Struggle for a Reformed Church* (Berkeley and Los Angeles: University of California Press, 1979), 233–48. Grindal's letter is printed in full in John Strype, *The History of the Life and Acts of . . . Edmund Grindal* (Oxford, 1821), 558–74. Cf. Christopher Hill, "From Grindal to Laud," in *Collected Essays of Christopher Hill*, 2:69: "Prophesyings, household religion, repetition of sermons, [and other religious exercises] . . . came near to forming independent congregations within the state church of a sort which the Cromwellian church was later to embrace."

9. Collinson, *Archbishop Grindal*, 244; cf. also A. L. Rowse, *The England of Elizabeth: The Structure of Society* (New York: Macmillan, 1951), 271. For the following section in the text, cf. M. M. Knappen, *Tudor Puritanism* (Chicago: University of Chicago Press, 1939), 257.

10. Cf. J. W. Allen, *A History of Political Thought in the Sixteenth Century* (London: Methuen, 1928), 180: "The Elizabethan Church had no defined constitution, form or character."

11. Cited in H. D. Traill and S. S. Mann, eds., *Social England* (London: Cassell, 1901–4), 3:434.

12. Allen, *History of Political Thought*, 179.

13. Ibid.

14. I find the parallels with the history of the revolution in Germany most consistently developed (apart from Cosin's pamphlet) by Ormerod. Ormerod, *Picture of a Puritane*, discusses the problem of authority on several occasions (9, 14–16, 26, 46, 63), criticizing butchers, cooks, tailors, and blacksmiths for thinking they are fit to interpret the Bible for themselves: "doe all speake with tongues? do all interprete?" (70).

15. Nashe, *Works of Thomas Nashe*, 2:232–41.

16. Hooker, *Works of Richard Hooker*, 3:146.

17. Cosin, *Conspiracie for Pretended Reformation*, 83 (wrongly paginated as 53).

18. Ibid., 6. This refers to William Hackett's "maner of praying."

19. Cooper, *Admonition to the People of England*, 118.

20. Reasons for such a weak defense of authority within the church may be found in such varied places as the foundation charter of the Reformation and the ideological pragmatism of Elizabeth's reign. One has only to recall, for example, the tenuous grounds on which Thomas Cromwell justified the break with Rome and thus the sovereignty of "high authority" for the Re-

formation Parliament (1529–36). The act of legitimation was based on the claim that "in dyvers sundry old authentike storyes and cronicles it is manifestlie declared and expressed that this realme of England is an Impier [Empire]," in which "the king of England and no one else held . . . authority, prerogative and jurisdiction" (from the first draft of the Act in Restraint of Appeals, SP 2/N, fols. 78–90, Public Record Office, *Letters and Papers of Henry VIII*, 4.120 [7], cited in Lehmberg, *Reformation Parliament*, 164).

21. Lewalski, *Protestant Poetics*, 4.

22. David Cressy, *Literacy and the Social Order: Reading and Writing in Tudor and Stuart England* (Cambridge: Cambridge University Press, 1980), 5.

23. Joel Hurstfield, *Freedom, Corruption, and Government in Elizabethan England* (London: Cape, 1973), 25.

Part II: Sign and Authority in Early Modern Fiction

1. John Lyly, prologue to *Midas*, in *The Complete Works of John Lyly*, ed. R. W. Bond (Oxford: Clarendon Press, 1902), 3:115.

Chapter 7: Contexts of Renaissance Humanism

1. Sidney, *Prose Works of Sir Philip Sidney*, 3:19. Further page citations appear in the text.

2. Hiram Haydn, *The Counter-Renaissance* (New York: Grove Press, 1960), 143.

3. Torquato Tasso, cited in Robert M. Durling, *The Figure of the Poet in Renaissance Epic* (Cambridge, Mass.: Harvard University Press, 1965), 125ff.

4. Guillory, *Poetic Authority*, viii–x and passim.

5. See Lisa Jardine, *Francis Bacon: Discovery and the Art of Discourse* (London: Cambridge University Press, 1974), 17–158. The quote is from *Love's Labour's Lost* 1.1.87.

6. Martin Elsky, *Authorizing Words: Speech, Writing, and Print in the English Renaissance* (Ithaca, N.Y.: Cornell University Press, 1989), 41–42. Further page citations appear in the text. Cf. Murray Cohen, *Linguistic Practice in England, 1640–1785* (Baltimore: Johns Hopkins University Press, 1977), 1–42.

7. Elsky, *Authorizing Words*, 75.

8. Ibid., 81.

9. For the crisis of humanism and "the unitary, integrated, plausible 'character,'" see Jonathan Dollimore, *Radical Tragedy: Religion, Ideology, and Power in the Drama of Shakespeare and His Contemporaries* (Chicago: University of Chicago Press, 1984), 63, and Timothy J. Reiss, *Tragedy and Truth: Studies in the Development of a Renaissance and Neoclassical Discourse* (New Haven: Yale

University Press, 1980), 40–41, for a humanist discourse that, in the drama, "cannot be translated into action," especially when "no socialized meaning can be given to an individual's utterance."

10. Nashe, *Works of Thomas Nashe*, 2:263.

11. Agnew, *Worlds Apart*, 54.

12. Julia Kristeva, *Desire in Language: A Semiotic Approach in Human Society* (New York: Columbia University Press, 1980), 60.

Chapter 8: Authority in Relations of Orality

1. Victor Turner, *Dramas, Fields, and Metaphors: Symbolic Action in Human Society* (Ithaca, N.Y.: Cornell University Press, 1974), 53.

2. Brian Stock, *The Implications of Literacy: Written Language and Models of Interpretation in the Eleventh and Twelfth Centuries* (Princeton: Princeton University Press, 1983), 9.

3. For the issue of authority qua truth-value in these early practical uses of literacy, see M. T. Clanchy, *From Memory to Written Record: England, 1066–1307* (Cambridge, Mass.: Harvard University Press, 1979), 21–26, 64–82; cf. Stock, *Implications of Literacy*, 529–31.

4. Pierre Clastres, *Le grand parler: Mythes et chants sacrés des Indiens Guarini* (Paris: Éditions du Seuil, 1972), 9, 21. See also Pierre Clastres, *Chronique des Indiens Guayaki* (Paris: Éditions Plon, 1972), and Pierre Clastres, *La societé contre état* (Paris: Éditions de Minuit, 1974). Clastres's collection of these chants follows and helps complete the work of such anthropologists as Curt Unkel (Nimuendaju), "Die Sagen von der Erschaffung und der Vernichtung der Welt als Grundlagen der Religion der Apapocuva-Guarini," *Zeit: Ethnologie* 46 (1914): 284–403, and Leon Cadogan, *Ayvu Rapyta: Textos Miticos dos Mbya-Guarini*, Universidade Boletim 227, Antropologia 5 (Sao Paulo, 1959).

5. Clastres, *Le grand parler*, 21.

6. Cf. Martin Fontius, "Das Ende einer Denkform," in *Literarische Widerspiegelung*, ed. Dieter Schlenstedt (Berlin: Aufbau, 1981), 189–238, esp. 194–97.

7. Clastres, *Le grand parler*, 124 (my translation); cf. 130. Further page citations appear in the text.

8. Jean-François Lyotard, *The Postmodern Condition: A Report on Knowledge*, trans. Geoff Bennington and Brian Massumi (Minneapolis: University of Minnesota Press, 1984), 18.

9. *Beowulf and the Fight at Finnsburg*, ed. F. Klaeber (Boston: D. C. Heath, 1922), cxxi–cxxii. Further line citations appear in the text.

10. Hans-Jürgen Diller, "Literacy and Orality in *Beowulf*: The Problem of Reference," in *Mündlichkeit und Schriftlichkeit im englischen Mittelalter*, ed. Willi Erzgräber and Sabine Volk (Tübingen, Germany: Narr, 1988), 25.

11. "Mine gefraege," l. 776; cf. ll. 837, 1955, 2685, 2837. (Here and in what follows, I have not undertaken an exhaustive listing.)

12. Cf. ll. 70, 666, 837, 1011, 1196, and so forth.

13. This term is from W. P. Ker, *Epic and Romance: Essays on Medieval Literature* (London: Macmillan, 1908), 21. This unifying sentiment clearly is on the defensive; in the poem there is, as a recent critic notes, "a marked and persistent hostility toward the epistemological foundation underpinning the practice of literacy. While *Beowulf* seems to acknowledge the psychological posture conditioned by, or at least compatible with, literate practices, the acknowledgment characterizes that posture as a clear, direct threat to the ordering structures—and thus to the basic survival—of the poem's central system of personal interdependencies. *Beowulf* confronts the psychological demands of the reading experience by persistently reaffirming those idioms of speech and patterns of interaction that require the open immediacy of spoken exchange" (Michael R. Near, "Anticipating Alienation: *Beowulf* and the Intrusion of Literacy," *PMLA* 108 [March 1993]: 321).

14. "Ge-frignan" has a more poetic form in "ge-fricgan"; cf. ll. 1826, 2889, 3002.

15. See *Beowulf, with the Finnesburg Fragment*, ed. C. L. Wrenn (London: Harrap, 1958).

16. Susan Stewart, "Scandals of the Ballad," *Representations* 32 (Fall 1990): 134–56; 150.

17. *Homilies of Ælfric: A Supplementary Collection*, ed. John C. Pope (London: Oxford University Press, 1967–68), 2:728.

18. Wilhelm G. Busse, "Boceras: Written and Oral Traditions in the Late Tenth Century," in Erzgräber and Volk, *Mündlichkeit und Schriftlichkeit im englischen Mittelalter*, 29.

Chapter 9: Minstrelsy and Author-Function in Romance

1. Chrétien de Troyes, *Erec et Enide*, vol. 3 of *Sämtliche Werke*, ed. Wendelin Foerster (Halle, Germany: Niemeyer, 1890), 1, ll. 9, 13–14. Further line citations appear in the text.

2. Rainer Warning, "Staged Discourse: Remarks on the Pragmatics of Fiction," *Dispositio* 5 (1980): 44.

3. Chrétien de Troyes, *Arthurian Romances*, trans. W. W. Comfort (1914; reprint, London: J. M. Dent, 1965), 1. On "conjointure" (in Latin, *conjunc-*

tura), see Foerster's note in Chrétien, *Erec et Enide*, 297–98, and Foerster, *Kristian von Troyes: Wörterbuch* (Halle, Germany: Niemeyer, 1914), 54, 86, where he freely reads the word as "connection," "relation," "opportunity," "juncture," and "conclusion." Cf. Tobler-Lommatzsch, *Altfranzösisches Wörterbuch* (Wiesbaden: Franz Steiner Verlag, 1956), 2.1:695–96.

4. Chrétien, *Arthurian Romances*, 91; cf. Chrétien de Troyes, *Cligés*, vol. 1 of *Sämtliche Werke*, ed. Wendelin Foerster (Halle, Germany: Niemeyer, 1884), 1, ll. 1–7.

5. Chrétien, *Arthurian Romances*, 1.

6. See John Stevens, *Medieval Romance: Themes and Approaches* (London: Hutchinson, 1973), 208–26.

7. It seems noteworthy that in the early modern theater, "fictionality" in the form of dramatic illusion required a comparable silencing of the actor's voice, so that players were admonished to "speak no more than is set down for them" (*Hamlet* 3.2.40). It was only when the player was made to stick to the text and to his or her impersonation as an autonomous role that closure in the representation of that role helped bring forth a "character," that is, the illusion of an organic consistency in a particularized ensemble of signs and meanings. Like the convention of the fictionalized narrator, this required a "staged discourse," which, as Rainer Warning suggests, was a basic element in the new pragmatics of fiction (see Warning, "Staged Discourse").

8. See Reinhard Mischke, *Launcelots allegorische Reise: Sir Thomas Malorys Le Morte Darthur und die englische Literatur des fünfzehnten Jahrhunderts* (Frankfurt am Main: Peter Lang, 1976), 192–98.

9. Cited in Thomas Malory, *The Works of Sir Thomas Malory*, ed. Eugène Vinaver (Oxford: Clarendon Press, 1967), 1:cxliii.

10. William Caxton, *The Prologues and Epilogues of William Caxton*, ed. W. J. B. Crotch, Early English Text Society, original series, vol. 176 (London: Oxford University Press, 1928), 86, 103–4, 109.

11. Cited in Malory, *Works*, 1:cxlvi (emphasis added).

12. Ibid., 1:12. Further page citations appear in the text. Here, the Winchester version corresponds to the opening of book 1, chap. 5, in Caxton's edition, cited above under the rubric "how Arthur was chosen kyng." See Thomas Malory, *Le Morte D'Arthur*, Everyman ed. (London: Dent, 1910), 10.

13. Cf. Hans Ulrich Gumbrecht, "Wie fiktional war der höfische Roman?" in *Funktionen des Fiktiven*, ed. Dieter Henrich and Wolfgang Iser (Munich: W. Fink, 1983), who perceives a chasm between "the signs of worldly reference and their interpretability in terms of 'sensus moralis'" (440; my translation). Small wonder when the resulting ambiguities have turned the most

persistent strand in Malory criticism into a series of questions about symbolization and the closely related notion of imaginative unity. See Robert M. Lumiansky, "The Question of Unity in Malory's *Morte Darthur*," *Tulane Studies in English* 5 (1955): 29–39; D. S. Brewer, "The Hoole Book," in *Essays on Malory*, ed. J. A. W. Bennett (Oxford: Clarendon Press, 1963), 41–63; Elizabeth T. Pachoda, *Arthurian Propaganda: "Le Morte Darthur" as an Historical Ideal of Life* (Chapel Hill: University of North Carolina Press, 1971); and Eugène Vinaver, *The Rise of Romance* (New York: Oxford University Press, 1971).

14. Cf. Malory, *Works*, 3:1285.

15. Helaine Newstead, "Malory and Romance," in *Four Essays on Romance*, ed. Herschel Baker (Cambridge, Mass.: Harvard University Press, 1971), 14.

16. Pachoda, *Arthurian Propaganda*, 32.

17. This suggests that the answer to the vexed problem of *sens* and *matière* may well be found in the complex and inconsistent uses of authority in romance writing. If, as in Eugène Vinaver's work, *sens* may be identified with *conjointure* while both entail a deliberate (and quite positive) tension as against *conte* and *matière*, this scheme of dichotomies can be challenged as providing too rigid and too static a sense of "duality" (Vinaver, *Rise of Romance*, 34–37). It might instead be argued that the *auctoritas* of the poet engages both the *conte* and its previous adaptations by superimposing on and drawing out of the authority of ancient matter some more symbolic and representational pattern of *conjointure*. This is how Wolfram and Gottfried respond to Chrétien; in Malory's case, too, what results is not a fixed state of duality but the interrogation and negotiation of two types of authorization.

18. For a position contrary to that of Vinaver, see Charles Moorman, *The Book of Kyng Arthur: The Unity of Malory's "Morte Darthur"* (Lexington: University of Kentucky Press, 1965), 91.

19. Eugène Vinaver, ed., *King Arthur and His Knights: Selected Tales by Sir Thomas Malory* (London: Oxford University Press, 1975), x.

20. Ibid., xvi.

21. Malory, *Works*, 3:1368; but see, in this connection, Robert M. Lumiansky, ed., *Malory's Originality: A Critical Study of "Le Morte Darthur"* (Baltimore: Johns Hopkins Press, 1964). Cf. Pachoda, *Arthurian Propaganda*, 62.

22. David F. Hult, "Author/Narrator/Speaker: The Voice of Authority in Chrétien's *Charrete*," in Brownlee and Stephens, *Discourses of Authority*, 96.

23. David F. Hult, *Self-fulfilling Prophecies: Readership and Authority in the*

First "Roman de la Rose" (Cambridge: Cambridge University Press, 1986), 94–95.

Chapter 10: Allegory and the Authorization of Folly

1. Walter Benjamin, *Gesammelte Schriften*, ed. Rolf Tiedemann and Hermann Schweppenhäuser (Frankfurt am Main: Suhrkamp, 1974), 1.1:342 (my translation).

2. Quintilian, *Institutio oratoria*, trans. H. E. Butler (London: Heinemann, 1920–22), vol. 3, book 8, part 6, sec. 44; cf. Jon Whitman, *Allegory: The Dynamics of an Ancient and Medieval Technique* (Oxford: Clarendon Press, 1987), 5, and Angus Fletcher, *Allegory: The Theory of a Symbolic Mode* (Ithaca, N.Y.: Cornell University Press, 1964), 2.

3. Whitman, *Allegory*, 2.

4. Stephen A. Barney, *Allegories of History, Allegories of Love* (Hamden, Conn.: Archon Books, 1979), 49.

5. Preface to *Allegory and Representation: Selected Papers from the English Institute, 1979–1980*, ed. Stephen Greenblatt (Baltimore: Johns Hopkins University Press, 1981), viii. For a parallel in the modern period, see Bainard Cowan, *Exiled Waters: Moby Dick and the Crisis of Allegory* (Baton Rouge: Louisiana State University Press, 1982), 11: "Allegory has arisen at moments in history when a people has found itself in a crisis of identity, its members seeing themselves as inheritors of a past tradition of such authority that the tradition is identified with their very name as a people, yet on the other hand finding much of that tradition morally or factually unacceptable."

6. Joel Fineman, "The Structure of Allegorical Desire," in Greenblatt, *Allegory and Representation*, 28.

7. Guillory, *Poetic Authority*, 58.

8. This is Paul de Man's term; see *Blindness and Insight: Essays in the Rhetoric of Contemporary Criticism*, 2d ed., Theory and History of Literature, vol. 7 (Minneapolis: University of Minnesota Press, 1983), 223.

9. See my recent study of *The Tide Tarrieth No Man*, "'Moralize two meanings' in One Play: Divided Authority on the Tudor Stage," *Mediaevalia* 18 (1995): 427–50.

10. Ernesto Grassi and Maristella Lorch, "Folly and Insanity in Renaissance Literature," *Medieval and Renaissance Texts and Studies* 42 (1986): 90.

11. Barbara Swain, *Fools and Folly during the Middle Ages and Renaissance* (New York: Columbia University Press, 1932), 132–33.

12. Desiderius Erasmus, *The Praise of Folly*, trans. Clarence H. Miller (New

Haven: Yale University Press, 1979), 139, 174. Further page citations appear in the text.

13. Mikhail Bakhtin brought this to the fore many years ago when he called *The Praise of Folly* "one of the greatest creations of carnival laughter in world literature." See M. M. Bakhtin, *Rabelais and His World*, trans. Hélène Iswolsky (Bloomington: Indiana University Press, 1984), 14.

14. Michael Bristol, *Carnival and Theater: Plebeian Culture and the Structure of Authority in Renaissance England* (New York: Routledge, 1989), 133. At the same time, laughter "tends towards dissolution of all forms of worldly and institutional knowledge" (132).

15. Desiderii Erasmi, *Opera omnia*, ed. Jean Leclerc (1703–6; reprint, Hildesheim: Georg Olms, 1962), 4:408. Further page citations appear in the text.

16. See Wells, *Dialectic of Representation*, 19–34. I have developed further the historical dimension of representativity in "Text, Author-Function, and Appropriation in Modern Narrative: Toward a Sociology of Representation," in *Critical Inquiry* 14 (Spring 1988): 431–47.

17. Walter Benjamin, *Schriften*, ed. T. W. Adorno and Gretel Adorno (Frankfurt am Main: Suhrkamp, 1955), 1:298: "dass jene Requisiten des Bedeutens alle mit eben ihren Weisen auf ein anderes eine Mächtigkeit gewinnen, die den profanen Dingen inkommensurabel sie erscheinen lässt." Here (291), Benjamin acknowledges his indebtedness to Karl Giehlow's pioneering work, *Die Hieroglyphenkunde des Humanismus in der Allegorie der Renaissance, besonders der Ehrenpforte Kaiser Maximilians I* (Vienna: Halm and Goldmann, 1915).

18. Ernest Gordon Rupp, ed. and trans., *Luther and Erasmus: Free Will and Salvation* (Philadelphia: Westminster Press, 1969), 93.

19. Benjamin, *Schriften*, 1:299.

20. Desiderius Erasmus, *The Praise of Folly*, trans. Sir Thomas Chaloner, Early English Text Society (Oxford: Oxford University Press, 1965), 3.

21. Walter Kaiser, *Praisers of Folly: Erasmus, Rabelais, Shakespeare* (Cambridge, Mass.: Harvard University Press, 1963), 36.

22. See the translator's notes of Clarence H. Miller in Erasmus, *Praise of Folly*, 73 n. 5.

23. See, for example, George Faludy, *Erasmus of Rotterdam* (London: Eyre and Spottiswoode, 1970), 12–16.

24. H. J. Hillerbrand, "The Origin of the Sixteenth-Century Anabaptism: Another Look," *Archiv fuer Reformationsgeschichte* 53 (1962): 152–80; see esp. 157–59.

25. Henning Graf Reventlow, *Bibelautorität und Geist der Moderne* (Göttingen, Germany: Vandenhoeck and Ruprecht, 1980), 105; for further parallels between Erasmus and the radical reformation, see 76, 79, 82–84, 95, 101.

26. J. Savignac, cited in Reventlow, *Bibelautorität und Geist der Moderne*, 80.

27. This point is made and discussed by Günter Bader, *Assertio: Drei Fortlaufende Lektüren zu Skepsis, Narrheit und Sünde bei Erasmus und Luther* (Tübingen, Germany: Niemeyer, 1985), 31.

28. Kaiser, *Praisers of Folly*, 35.

29. Peter G. Bietenholz, *History and Biography in the Work of Erasmus of Rotterdam* (Geneva: Droz, 1966), 27.

30. Peter Saccio, *The Court Comedies of John Lyly: A Study in Allegorical Dramaturgy* (Princeton, N.J.: Princeton University Press, 1969), 5.

31. These "conditions of possibility" for the new subjectivity in reading are hinted at by Rosalie Colie when she writes that Folly "has abandoned the reader to make his own decisions about value. . . . Folly has left it up to each reader to interpret her words as he can and as he must." Victoria Kahn writes (more stringently) that "while the *Encomium* leaves the interpretation to the reader, it also forces him to question the possibility of an interpretation that would be grounded in the reader's prudence or a rhetoric that would appeal to the reader's free will." Cf. Rosalie Colie, "Problems of Paradoxes," in *Twentieth-Century Interpretations of "The Praise of Folly,"* ed. Kathleen Williams (Englewood Cliffs, N.J.: Prentice-Hall, 1969), and Victoria Kahn, *Rhetoric, Prudence, and Skepticism in the Renaissance* (Ithaca, N.Y.: Cornell University Press, 1985), 90.

Chapter 11: New Authority in Signification

1. Richard Sherry, *A Treatise of the Figures of Grammer and Rhetorike* (London, 1555), fols. iiiv–iiiir, cited in Elsky, *Authorizing Words*, 58. Elsky, in his incisive discussion of authority in humanist discourse, notes: "This mental discourse . . . assigns names to things, not arbitrarily, but according to their properties."

2. Elsky, *Authorizing Words*, 209, 212; compare Bacon's awareness of historicity in authority as at least indirectly promoting new space for 'discovery'; this complements Burton's contrary anxiety, according to which, as Elsky notes, the "very authenticity of speech and writing" in print "makes it inevitable that, with the passage of time, their authority diminishes" (223).

3. Michel Foucault, "What Is an Author?" in *Textual Strategies: Perspectives*

in Post-Structuralist Criticism, ed. Josué V. Harari (London: Methuen, 1980), 148.

4. For this concept of 'appropriation,' see Karl Marx, *Grundrisse: Foundations of the Critique of Political Economy*, trans. Martin Nicolaus (Harmondsworth, England: Penguin, 1973), 485–87. For a more extended discussion of the impact on representation, see my "Text, Author-Function, and Appropriation in Modern Narrative," esp. 432–47.

5. Agnew, *Worlds Apart*, 59; see also Douglas Bruster, *Drama and the Market in the Age of Shakespeare* (Cambridge: Cambridge University Press, 1992).

6. Agnew, *Worlds Apart*, 58.

7. I am using (and adapting to this present context) Wolfgang Iser's suggestive use of these terms; see "Indeterminacy and the Reader's Response in Prose Fiction" in *Aspects of Narrative: Selected Papers from the English Institute*, ed. J. Hillis Miller (New York: Columbia University Press, 1971), 1–45, and Wolfgang Iser, *The Act of Reading: A Theory of Aesthetic Response* (Baltimore: Johns Hopkins University Press, 1978), 68–70, 92–93, and passim.

8. Agnew, *Worlds Apart*, 59. The "placelessness" of this early modern fiction correlates to what David Margolies, in *Novel and Society in Elizabethan England* (London: Croom Helm, 1985), 34–43, calls the "objectification of the text," even though the latter—involving "an acceptance of print as a medium"—must be considered "broader than commercialisation" (38).

9. This is Sidney's phrase. See *Prose Works of Sir Philip Sidney*, 1:206, and the text at note 29 of the introduction, above.

10. François Rabelais, *Oeuvres complètes*, ed. Pierre Jourda (Paris: Garnier Frères, 1962), 1:40–42. The translation is from François Rabelais, *Gargantua and Pantagruel*, trans. J. M. Cohen (Harmondsworth, England: Penguin, 1955), 57–58.

11. Walter Benjamin, *The Origin of German Tragic Drama*, trans. John Osborne (London: Verso, 1977), 164.

12. Terence Cave, *The Cornucopian Text: Problems of Writing in the French Renaissance* (Oxford: Clarendon Press, 1979), 99, 100–101.

13. A. J. Minnis, *Medieval Theory of Authorship: Scholastic Literary Attitudes in the Later Middle Ages* (London: Scolar Press, 1984), 11; cf. Nicholas Watson, *Richard Rolle and the Invention of Authority* (Cambridge: Cambridge University Press, 1991), 265, where the positive "quest for authority" involves not only the "remorseless self-referentiality" of a mystic but an early search for such "poetic fame" as a distinguishing mark of the author's name.

14. Michel Foucault, *Madness and Civilization: A History of Insanity in the Age of Reason*, trans. Richard Howard (New York: Pantheon Books, 1965),

26–27. The point is that what we have is *not* "a self-multiplication of significance" (26; "une multiplication du sens par lui-même"), but that interlocking of discursive and nondiscursive activities, characteristic of the narrative of *Aneignung* in modern history, which results in that "conversion fondamental du monde des images: la contrainte d'un sens multiplie le libere de l'ordonnance des formes" (*Folie et déraison: Histoire de la folie à l'âge classique* [Paris: Librairie Plon, 1961], 22–24).

15. Jardine, *Francis Bacon*, 4.

16. Ibid., 16, 27.

17. Cave, *Cornucopian Text*, 100.

18. Plotinus, *Enneads* 5.8.6, cited in Walter R. Davis, *Idea and Act in Elizabethan Fiction* (Princeton: Princeton University Press, 1969), 37.

19. Rabelais, *Oeuvres complètes*, 1:8.

20. Ibid., 1:6.

21. Cf. Bakhtin, *Rabelais and His World*. It is one thing to challenge the adequacy of a canonized reading of Rabelais within the confines of the dominant literary "official culture" (at which Bakhtin is brilliantly successful), but it is an entirely different matter to claim that "the organized human collectivity" (301) of popular culture is what in the original Russian edition is called "the most essential in Rabelais's work," that is, the main "stream" (*potok*) or tradition (*Tvorchestvo François Rabelais i narodnaya kultura srednevekovia i Renaissanca* [Moscow: Khudozestvennaya Literatura, 1965], 516). Bakhtin is on much safer ground when developing a concept of "heteroglossia" as, broadly, a cultural and linguistic mode of polyvalence, with important and far-reaching implications for a noncanonical, unofficial dissemination and circulation of authority *between* oral and literary types of articulation. See, especially, Mikhail Bakhtin, *The Dialogic Imagination*, trans. Michael Holquist and Caryl Emerson (Austin: University of Texas Press, 1981), 262–75, 426.

22. Rabelais, *Oeuvres complètes*, 1:5.

23. Glyn P. Norton, "Rabelais and the Epic of Palpability: Enargeia and History (Cinquiesme Livre: 38–40)," *Symposium* 33 (1979): 171–84.

24. See Floyd Gray, "Ambiguity and Point of View in the Prologue to *Gargantua*," *Romanic Review* 56 (February 1965): 12–21.

25. Rabelais, *Oeuvres complètes*, 2:454; Rabelais, *Gargantua and Pantagruel*, 705.

Chapter 12: Historia *in* Fabula

1. Sidney, *Prose Works of Sir Philip Sidney*, 3:10, 16. Further page citations appear in the text.

2. Davis, *Idea and Act in Elizabethan Fiction*, 236.

3. Nashe, *Works of Thomas Nashe*, 2:201. Further page citations appear in the text.

4. Hayden White, "The Value of Narrativity in the Representation of Reality," *Critical Inquiry* 7 (Autumn 1980): 6–31.

5. G. R. Hibbard, *Thomas Nashe: A Critical Introduction* (Cambridge, Mass.: Harvard University Press, 1962), 145.

6. Crewe, *Unredeemed Rhetoric*, 22. In his stimulating discussion of the subversive function of "rhetorical excess," Crewe himself notes that "Nashe succumbs to history" (25). There is no point, then, in minimizing the "mass of recorded experience" rendered, often enough, with "the immediacy of spoken discourse" (Davis, *Idea and Act in Elizabethan Fiction*, 216, 218), which went hand in hand with Nashe's "powers of observation" (Hibbard, *Thomas Nashe*, 80). This constitutes a new type of authority in the narrative and, as I attempt to show, inspires at least one of the functions of Nashe's rhetoric.

7. White, "Value of Narrativity," 8.

8. Hibbard, *Thomas Nashe*, 223–25. The terms are Sidney's (in *Prose Works of Sir Philip Sidney*): 3:18.

9. See Crewe, *Unredeemed Rhetoric*, 71.

10. Charles S. Peirce, *Collected Papers* (Cambridge, Mass.: Harvard University Press, 1931–58), 2:227–29. If a "sign, or *representamen*, is something which stands to somebody for something in some respect or capacity," then it produces in the mind of the recipient "an equivalent sign, or perhaps a more developed sign. That sign which it creates I call the *interpretant* of the first sign" (227).

11. William Nelson, *Fact or Fiction: The Dilemma of the Renaissance Storyteller* (Cambridge, Mass.: Harvard University Press, 1973), 19.

12. Leonard J. Davis, "A Social History of Fact and Fiction: Authorial Disavowal in the Early English Novel," in *Literature and Society: Selected Papers from the English Institute*, ed. Edward W. Said (Baltimore: Johns Hopkins University Press, 1980), 144, 121.

13. Erich Auerbach, *Mimesis: The Representation of Reality in Western Literature*, trans. Willard R. Trask (Princeton: Princeton University Press, 1953), chap. 13.

14. Mihoko Suzuki, "'Signorie over the Pages': The Crisis of Authority in Nashe's *The Unfortunate Traveller*," *Studies in Philology* 81 (Summer 1984): 354.

15. Gabriel Harvey, *Third Letter*, in *Elizabethan Critical Essays*, ed. G. Gregory Smith (Oxford: Clarendon Press, 1904), 2:278, 431.

16. Gabriel Harvey, *Pierce's Supererogation*, in Smith, *Elizabethan Critical Essays*, 2:257–59.

17. Ibid., 277; cf. 255, where, in reference to Nashe's "Mercuriall fingers," he ridicules "the Archmistery of the busiest Modernistes."

18. Nashe's departure from the traditional mode of dedication can be read in the light of Montaigne's essay on the same subject (*The Complete Essays of Montaigne*, ed. Donald M. Frame [Stanford, Calif.: Stanford University Press, 1957], book 1, chap. 23; cf. book 1, chap. 25), where "appropriation" is the concept by which any authority that is simply given ("preordained") through precedence or custom is severely criticized or superseded by a more "independent judgment of the outside world" based on that "measure of truth and reason" derived from things themselves. Montaigne here has broader ideals in mind than does Nashe, but the latter's explicit reference to the commodification of poetry, which means a move from the "blinde custome . . . of antiquity" toward "papers as *goods* uncustomed," is in closer touch with the formidable realities of the late-sixteenth-century market for printed products.

19. Suzuki, "Signorie over the Pages," 369. For the issue of the rise of radical Protestantism, see chap. 6 above.

20. Agnew, *Worlds Apart*, 12.

Chapter 13: Textual Ownership and the New Reading

1. Sidney, *Prose Works of Sir Philip Sidney*, 1:3.

2. Cervantes, *Don Quijote de la Mancha*, 1:7 (my translation).

3. Gombrich, *Art and Illusion*, 313: "All representations are grounded on schemata which the artist learns to use."

4. Iser, *Act of Reading*, 91.

5. Marx, *Grundrisse*, 485. I have developed an approach to this mode of appropriation at some length in *Realismus in der Renaissance: Aneignung der Welt in der erzählenden Prosa* (Berlin: Aufbau, 1979), 47–182.

6. This is Merleau-Ponty's phrase, cited in Iser, *Act of Reading*, 91.

7. Cervantes, *Don Quijote de la Mancha*, 1:7–9. The English translation is from Miguel de Cervantes Saavedra, *The Adventures of Don Quixote*, trans. J. M. Cohen (Harmondsworth, England: Penguin, 1950), 25.

8. Cervantes, *Don Quijote de la Mancha*, 5:20.

9. Ibid., 76.

Epilogue: Ambivalent Representations

1. Michel Foucault, *The Order of Things: An Archaeology of the Human Sciences* (New York: Vintage, 1973), 209. Further page citations appear in the text.

2. Ibid., 61: "When the *Logique de Port-Royal* states that a sign can be inherent in what it designates or separate from it, it is demonstrating that the sign, in the Classical age, is charged no longer with the task of keeping the world close to itself and inherent in its own forms, but, on the contrary, with that of spreading it out, of juxtaposing it over an indefinitely open surface."

3. This is Louis Montrose's phrase; see Montrose, "New Historicisms," 396.

4. Michel Foucault, *Power/Knowledge: Selected Interviews and Other Writings, 1972–1977,* trans. Colin Gordon et al., ed. Colin Gordon (Brighton, England: Harvester Press, 1980), 119.

5. For Heidegger's concept of early modern *Weltbild,* see "Age of the World Picture."

6. Anthony Fletcher and John Stevenson, eds., *Order and Disorder in Early Modern England* (Cambridge: Cambridge University Press, 1985), 10.

7. Peter Clark, *English Provincial Society from the Reformation to the Revolution: Religion, Politics, and Society in Kent, 1500–1640* (Hassocks, Sussex, England: County Council, 1977), 111, 142, 144.

8. A. Hassell Smith, *Country and Court: Government and Politics in Norfolk, 1558–1603* (Oxford: Oxford University Press, 1974), 277.

9. Ibid., 334. These and the following points are based on what I continue to find useful in my *Drama und Wirklichkeit in der Shakespearezeit,* of which there is a highly condensed version in English, subtitled "Towards a Historical Approach to Shakespeare," in *Shakespeare in a Changing World,* ed. Arnold Kettle (London: Lawrence and Wishart, 1964), 17–42.

10. Fletcher and Stevenson, *Order and Disorder,* 11.

11. John Lyly, prologue to *Midas,* in *Complete Works,* 3:115.

12. Azade Seyhan, *Representation and Its Discontents: The Critical Legacy of German Romanticism* (Berkeley and Los Angeles: University of California Press, 1992), 4. For W. J. T. Mitchell's phrase, see his "Representation," in *Critical Terms for Literary Study,* ed. Frank Lentricchia and Thomas McLaughlin (Chicago: University of Chicago Press, 1990), 21.

13. Christopher Braider, *Refiguring the Real: Picture and Modernity in Word and Image, 1400–1700* (Princeton: Princeton University Press, 1993), 3.

14. Ibid.

15. Guillory, *Poetic Authority,* ix: "My hypothesis is that the authority of the imagination . . . is completely implicated in the efflorescent death of inspiration."

16. For citations in this paragraph, see above, chaps. 11 and 12.

17. Paul Ricoeur, "Imagination in Discourse and Action," in *Rethinking*

Imagination: Culture and Creativity, ed. Gillian Robinson and John Rundell (London: Routledge, 1994), 130.

18. Marsilio Ficino, *Théologie Platonicienne de l'immortalité des âmes,* ed. and trans. Raymond Marcel (Paris: Les Belles Lettres, 1964–70), 2:223. (The English translation is mine.)

19. Ibid. Note the poetics (and the pathos) of appropriation (225): "Quam mirabilis per omnem orbem terrae cultura! Quam stupenda aedificiorum structura et urbium! Irrigatio aquarum quam artificiosa!"

20. Bacon, *Works,* 3:382; further page citations appear in the text.

21. Ricoeur, *Rethinking Imagination,* 130.

22. Ibid., 130–31.

23. Cornelius Castoriadis, *The Imaginary Institution of Society,* trans. Kathleen Blamey (Oxford: Polity Press, 1987), 371. Further page citations appear in the text.

24. Cornelius Castoriadis, *L'institution imaginaire de la société* (Paris: Editions du Seuil, 1975), 325. Further page citations appear in the text. For a partial summary that Castoriadis wrote in English, see chap. 3 ("The Social-Historical") in *Philosophy, Politics, Autonomy,* ed. David Ames Curtis (New York: Oxford University Press, 1991), 33–46.

25. Castoriadis elsewhere goes as far as claiming *tout court* that these "social imaginary significations . . . determine at the same time the representations, the affects, and the intentions dominant in a society" ("Social-Historical, 42). The difference, here especially obvious, between Romantic theory and Castoriadis's "social-historical" reading of the "radical imaginary" is well brought out by Wolfgang Iser, *The Fictive and the Imaginary: Charting Literary Anthropology* (Baltimore: Johns Hopkins University Press, 1993), 186–222.

26. Roger Chartier, *The Cultural Uses of Print in Early Modern France,* trans. Lydia G. Cochrane (Princeton: Princeton University Press, 1987), 182. This study pinpoints the central paradox that "relative uniformity brought about by the higher volume of book circulation did not by any means stifle the variety of the 'figures for reading' ": while "differences in book production attenuated," the "uses of the printed word" were linked to "a desire for an increased differentiation in the modes of appropriation of typographic materials" (239).

27. See Castoriadis, *L'institution imaginaire de la société* (307) on the underlying dialectic of *séparation* and *réunion.*

28. Braider, *Refiguring the Real,* 184.

29. Christopher Marlowe, *Tamburlaine the Great,* in *The Complete Works of*

Christopher Marlowe, ed. Fredson Bowers (Cambridge: Cambridge University Press, 1973), prol. 7; 1:77.

30. Joseph Hall, *Virgidemiarum,* 1.1.44, in *The Works of Joseph Hall,* ed. Philip Wynter (1863; reprint, New York: AMS Press, 1969), 9:58.

31. See note 38 to the introduction. I have further approached the terrain of a follow-up study of the theater in "Performing at the Frontiers of Representation," in *the Arts of Performance in Elizabethan and Early Stuart Drama: Essays for G. K. Hunter,* ed. Murray Biggs et al. (Edinburgh: Edinburgh University Press, 1991), 96–112; "Bifold Authority in Shakespeare's Theatre," *Shakespeare Quarterly* 39 (1988): 401–17; and "Thresholds to Memory and Commodity in Shakespeare's Endings," *Representations* 53 (Winter 1996).

Index

Index

Index

Lumiansky, Robert M., 227 n. 13, 228 n. 21
Luther, Martin, 14, 30, 31–41, 42–46, 48, 50, 52, 67, 68, 91, 140, 144, 164, 168
Lyly, John, 2, 10, 86, 103, 146, 174, 195–97
Lyotard, Jean François, 115–16

MacCaffrey, Wallace, 55
MacCulloch, Diarmaid, 87
Maclure, Millar, 83
Malory, Thomas, 15, 124–31, 149, 150, 155, 180, 198
Man, Paul de, 135
Marcus, Leah S., 209 n. 1
Margolies, David, 232 n. 8
Marlowe, Christopher, 109–10, 204–5
Marprelate, Martin, 60–61, 85, 90–91, 93
Marx, Karl, 149, 181, 210 n. 10, 218 n. 10, 232 n. 4
Mary (Queen), 58, 60
McConica, James K., 213 n. 4
McGrath, Alister E., 45
McKeon, Michael, 16
McKerrow, Ronald B., 175
Medwall, Henry, 65–66
Merleau-Ponty, Maurice, 182
Miller, Clarence H., 142, 143, 230 n. 22
Miller, Jacqueline T., 212 n. 31, 221 n. 11
Milton, John, 3, 107
Minnis, Alastair J., 154
Mischke, Reinhard, 227 n. 8
Mitchell, W.J.T., 196
Montaigne, Michel de, 148, 235 n. 18
Montrose, Louis, 10, 191–92
Moorman, Charles, 228 n. 18
More, Thomas, 68–69, 108, 147, 164
Mori, Gui de, 132
Mulcaster, Richard, 109

Munday, Anthony, 212 n. 32
Müntzer, Thomas, 53, 79, 96

Nashe, Thomas, 3, 4, 10, 17, 20, 29, 92–93, 95–97, 103–4, 111, 112, 150, 160–79, 180, 181, 198, 203
Neale, John Ernest, 13
Near, Michael R., 226 n. 13
Nelson, William, 170
Newstead, Helaine, 128
Norton, Glyn P., 158

O'Day, Rosemary, 218 n. 14
O'Donovan, Joan Lockwood, 27–28
Ormerod, Oliver, 78–79, 92, 204

Pachoda, Elizabeth T., 129, 227 n. 13, 228 n. 21
Parker, Thomas M., 61
Patterson, Annabel, 84
Peirce, Charles Sanders, 167
Perkins, William, 88–89, 99
Petrarch, Francis, 171, 172
Plotinus, 156–57
Pratt, Mary Louise, 211 n. 16
Pulci, Luigi, 182

Quintilian, 133

Rabelais, François, 3, 10, 17, 20, 35, 103–4, 112, 136, 146, 150–59, 172, 181, 183, 203
Rasmussen, Carl J., 213 n. 4
Reiss, Timothy J., 224 n. 9
Reventlow, Henning Graf, 144
Ricoeur, Paul, 198, 200–201
Ridley, Jasper, 214 n. 5
Roberts, Henry, 212 n. 32
Rowse, Alfred Leslie 223 n. 9

Saccio, Peter, 146
Salzman, Paul, 212 n. 32

Index

Savignac, Jean, 144
Scarisbrick, John J., 58, 214 n. 13
Scotus, John Duns, 176–77
Seyhan, Azade, 196
Seymour, Edward (Duke of Somerset), 57, 61, 69–77
Shakespeare, William, 1, 8, 9–10, 12, 14, 17, 21, 27, 35, 64, 65, 73, 82, 83, 87, 99, 109, 110, 138, 142–43, 145, 146, 153, 160, 162, 163, 169, 182–83, 195–96, 198, 200, 201, 204–5
Sherry, Richard, 147–48
Shuger, Debora K., 209, 4
Sidney, Philip, 10, 14–16, 17, 105–7, 146, 147, 150, 161–64, 180, 183, 187, 198, 203
Siemon, James R., 73
Sinfield, Alan, 221 n. 17
Smith, A. Hassel, 194
Socrates, 157–58
Spenser, Edmund, 3, 107, 135
Stapleton, Thomas, 59
Stevens, John, 227 n. 6
Stevenson, John, 194–95
Stewart, Susan, 119
Stock, Brian, 114
Surrey, Henry Howard, Earl of, 164, 168
Sutton, Christopher, 64–65
Suzuki, Mihoko, 175
Swain, Barbara, 136–37

Tarlton, Richard, 90, 173
Tasso, Torquato, 106
Thompson, W.D.J. Cargill, 216 n. 7
Thomason, John A. F., 220 n. 9
Travers, Walter, 88
Troyes, Chrétien de, 121–24, 130, 131

Turner, Edith, 73, 220 n. 5
Turner, Victor, 73, 112, 220 n. 5
Tyndale, William, 67, 68–69

Unkel, Curt, 225 n. 4

Valla, Lorenzo, 108
Vinaver, Eugene, 130, 227 n. 13, 228 n. 17
Viret, Pierre, 45
Virgil, 106, 159
Vivés, Luis, 108

Warenne, Earl, 114
Warner, William, 212 n. 32
Warning, Rainer, 121, 227 n. 7
Watson, Henry, 136
Watson, Nicholas, 232 n. 13
Weber, Max, 2, 73
Weiner, Andrew D., 213 n. 4
Wells, Susan, 138, 215 n. 3, 230 n. 16
Whigham, Frank, 56
White, Hayden, 164
White, Paul W., 28
Whitgift, John (Archbishop of Canterbury), 60, 79, 84, 90, 94
Whiting, Robert, 58
Whitman, Jon, 134, 229 n. 2
Wickram, Jörg, 17
Williams, Penry, 217 n. 3
Wilson, John Dover, 90
Wolsey, Thomas (Cardinal, Archbishop of York), 27
Wyclif, John, 12

Young, Robert, 10

Zwingli, Huldrych, 30

LIBRARY OF CONGRESS CATALOGING-IN-PUBLICATION DATA

Weimann, Robert.
Authority and representation in early modern discourse / Robert Weimann ;
edited by David Hillman.
p.   cm.
Includes bibliographical references and index.
ISBN 0-8018-5190-4 (alk. paper). — ISBN 0-8018-5191-2 (pbk. : alk. paper)
1. European literature—Renaissance, 1450–1600—History and criticism.
2. Mimesis in literature.   3. Authority in literature.   I. Hillman, David
(David A.)   II. Title.
PN721.W45   1996
809'.031—dc20   95-38124